GETTING OFF THE MERRY GO-ROUND

YOU CAN LIVE WITHOUT COMPULSIVE HABITS

Carla Perez, M.D.

Impact ⁂ Publishers®
San Luis Obispo, California 93406

Impact Publishers and colophon are registered trademarks
of Impact Publishers Inc.

Library of Congress Cataloging in Publication Data

Perez, Carla
    Getting off the merry-go-round : you can live without compulsive
habits / Carla Perez.
        p.   cm.
Originally published by Simon & Schuster,   New York,   1991.
Includes bibliographical references and index.
ISBN 0-915166-85-2   (pbk.)   :
1. Compulsive behavior—Popular works.   I.   Title.
RC533.P36   1994
158'.1—dc20
                                                        93-50887
                                                        CIP

Printed in the United States of America on acid-free paper
Cover design by Sharon Schnare, San Luis Obispo, California
Author photograph by Rick English Photography, San Francisco, California

Published by **Impact 〰 Publishers**®
POST OFFICE BOX 1094
SAN LUIS OBISPO, CALIFORNIA 93406

I want to dedicate this book —

To my husband, Virg, for always being there with patience, humor, and gentle nudging to use the word processor instead of my typewriter left over from high school days.

To my children — Andrea, Michelle, Francesca, and Mario — for enriching my life, giving me wonderful ideas, listening to endless readings of yet another draft, and eating instant dinners that I didn't prepare because I was busy being a writer.

To all of you who struggle to get off the compulsive merry-go-round.

* * *

A compulsive life

is like listening to a bad joke.

You impatiently wait for the punch line.

And it is never good enough.

* * *

Contents

Preface 1

Part I "THE SECRET REBELLION"

Chapter 1: Compulsive Living — A Complex Enemy 7

Chapter 2: "Why Do I Do This To Myself?" 30

Chapter 3: The Source Of Compulsive Living 64

Part II BREAKING FREE

Chapter 4: Setting The Stage For Recovery 90

Chapter 5: Tools To Get In Control 125

Chapter 6: A Two-week Detox Program 150

Chapter 7: Not Shooting Yourself In The Foot —
Relapse Prevention 164

Part III ATTACK PLANS FOR SPECIFIC PATTERNS 177

Chapter 8: Driven Preoccupations, Thought Patterns,
And Fears 179

Chapter 9: Compulsive Work Activities,
Procrastination, Escapes 190

Chapter 10: Relationship And Sexual Fixations 202

Chapter 11: Eating, Food, And Weight Obsessions 212

Chapter 12: Money Addictions — Spending, Gambling,
Shoplifting 227

Chapter 13: Substance Abuse — Alcohol, Drugs,
Cigarettes 240

Part IV RE-ENGAGING WITH THE WORLD

Chapter 14: Beyond Compulsive Living 252

Chapter 15: When To Get Psychotherapy 263

Appendix: References and Addresses 273

Index 283

PUBLISHER'S NOTE

Acknowledgements

A special thanks to Ron Jones and Nate Shafler who helped me shape the original book proposal; to Brad Bunnin and Peter Beren who believed I could write; to kind friends who have taken time from their busy lives to read and edit various drafts, giving useful suggestions and much encouragement to me in my new role as writer and sometimes helping me keep my foot out of my mouth: Arlan Cohn, Steve Elias, Myra Green, Lela Groom, Barbara Harriman, Kit Lynch, Dennis Posadis, Michael Robertson, Gene Rusco, Janellan Smith, Jim Taranto, Lisa Willander and Joan Zweban; and to John Bradshaw for his generous support.

And thank you, Bob Alberti, for your most helpful additions. I feel fortunate to have a publisher/editor who is also an insightful psychologist.

My greatest appreciation to all of you.

PREFACE

Those who sin, grin — temporarily.
— A. Alexandre

Compulsive merry-go-rounds, like all merry-go-rounds, wait eagerly for us to jump on board. And so we do. The ride starts innocently enough. The price sounds right as the hidden costs are nowhere to be seen.

Browsing along the platform, it's not clear why particular horses are so fascinating. Shall you try alcohol, drugs, cigarettes, overeating, or overspending? Perhaps a whirl with dead-end relationships, obsessive sex, driven work, or some other colorful escape? The gaudy painted beasts beckon relentlessly. "Climb on me. Climb on me," they seem to say, "Come to the land of permanent bliss." Wanting so much to trust something other than yourself, you brush aside your trepidation and mount a horse that's nearby.

The merry-go-round becomes a temporary haven of comfort, greater than any that you'd dared imagine. Seduced by the gentle mesmerizing music and promises of eternal joy, you sit back and let your mind go blank. Up and down, up and down you go. Surely the ride will take you somewhere, to a place that holds no fear.

But just as you are snugly seated, it becomes apparent that you are going nowhere, round and round, faster and faster, but going nowhere. You might switch from horse to horse — back to old ones, on to new ones — only to find the pace of the merry-go-round quickening and your stomach sickening.

What have you gotten yourself into? The bobbing horses pay no heed to your growing qualms. They chew up your spirit and sense of right and wrong, and spit out pieces of your broken life for all the world to see. But once you are a captive of the compulsive merry-go-round, you lose sight of who you are and what you want. Help!

A dramatic, exaggerated picture of what happens, yes — but a real and all too familiar one.

* * *

I gravitated toward working with patients battling various forms of compulsive living long before I realized that it related to a need to better deal with my own self-destructive patterns: a preoccupation with my weight, constant worries about pleasing and taking care of everyone and everything, and obsessive busyness. There were plenty of times when my life was in control, but more often than not I lapsed into familiar harmful patterns or developed new ones. I wasn't a heroin addict or stricken with gambling fever, but I was on a compulsive merry-go-round that was detrimental to my well-being and peace of mind.

When I looked for answers, I found no more than bits and pieces of the compulsive puzzle. Books, programs, and therapies that focus on particular patterns — around food, work, being perfect, etc. — don't go far enough. Specific approaches to recovery also fall short: Behavioral resources address learning new ways to react to given circumstances; cognitive resources target changing how you feel about yourself and about certain situations; psychoanalytic resources seek understanding of the roots of the self-destructive patterns. No single resource adequately explained the entire problem. So I stumbled about for years. I felt like I had an illness and was treating its symptoms, but not dealing with the primary infection that caused it.

At the same time, I discovered that the struggles of friends and patients in trouble with other substances and behavior patterns closely resembled mine. My life slowly began to fall into place, but it was saddened by the deaths of a much-loved brother and sister. It was not until some years after their deaths that I realized: Not only had both of them been heavy smokers with weight concerns, but they were alcoholics as well. This, too, made me ponder the issues of my life and others who get sidetracked into compulsive patterns, and how the patterns are interrelated. Gradually the pieces of the puzzle began to come together.

I started writing to get a better grasp of the whole situation — first for myself and then for friends and patients. As the material grew, it struck me that it was worth trying to get it out to the public at large. And so this book evolved.

Your problems could center around work, fears, compulsive relationships or sex. They may concern food, money, alcohol, drugs or cigarettes. Habits can range from merely bothersome to life-threatening — from "soft-core" addictions to hard-core ones. Regardless of which compulsive patterns plague you, all of them deflect your energy and rob you of genuine happiness. Life is difficult enough without such needless suffering. You deserve far better. You deserve freedom from self-destructive habits. You deserve to feel good about yourself.

Your past trials and tribulations offer the first and most important lessons toward your becoming an expert in your own treatment. *Getting Off the Merry-Go-Round* will provide you with the next step, a comprehensive framework in which to understand and integrate your past experience with other vital information and support. It will also serve as a concise resource and practical guide for navigating through the jungle of programs and "how to" books that are currently on the bookstore and library shelves, so that you can make the best use of them. You will then be able to create your own custom-designed recovery program.

The book offers a total approach — a blueprint for mastering the problem — divided into four major parts and fifteen chapters to guide you through your recovery process:

Part I: "The Secret Rebellion" will help you understand how your compulsive patterns originated, and what keeps them going.

Chapter 1: "Compulsive Living — A Complex Enemy" defines compulsive living and gives insight into why it has such a stronghold on our lives.

Characteristics of compulsive living are spelled out. The specific habits vary, but their underlying dynamics don't. In unhealthy ways we use our habits to take care of ourselves:

- To deal with our feelings and needs;
- To lessen our fear of being out of control;
- To counterbalance our oppressive guilt; and
- To declare our independence.

Chapter 2: "Why Do I Do This To Myself?" points out that habits are held in place by particular precipitating factors that trigger us into old feelings of helplessness and pain. These feelings then lead us into self-defeating cycles kept in perpetual motion by our responses to discomfort. We will also analyze the kinds of rationalizations and mental games we use to avoid change.

Chapter 3: "The Source Of Compulsive Living" examines the origins of our habits, and the social pressures and seductions that fuel them. Compulsive patterns are vestiges of childhood struggles that have never been properly resolved — pseudo-solutions to life that once worked but later ran amuck. The society in which we live exploits and plays into our weaknesses with escapes disguised as easy comfort. We are urged to eat, drink, spend, and work harder when life hurts too much.

Part II: "Breaking Free " offers basic training to get you started on the way to recovery.

Chapter 4: "Setting The Stage For Recovery" looks at ways to get in gear for change:

- by taking stock of how compulsive living is affecting your life;
- by getting a perspective on the whole recovery process; and
- by becoming familiar with the kinds of necessary support that are available.

Chapter 5: "Tools To Get In Control" presents concrete plans for each stage of the recovery process. The goal is to get and keep yourself in check for all compulsive patterns. You need to attack both the symptoms and their underpinnings. An effective comprehensive healing process must be multi-dimensional and include:

- finding new means of coping and relating to others; and
- developing more appropriate ways of thinking about yourself and your life.

Chapter 6: "A Two-Week Detox Program" offers you a plan for immediate intervention — a way to break your destructive routine and begin your path to recovery.

Chapter 7: "Not Shooting Yourself In The Foot — Relapse Prevention" will help you combat common rationalizations that frequently impede recovery programs, and remain vigilant against other hazards that might sabotage your progress.

Part III: "Attack Plans For Specific Patterns" shows you how to deal with each of the six major compulsive habit areas.

8 • Driven Preoccupations, Thought Patterns, And Fears
9 • Compulsive Work or Activities, Procrastination, Escapes
10 • Relationship And Sexual Fixations
11 • Eating, Food, And Weight Obsessions
12 • Money Addictions — Spending, Gambling, Shoplifting
13 • Substance Abuse — Alcohol, Drugs, Cigarettes

Each chapter of Part III covers possible varieties of compulsive living in a given category, and then goes on to spell out explicit strategies for change. This includes modifications of material already presented in Part II, as well as an evaluation of supplementary resources for particular compulsive habits.

Part IV: "Re-Engaging With The World" bridges the gap from your recovery program back to the "real world."

Chapter 14: "Beyond Compulsive Living" suggests ways to actively move on with your life and to let go of outdated parts of your past that keep derailing you.

Chapter 15: "When To Get Psychotherapy" will help you decide when psychotherapy could be helpful.

* * *

To get off the compulsive merry-go-round requires nothing short of a thorough psychological overhaul. You must shift from thinking of yourself as being a helpless pawn of life into an awareness that it is *you* who actively participates in life's unfolding. What happens to you is *not* just chance. It is very much influenced by how you feel about yourself and the actions you decide to take.

No stone can be left unturned if you are to succeed in this process of self-liberation.

I have tried here to be straightforward and hit hard, yet be supportive and encouraging. People in trouble or heading for it need to be both shaken up and given a lift.

You may feel a bit discouraged while reading Chapters 1, 2 and 3 about the habits and their origins, but there is a reason for this. I have consciously painted a realistically bleak picture of life in the compulsive lane. I want to make you aware of how self-destructive you can be when your habits get out of control. But don't despair, read on. The rest of the book will bring you to a place of alternatives and hope, and help you find a happier way to live.

Throughout the book, I have sprinkled vignettes that reveal different versions of compulsive living. These stories come from patients, friends, relatives, as well as first-hand experiences of my own. Though I have changed details to protect individuals' privacy, the vignettes represent real situations of real people. When a habit that I describe is not one that you have, I urge you to be patient. The particulars of the pattern might sound unfamiliar, but right beneath the surface it's all the same.

Some of you may be surprised at my occasional levity in seemingly heavy situations. I can only tell you my firm belief that no matter what horrors one has been through, you can't cry all the time. In fact humor sometimes saves the day.

I might add that there may be people in your life who not only don't understand your problems but, worse yet, actually undermine your efforts to change. Ironically, many of these people are really like you — they just don't realize it. Reading this book also can help them become more enlightened and more sympathetic to and supportive of your journey.

I've tried to write in a readable style that does not sacrifice psychological accuracy, and give you the book that I wish had been available for me.

COMPULSIVE LIVING —
A COMPLEX ENEMY

1

You can run, but you can't hide.
— Sheldon Kopp

Compulsive living comes in many forms and infinite variations: When asked what brought her into therapy, Mona, a thirty-five-year-old legal assistant stated her frustrations, "It's only when I'm thin enough, when some man is giving me attention, when I'm accomplishing a lot that I temporarily feel okay. There must be more to life than this."

Already in recovery for alcohol abuse, a forty-three-year-old visibly depressed executive in an advertising firm related his agony, "It's been an uphill struggle but I thought I'd done a complete turnabout. I work hard. I jog like crazy. I eat all the right foods. I'm in the greatest physical shape I've ever been in — and I feel wretched. Formerly I ran to cigarettes and alcohol. Now I'm on a different treadmill."

Over lunch one day, a longtime friend said, "I can't say I'm not happy. I have everything I always thought I wanted. Yet one day just blends into the next as I do what I need to, to get through it. Work used to be challenging, but now it isn't. I don't know when it happened, but somewhere along the way I've lost me. What's scary is that weeks and months and years go by and I'm not doing anything about it."

These particular stories may not exactly match yours, but there might be uncomfortable similarities that gnaw at your complacency:

• You may simultaneously be caught into a number of on-going, self-destructive life patterns where good intentions, promises to yourself or loved ones, even therapy haven't significantly altered the situation.

• You may center your life around trying to be perfect, forever pleasing others, being a super-achiever, and always over-committing yourself.

• You may obsessively procrastinate or escape into television, books, good causes or other diversions. Endless plans and projects remain in limbo.

• You may have fears or phobias that seriously curtail areas of daily living. Perhaps you drink or take drugs to lessen anxiety about these fears.

• You may be preoccupied with your weight and being thin — eternally nibbling, forever dieting, and losing the same poundage an embarrassing number of times.

• You may feel stuck in a self-destructive relationship. This could be to a mate, parents, a friend, children or others. Rationally you know the relationship isn't good for you, but you can't change it or let it go.

• You may be a workaholic, possibly troubled by high blood pressure, the fear of a heart attack or the feeling that life is sheer drudgery.

• You may have trouble controlling your spending, frequently living beyond your means. While you spend, you feel no pain. But afterwards, you feel guilty and ashamed about your battered bank account.

• You may be engaged in compulsive promiscuity, infidelity or flirting. This may have grave consequences for the rest of your life.

• You may habitually get "highs" through gambling or shoplifting.

• A Twelve-Step Program or other support group for alcohol,

drug or other abuses might have helped you gain control over your main compulsive habit. But new self-destructive patterns may have surfaced to replace old ones.

It is discouraging enough to try to wage war against troublesome patterns once we recognize and face them. It is far more infuriating to find that even when specific habits are conquered, the compulsive urge goes on.

Incidentally, when I use the words "obsessive" and "compulsive," I am *not* referring to obsessive-compulsive disorder, now labeled OCD and illustrated by Lady MacBeth's obsessive hand washing in the Shakespeare play. Compulsive living is related to OCD a bit like a cat is related to a tiger. In this book, we are sticking with the domestic animal. But make no mistake — its claws are sharp. They can torment and do much damage.

Is My Bad Habit Really Destructive?

As you read, a basic question may swim around in your mind — a variation of, "Aren't we entitled to have at least a few bad habits? Must we live 'vicelessly'?"

After looking over a draft of this manuscript, one of my friends started worrying. He thought his life was in pretty good order. He has happy relationships and satisfying work. But the book made him aware of some of his patterns — having a regular evening drink, overeating when he is stressed, often becoming buried in work. Was he worse off than he thought? Should he change his habits immediately?

Indulging or even overindulging in a substance or an activity does *not* necessarily signify the presence of compulsive living. The reality of life is that most of us occasionally detour into a self-destructive pattern to cope with daily tensions. After all, do you know many people who *never* misuse alcohol, food, spending, work, television, or some other escape?

But indulging becomes compulsive:

• when you *regularly* use a substance or activity to get through the day and to avoid dealing with discomfort;

• when you indulge rather than face personal or work-related problems;

• when you indulge more and more and enjoy it less and less;

• when the rest of your life is compromised by the habit;

• when stopping the pattern is difficult, even though the habit adversely affects your health, work, or relationships;

• when your self-worth depends on your feeling in control, and whether the consequences of a pattern are visible to others;

• when you spend sleepless nights worrying about the situation.

Others might not be aware of your difficulties, but at some level, you are. In the *Rubaiyat,* when Omar Khayyam said, "A loaf of bread, a jug of wine and thou," I suspect he meant you should embellish, not embalm, your life.

Blatantly Obvious Or Well Concealed

Few of us would have trouble identifying compulsive patterns at their most excessive, the "you're gonna die" obsessions of

• The down-and-out alcoholic or substance abuser;
• The chain-smoker who coughs incessantly;
• The overweight individual who eats all day long;
• The gambler who has hocked his house.

Subtler patterns of compulsive living are often overlooked and/or denied:

• You may obsess about whether a particular individual in your life is angry at you.

• You may constantly worry about how you look.

• You might feel so hooked on a standard of living that you allow yourself to become trapped into a job which you've grown to hate.

• You may rely on legal drugs.

Many of us close our eyes to such problems. We limp along, while our lives go by without us.

As we discuss compulsive living, you will see that all of these habits are used to compensate for underlying insecurities and anxieties. For some people, the compensatory habits completely overshadow everything else and the underlying anxieties may be unnoticed. For other people, the underlying anxieties so dominate the picture that full-blown phobias emerge.

A Never-Ending Story

Why is it so difficult to moderate habits that, left unchecked, create havoc in our lives? Unfortunately both the problem and the solution are extremely complex:

- Patterns of compulsive living have roots in childhood. They were initially used to nurture us and to handle what felt uncomfortable.
- With time, they increasingly become a way of existing, kept alive by familiarity and distorted thinking.
- Tenaciously intertwined into all aspects of our lives, they choke our normal growth and our capacity to experience life fully.
- When we try to change, we not only struggle against our own resistance, but also with society's confusing demands and pressures. These directly or indirectly reinforce our patterns.
- To get off the compulsive merry-go-round, you must properly assess all its intricacies — the underlying compulsive condition from which your habits arise, as well as the interrelated self-destructive patterns that are manifestations of it. You need to deal with the entire problem.

Onward

Although we arrive in life on different ships, we are all "in the same boat." Each of us must come to terms with many challenges:

- Identifying and juggling the stresses of life;
- Figuring out what to accept and what to change, in ourselves and in our environment;
- Living each day with dignity and sanity, finding healthy means to cope;
- Discovering how to enjoy our lives and make them meaningful.

Compulsive living, in whatever form it appears, is certainly *not* the answer. You will see that it is a frustrating rut that leads nowhere — an ineffective attempt to fill your personal needs at an emotional price that is too devastating.

As you start to heal yourself, you can begin to ask directly for what you want. In so doing, you will finally be able to get off the compulsive merry-go-round, and get on with your life.

Compulsive Patterns — Up Close And Personal

> *When choosing between two evils, I always like to try the one I've never tried before.*
>
> — Mae West

To look at her, you would never guess she had a worry in the world. She was warm, attractive and dressed in the latest style. What didn't show was the fact that five days previously she had made a serious suicide attempt. Why did this seemingly happy, young married mother who appeared to have so much feel that life wasn't worth living?

Here is her story:

> It's very painful to talk about this. I don't know where to start.
>
> I come from an upwardly mobile family. Though we didn't have a lot, my parents always made ends meet and tried to help me. This often caused harsh words between them. Mother incessantly wanted us to look our best. Father worried about money, complaining that she was extravagant and we'd end up in the poor house.
>
> Appearances were very important to my mother, and soon became so to me. I was in the top of my class in school and very popular. I married shortly after college. My husband is a good man and cares deeply about our family. We'd be fine if it weren't for me and what I've done.

It's hard to say what came first, the tension between my husband and me, or my increasingly out of control spending. All I know is that I was buying more and more furniture and other items for our house, and more nice clothes for myself and the children. My husband and I were starting to bicker on a daily basis about everything, including money.

I'd always liked shopping for pretty things, but gradually the stores became a refuge — I couldn't wait to get in the car and go to the malls. When I was there, I could forget everything else. Afterwards I'd arrive home in a sort of delirium, and usually squirrel away my purchases in a closet. I used to shop with friends or meet someone for lunch, but that fell by the wayside. I got so I'd rather go alone.

This must sound crazy to you. I can't say it makes sense to me. Debts were piling up. I was juggling like mad to try to keep my head above water. And at the same time, I kept buying more clothes and things for the house — not "nickle and diming it away," rather "hundreds of dollaring" it away.

Buying and shopping and worrying about how to pay off the debts consumed my days and even my nights. I couldn't sleep well. Communication with my husband really suffered as I became secretive about how far I'd run up the accounts and the incredible balancing act I was doing with the credit cards. I got in the habit of always grabbing the mail first and quickly pulling out the bills. I'd pay a monthly token amount on each and totally hide the extent of our debts from my husband. I kept fooling myself that somehow I could get caught up. My parents bailed me out several times, unbeknownst to my husband.

The last straw was when I got so desperate, I went to my boss and asked for a very large advance on my salary. Things might have been all right, but it has become clear that my boss expects something in return — and it's not money. Now the situation in the office has become a mess. I feel like I'm drowning both at work and at home. I can't live with this. My family doesn't deserve it. I honestly feel they'd be better off without me.

When we open Pandora's box of compulsive living patterns, "bad" habits fly out in all directions — some packaged in socially acceptable disguises, others look quite grotesque. They are as unlimited as the human beings who inhabit them. But, lo and behold, when the wrappings of each pattern are peeled away, the inside contents are surprisingly similar. If we look closely, common themes can be identified, dependent on what stage the whole process is in.

Unlike pregnancy, which is an all-or-none situation, compulsive living has a whole range of intensities. In order to gauge to what degree its patterns have you under their thumb, here are some questions to ponder. Each highlights a different aspect of the problem and includes examples of various habits. The earlier questions apply to a relatively benign involvement with compulsive patterns, whereas the latter ones depict situations of far more dire consequences. There are no right or wrong answers — just food for thought to get you in gear for future action.

Compulsive Patterns As An Integral Part Of Your Existence

• *Do you habitually use particular patterns to get through the day and/or to avoid discomfort? Have they become a regular source of gratification?*
It is not the occasional drink when you are tense that gets you into trouble, but rather a pattern of regular drinking which becomes a central part of your life. It is not unusual that you absorb yourself in work or daydreaming when life at home is upsetting, but when these activities become an overriding way to handle your feelings. It is not that you sometimes go on an eating or a shopping rampage, it's that such sprees are a customary and often automatic means of handling the pressures of life. It is not that you simply enjoy having particular people in your life, rather that you need these relationships to feel all right. You feel lost without them.

• *When you are not kidding yourself, are you bothered by your patterns?*
How much particular habits annoy and embarrass you will influence your manner of indulging in them.

Some people's involvement in compulsive patterns seems

uncolored by shame or guilt. In this case, the difficulty of trying to maintain control may be frustrating, but it is not hidden. A forty-five year old salesman nonchalantly told me of his battle of the bulge:

> *I've always been big, since I was a kid — a good eater, the perfect son, kind of the family garbage can, finishing all the leftovers. Unfortunately my Mom was a great and bountiful cook. I started to get really heavy in junior high. But I was active enough in sports to not let it get totally out of bounds.*
>
> *Since I have gotten out of school, my weight has been a real struggle. It's gone even higher now that I'm more settled — I'm a good seventy pounds over what I'd like to be. I'm married, my business is going well, but I don't like the way I look. When I'm working, food is not on my mind. Often I even work right through lunch. However, if I do take lunch, I eat far more than I intended, usually quite rich food.. I seem to have to clean up whatever food is around. The evenings get filled with TV, a few drinks, chips and other snacks. Every few years I go on an all-out exercise program and fanatically lose a few pounds. But I never stick with it.*

Also, you may engage in patterns quite openly if you are busy denying or *not* seeing the effect of your habits on your health, relationships and work. You rationalize your habits to yourself and to others, with no attempt to hide them. You drink or overeat in front of everyone; boast about how much you work, spend or womanize; wax on endlessly about how you are devoted to the "heel," even though he keeps deceiving you.

On the other hand, if you are uncomfortable about your habits and how they are affecting the rest of your life, you may indulge in a secretive, sneaky fashion, behaving "normally" in public and chaotically in private. You carefully conceal your patterns of bingeing, drinking, womanizing, using Valium, staying involved with your horrible "ex." Your cookies are sequestered under the bed, your liquor in the closet with the empty bottles well hidden in the trash, and your "liaison" in another city. You are so troubled by your ongoing struggle to gain control of your habits that you attempt to keep the problem and all its frustrations to yourself.

In contrast to the salesman just described, here is an entirely different style of handling an eating difficulty. A bright slender mid-thirties woman was very uncomfortable with her struggles.

I feel terrible about my crazy eating and what I do to stay thin. I forever gorge on food. But I don't get fat and no one ever sees me binge, not even my boyfriend. I'd be mortified if they did. This is embarrassing to describe. I never binge on work days because I need the time to throw up afterwards — a weight gain terrifies me and I don't like to feel stuffed. So I only eat when I have ready access to a bathroom and I don't have to think about any other commitments.

Sometimes I wonder what people would think of me if they knew about my craziness. They'd think I was some kind of freak and had gone off the deep end. I'm always so responsible in public.

• *Are you becoming less discriminating in your indulgences?* Initially the habits or behavior gave you pleasure and provided a pleasant distraction. You looked forward to involving yourself in the particular pattern on specific occasions. The indulgences were handled with care and discretion, not driven by the stress within you. You may or may not be able to remember when this was true.

As you become dependent on your compulsive patterns, the sought after pleasure is more elusive. Rather than being used to feel good, your habits increasingly serve to help you *not* feel bad. You are less aware what feelings even trigger the patterns. The habits become relatively autonomous and self-reinforcing.

"I used to be very choosy about what man was in my life, and be strictly monogamous," said a thirty-year-old buyer for a major department store. "Now long-term relationships make me feel fenced in. I don't like being at the mercy of one man. But I feel so 'blah' and empty when I have no man in my life that I end up flirting outrageously with all sorts of people. This gives me some kind of a 'high.' It's hard to explain. It's like I can be with a man but not too close — safe.

What I mainly like is the feeling of becoming quickly close, instantly intimate. Riding on airplanes, which I do as part of my work, provides me with the perfect opportunity to become totally vulnerable with a perfect stranger whom I'll probably never even see again. Sure, sometimes things lead to going to bed together, but that's not the main point of what I'm after. Rather it's that open and complete sharing of even personal details of my life, a fleeting connectedness where momentarily we're really special to each other, a quick tragi-romantic 'in love' that won't go anywhere. This is ridiculous, but I even get a 'high' out of an encounter as brief as locking eyes with someone while I'm walking down the street. It makes me feel all woman, like I own the world.

I don't think of myself as promiscuous — I never sleep with someone who I'm not at least temporarily madly in love with. But all of this makes me uneasy, especially with so many horrible illnesses around."

• *Are you needing more and more of your patterns in order to feel all right?*

When you are not involved in your compulsive pattern, you may feel unsafe, tense, empty, swallowed up by overwhelming feelings, dead inside, or practically nonexistent. Hence you literally live for the next "fix" — whether it be alcohol, drugs, nicotine, food, work, sex, to be with a particular person, to engage in your preoccupying cause, or some other process or experience. Ever greater usage of your compulsive patterns may be needed to satisfy you and make you feel all right.

Right on time for his appointment, a middle-aged lawyer immediately launched into a description of his driven life:

In the past, when I was working well I felt a wonderful inner peace and sense of fulfillment. But this feeling has become the exception, and the majority of the time I'm working I just feel that I'm not doing it well enough. Even when I'm with friends I find my mind drifting back to work projects, redoing them endlessly in my thoughts, but not in a way that necessarily leads to any conclusion. And if I don't stop myself, it grows into this awful anxious feeling — that I'm accomplishing nothing, I should be working, I'm getting behind, I'll never get caught up.

I used to be able to take time off, but lately it's getting harder and harder. Sometimes when I work to the point of exhaustion, I can finally allow myself to stop, without having the guilty little voices of my conscience drive me nuts about all that I can and should be doing. I've gotten into the habit of having a couple of drinks in the evenings to help me unwind.

I'm beginning to dread any sort of extended free time. I can't seem to let go of work. I dwell on it in my mind, even though I know it's sabotaging my social life. My work is enslaving me and I don't know what to do.

• *Are you fooling yourself about how out of control your life has become?*

To avoid having to take full responsibility for yourself, you may go to great lengths to maintain the illusion of being in control. You minimize your indulgences to yourself and to others; you make and break promises to yourself and/or to others to change; you repeatedly attempt and fail to set limits for yourself; you follow rigid rituals, setting others up as monitors and rescuers. As an extreme example, rather than directly facing and dealing with her out-of-control eating, a woman I knew had her roommates literally lock her into her room at night so she wouldn't raid the refrigerator.

You stay away from doctors, friends or relatives who might confront you with the consequences of your habits. You avoid the scale or the mirror that will show your weight gain. You drink only white wine and tell yourself that since it is not whiskey, you don't have a problem. You let a mate handle all the money in the family, so that you won't be in danger of overspending it. You close our eyes to reminders of undone chores. You try not to think about all you are missing in life. More and more energy gets swallowed into putting up a good "front" — primarily to reassure yourself. You try to look sober, cool, collected, responsible, and in control, acting as if there are *no* problems.

Or, if you are aware of having problems, you may choose to see your predicament as simply being "bad luck," and that there's basically nothing you can do about it.

During the course of therapy, a carpenter in his late forties recounted his prerecovery days:

The years progressed and so did my drinking. There were blatant acts of anger, violence, irresponsibility. I felt outright terror and increasing self-hate. Though I had always prided myself on being compassionate, I found myself assaulting others with verbal abuse. I even got into a couple of fist fights. As if that weren't enough, I also got into automobile accidents, suffered countless injuries, including a couple of broken bones. I started to lose jobs, relationships, and worst of all, my own self-respect.

My drinking got more and more out of hand, and my life more and more chaotic. I had a lot of blackouts. I couldn't remember whole conversations, evenings, days. Twice I had terrifying hallucinations.

I was oblivious to how wild and self-destructive my behavior was becoming. I ignored advice and ultimatums from others. I simply saw these constantly occurring misfortunes as part of life — fate's choice in dealing the cards, not my fault.

How Your Patterns Impact On Relationships

• *Do your patterns inappropriately draw people in, to enable you to indulge or to rescue you from the consequences of your indulgences?*

When you are "under the influence," you may use extremely poor judgment and can be highly undiscriminating about the company you keep. If you are sufficiently desperate to obtain some illegal substance or to participate in a socially unacceptable activity, you might befriend people whom you ordinarily would never pick as associates — those who supply or share your substances or activities. This gives an illusory feeling of belonging. But people actually play second fiddle to the "high" of partaking in your compulsive patterns.

You may get together with others more as an excuse to indulge than as an opportunity to visit. If you are honest with yourself, alcohol, food, and/or some other substance or activity has top billing over the joy of interacting. When a fifty-two-year-old friend of mine gave up drinking and smoking, he realized he had little in common with his wife and eventually left her. Another example was a patient telling me that since she had stopped clouding her social life with compulsive eating, her relationships with several friends no longer were fun.

Furthermore, if you addictively need others to compensate for not feeling good enough about yourself, you stay stuck in symbiotic relationships. A thirty-year-old woman physician found herself in two relationships that turned disastrous. She said,

> I end up pouring all my hard earned money into support-ing child-like dependent men and calling it love. They use me as a meal ticket while they stay busy "creatively" being irresponsible. If it weren't so pathetic, I'd laugh. Here I am trying to lose myself, and all they want to do is find themselves — and I pick up the tab while they do it. Yet I'm never the one who leaves. Being alone feels too empty.

People who otherwise might be on the fringe of your life can become integral and prominent parts of it to offset your irrespon-sibility. In fact they may become indispensable. You might use friends to provide cover stories for your alcohol, drug, sex, or gambling escapades. Debts can bind you inextricably to parents, relatives, a mate, a colleague, the bank, an unfulfilling job, or someone or something else. Due to these unhealthy involvements, you stay dependent on others, never free to be yourself, and become a perpetual child.

• *Are your patterns interfering with important relationships?* Your habits can buffer you from true intimacy. You might physically be with someone, but in reality be numbed by food, alcohol, cigarettes, drugs, or involvement with another activity. Because of your detachment, it doesn't matter if the other person is really there for you, or in many instances, even *who* the other person is.

> Every day after work I'll just plop down with a drink and watch anything that's on. My wife and children become back-ground. Family interaction is only during commercials. Sometimes I won't even switch channels to make a choice. I feel like I'm in a strange trance, totally mesmerized, and the next thing I know it's after 11:00 p.m. If my family walked out, I'll bet I wouldn't even know it for days.

That is forty-six-year-old executive and television junkie describing his evenings.

It should be noted that some compulsive patterns can be

completely hidden — no substance is ingested nor activity practiced. But your mind can be far away — preoccupied with work, an obsession, worrying, daydreaming. This results in your being emotionally removed into a detached, unavailable state. Your habits then remain quite invisible to others.

A newly married woman who consulted me was having difficulties because of just such a habit. She had grown up with an abusive alcoholic father and remembered using daydreaming as a safe refuge to help her tolerate the intolerable of her childhood.

> *No matter what chaos was going on, I could always retreat into the calmness of my fantasies. I'm sure it saved me from going insane. But the reason I came to see you is that often when my husband is talking, I find myself doing the same thing. My thoughts are miles away and I'm not even aware that it has happened. My husband gets furious, we get into a big fight, and I end up in the bedroom alone crying.*

• *Have people in your life complained that you overuse particular substances, obsessively engage in particular activities, or are forever absorbed in particular preoccupations?*

Your wife may be annoyed at the quantity of time you spend working or jogging. Your family may be upset because you are constantly out playing bridge. Your boyfriend may be put out because you are incessantly on the phone. Your son may be hurt because you are eternally preoccupied with your own thoughts. Friends may be exasperated that you are usually too busy to have lunch with them. Your husband may be worried about the amount you drink. Your girlfriend may be livid because you are constantly eyeing other women. Your children may be troubled about your health because you smoke two packs of cigarettes a day and cough a lot. Your cousin may be angry because you continually borrow money. Your boss may complain that you never get reports in on time. Your daughter may be distressed because you are rarely home in the evenings, forever out at meetings. Your friends may be alarmed when you stay in a relationship that is very upsetting to you.

Their concerns are getting to you. Sometimes you find yourself being quite defensive about how you are living your life — it's none of their damn business.

• *Are you playing games to avoid other people seeing the consequences of your patterns?*
In other areas of your life, you might function responsibly and in socially accepted ways. But in regard to particular patterns, you may have little insight, use poor judgment and behave like an irresponsible, rebellious child. You hide your letters from a lover at a friend's house; your phone bill to the bookie or drug dealer under a cohort's credit card number; your absences from your spouse under an elaborate lie; your creditors' due notices in a separate post office box.

In talking about his long-term marriage to what he described as an "intrusive wife," a forty-year-old salesman hesitantly told me of the patterns that he had gotten into:

> Over the years, I felt less and less that I owned my own life, like my wife was keeping track of every nickel I spent. Thank God because of work I'm often on the road. A lot of money just seems to slip through my fingers. I told my wife the new computer that suddenly appeared had been given to me as a bonus. A great deal of the money has gone for two pieces of real estate that she doesn't even know anything about. She would kick up a storm. But it's my money. I never had anything as a kid. I work hard now. I deserve to buy whatever I want to.
>
> I finally decided to get a separate post office box so there's no way she knows what I've bought. Nor does she know that I'm way over my head with bills that I have no idea how to pay off. I hate to think what would happen if she ever found out.

You camouflage your weight gain with particular clothes; your red eyes with Visene; your smoker's pallor under heavy makeup; your hangover with coffee and "uppers."

> I never go to bed at night without carefully planning the next twenty-four hours — how to stay sober enough so that my husband and children won't notice, and how to avoid

making a disastrous error at work. I'm almost as dependent on coffee as I am on alcohol. Somehow I make it through each day and hang on until I can have the next drink to stop my jitters. I welcome any occasion or excuse that justifies my indulging. As they always say, "It must be 5:00 o'clock some-where," so it's time for a drink. I just pray that others won't realize what's going on.

So speaks a thirty-one-year-old nurse and mother of three boys.

Compulsive Living Dominating Your Life

• *When you take an honest look at the negative and possibly devastating repercussions that habits have on your life, do you still continue to indulge?*

You are in debt and compulsively spend more. You are overweight and keep on overeating, especially when you are frustrated at not losing more weight after having followed the latest diet regime for two days. You continue to binge and purge, even though you know about potential cardiac arrhythmias and that the enamel of your teeth has already started to dissolve. You don't stop smoking even after you have had a heart attack or a relative dies of lung cancer. You are about to lose your job because of poor functioning, but your drinking persists and you keep getting to work late each day. A spouse says he or she will leave if you aren't home more, and you still regularly stay late at the office and pick up other partners. You are fed up with not getting anything done, and yet you remain glued to the television set.

Compulsive drives dissolve your judgment, your willpower and your conscience.

When I was in my early twenties, I won it big at the casinos. I figure if I did it once, I ought to be able to do it again, even though rationally I know the odds are against me. Over the years I've lost more than I even want to remember, but I know if I stick with it, at some point I'm going to make it big again. I know I can beat the odds.

I just love all the action and excitement. I get drawn to it like a moth is attracted to a light bulb. When I'm gambling, I don't feel hungry or tired. I can go on forever. Again and again

I've resolved to stop when I'm ahead, or to keep my losses to a fixed minimum. But when I'm in the thick of it, it's like another spirit takes over and I can no more pull out than cease breathing. And when I'm away from the action too long, I get edgy and tense and start to dream about being back at the tables. I'm like a starving man who hasn't eaten for weeks. At those times I even con friends to get money for a game.

It's created havoc with my wife and me. Not only have I spent money that together we had saved up for vacations, I've also used rent money and at times put us in serious debt. She's going to give up on me at some point. I've already lost countless friends through un-repaid loans.

The frustrations of not being able to stop gambling were so described by a middle-aged married man.

You know that the latest purchase, the new sexual escapade, the food consumed, the return to a hopelessly unfulfilling relationship does not help your life at all. In fact it clearly worsens your problems. Yet you can't disengage yourself from the same fruitless scenarios.

I remember the first time I was introduced to laxatives, I wished I had found out about them long before — I could binge and not gain an ounce. Then when I was two or three years into laxative abuse, I became concerned about what the fine print on the laxative box said regarding negative side effects. So I told a friend I was using laxatives. I can still hear her saying to me, "Don't worry. What it means is that it might hurt a person if they were continually using them for twenty years." Well, it has now been eighteen years. I can't stop.

This was told to me by a frightened forty-year-old teacher:

You could have been in excellent therapy, be well aware of the dynamics of your childhood, and clearly see how your compulsive habits started. You may also have brilliant insights into why and when you use your patterns. This in no way puts a lid on your indulgences, nor your desire to compulsively escape or experience a particular kind of "high." In fact, your understanding of why you engage might make you even more

*angry at yourself for not being able to stay in control — like
you are a failure and "no good" regardless of your strengths
and accomplishments in other areas.*

• *Are your patterns and their consequences absorbing ever
greater amounts of time, energy, and/or money?*

As was seen in a number of previous examples, your whole day can
get elaborately planned around compulsive habits. Ramifications
of this may be constantly on your mind.

At thirty-six, Margie was bright, extremely pretty, and had a
wonderful sense of humor. You would have thought that men would
be no problem for her. Not so. She was obsessed with the current
"love of her life":

> *Everything I do or see makes me wish he were here
> sharing it with me. It's all I can do to stop myself from running
> to the phone to invite him to join me, or to tell him about things
> afterwards. It's scary how dependent I have become on him.
> I always thought of myself as so self-sufficient. Now it's like
> I've fallen into a bottomless morass of vulnerability. I'm start-
> ing to wrap my whole life around him. I pick my clothes and
> my whole day in terms of what I think he'll like. I get so that I
> don't want to do anything myself. I just want to be wherever
> he is. I don't care about my own interests — me who always
> felt so independent.*
>
> *When we are together, we seem to have such fun and
> share so much. He must enjoy it as much as I do. Saying
> good-bye is so painful, especially as I don't know when I'll
> next see him. If too much time passes, I start to get a horrible
> sinking feeling that I'll never hear from him again, that he's
> mad at me or just lost interest, or that he has disappeared. I
> feel abandoned, incomplete. In my mind I do endless re-runs
> of our last time together, looking for what I did wrong or how
> it could have gone differently. I keep trying to remember ways
> that I might have been insensitive or stupid in whatever I said
> or didn't say. I feel so confused. Sometimes I think that
> perhaps it's me that got things mixed up. Maybe he did say
> something definite about getting together again and I forgot.
> I start praying that he'll call and not be angry or upset with me,
> or think I'm just a bother.*

I hungrily wait in ear shot of the phone, sometimes planning my entire schedule around being near it. My day is ruined if he doesn't call. When a call finally does come, I feel like a sentenced convict that has been given a reprieve. Suddenly life is beautiful again. Nothing else matters. The void within me is no longer there. But the feeling doesn't last. If too much time again goes by, I am back in the black hole. It's as if I need a regular fix of constant reassurances to know that I'm okay, and that he's still there and hasn't forgotten me.

I can't get him out of my thoughts. I know he's been hurt by women in the past, and is probably afraid of getting hurt again. But I'd do anything for him. I'm sure I could make him happy. Oh God how I love him. I can't imagine life without him

The above may sound a bit reminiscent of an abandoned child, feeling lost without parents nearby. *As you will later see, all compulsive patterns at some level are indeed adult variations of that old basic scenario.*

No longer a "side dish," a habit can become the main entree, the be-all and end-all of your existence. The thought of leading your life without your "habit" feels desolate and empty, like you'd never be able to have fun again if you couldn't indulge. If it goes to excess, you almost exclusively stay in environments and associate with people who indulge in or support your habit, and you spend less and less attention on your family and other friends.

You may feel as if you are leading a double life — what you present to others as opposed to your increasing preoccupation with your compulsive pattern. The latter may gradually become the only life that feels real. You literally live for the next indulgence, the central axis around which the rest of your life is organized.

• *Is your career, your family, or your marriage in jeopardy? Have you victimized other people? Have moral and/or legal boundaries been crossed?*

The worst scenarios for compulsive living can unfortunately be tragic. Regardless what form the patterns initially took, if unchecked, they steadily and unmercifully take over like a cancer, infiltrating all of your thinking, activities and relationships. Attention to other areas of life tapers off radically. Simple daily routines feel like major chores. Letters remain unwritten, bills unpaid, and your appearance ignored. This can be accompanied by a physical, emotional, social, and even moral deterioration, leaving you quite debilitated:

• If alcohol or other chemical substances have been abused, there may be damage to your liver, brain, nasal septum, skin, reproductive system.

• Family relationships and friendships may have been under-mined, strained, or disrupted.

• Debts may have been accrued to support a habit; credit cancelled; checks forged; money stolen. Overwhelming pressures may exist for repayments. All of this may have lead to bankruptcy or poverty.

• Laws may have been broken with resultant legal entangle-ments and court orders. There may also be threats of fines or imprisonment and felony charges.

Thirty extra pounds grows to 150. Alcohol problems contribute to losing jobs and relationships. Simple fears spread to phobias that prevent you from doing any work. Occasional infidelity becomes compulsive sex with numerous partners. A not-good-enough relationship becomes one where abuse is tolerated. Small debts lead to the embezzlement of thousands of dollars and the threat of imprisonment. Dabbling in drugs progresses to dealing.

In other words, you may be living in a disaster zone wherein consequences of your indulgences are putting your health, your happiness and possibly your life in peril.

> *Friends I knew first tried cocaine for a fun high or to get rid of boredom. Not me. I started using cocaine primarily just to get through the day. I often had to deal with salesmen, and I've always been pretty shy. Lots of people take coffee breaks. I took coke breaks. I got my coke from a reliable source, and it remained a controllable part of my life for a number of years. I could concentrate better. I could work longer hours. My mind was more alert and worked faster, maybe in part because emotionally I stayed numb.*
>
> *I didn't need it. I just didn't like to be without it. In fact the*

*more I used it, the more I found I couldn't work nearly as long
or as well without it. It gave me the extra push that I learned
to count on. Yes, sometimes I guess I overdid it and felt
uncomfortably wired. At those times I was always able to get
some doctor to prescribe Valium to calm me down, telling him
some cock and bull story about extra stress at work.*

But things changed.

*I got promoted to vice president of my company. The work
demands grew and so did my own inner pressures to succeed, side by side with my insecurities as to whether I'd be
able to. My coke usage skyrocketed, especially whenever I
felt on the line to perform. It got so that I was scared to go into
a sales meeting without a few snorts.*

*Then everything went downhill in my life. Instead of me
performing better, I became a paranoid basket case. I got fired
from my job. My ten-year marriage went on the rocks and my
wife eventually walked out. I got in a series of short lived,
dead-end relationships — in too many of which we shared
nothing more than cocaine.*

*Nights felt overwhelmingly lonely. I began to freebase. I
couldn't stand the lows when I'd come off of it. I became like
a wild desperate animal looking for more. My life progressively was a nightmare.*

*At this point I'm totally dependent on my dealer. I've gone
through all my savings and my current debts are way out of
hand. In the last couple of weeks I've indiscriminately injected
into my veins whatever I could get my hands on. I'm terrified
of what's going to happen. If I don't get help I'm going to die.
That's why I'm here.*

The above saga is pieced together from my memories of what
was told to me by a man in his late thirties, looking worn and
prematurely gray, at three o'clock one morning many years ago. I
was a resident on call in the crisis clinic of a local hospital. The man
refused immediate hospitalization, saying that he first needed to
clean up some matters at home. He promised to come back several
hours later to talk about what course of action would be best for
him. He never showed up. When I called the phone number he had
given me, I was told that he was no longer staying there. I never

heard further from or about him. To me this was an unusually sad story. It was one of such a wasted life, unlikely to have had a good ending.

• *Are you depressed about particular patterns of your life? Do you feel trapped and afraid that there is no way to change? Or worse, have you felt so hopeless that you contemplated, or actually attempted suicide?*

A strikingly beautiful young woman described reaching a point where she would go to any extreme to get cocaine.

> I literally picked up strange men and did things with them that violated every thread of decency I thought I had. When I looked at what I was doing, I wanted to die. I had lost all self-esteem. I felt like I was the scum of the earth. I got increasingly careless in my drug usage and almost did myself in one night. If a friend hadn't taken me to the emergency room and talked me into going to Cocaine Anonymous, I would be dead today.

• *Have the preceding questions hit too close to home? Did you think about areas of your life that you wish would just go away?*

Compulsive patterns may indeed have you in their clutches. For it is not *what* an indulgence is per se that makes it compulsive. Of far greater importance is *how, when* and *why* it is used, what else is being avoided, and how the rest of your life is affected. At maximum you can lose your life. At minimum you can lose your enjoyment of life — and that is a tragedy in it's own right.

The good news is that your enemy is *not* invincible. The bad news is that it *is* formidable. Have faith. Though compulsive habits won't magically disappear, by learning more about them you can become captain of your own fate.

"WHY DO I DO THIS TO MYSELF?"

Coping On The Outside, Hurting On The Inside

I'm in too much pain to allow the rest of my life to exist.
— A workaholic

*W*hen my oldest was four years old, upset about something and still sucking her thumb, I asked her how it felt. I hoped to finally get a bit of wisdom that would unlock the compulsive riddle. She sat a moment, looked thoughtful and said, "Good." Though I had counted on far more specifics, perhaps that's as much of an answer as we'll ever get.

Why do rational people engage in self-destructive habits when the human cost is so high? It may not immediately be apparent. To shed light on this quandary, we must investigate further.

On the outside, most of us who are caught into compulsive patterns seem to have so much. We're responsible, conscientious hard workers — always there to help. Others think we have it all together. They don't know what's going on underneath the surface, as our inner pain and struggles are frequently quite well hidden.

Though we may *appear* to be carrying off everything effort-lessly, inside we're often hurting too much and not enjoying life enough. When pressures get uncomfortable, we're driven by patterns that don't seem to make sense. Sometimes we stuff down our tension with the overuse of substances. Other times we inappropriately lean on relationships. Still other times, we compulsively escape into work or activities. Our paths of temporary relief differ. But common to all is that they serve as a catch-all way to feel better.

The following are functions that compulsive patterns can fill:

- self-nurturing, comfort, as a barrier against isolation;
- maintaining our identities, compensating for insecurities;
- tranquilizers — lessening uncomfortable feelings;
- relaxation, recreation, filling time;
- excitement, combating boredom and depression;
- a means of avoiding dealing with other life issues.
- a form of ongoing rebellion.

Though there is some overlap in these functions, for greater clarity I want to discuss each separately. When you enter the recovery process, the more you are aware which function a specific habit is filling at a given moment, the easier it will become to nip compulsive indulging in the bud. For you will then be able to address the need directly and shift into non-compulsive solutions, thereby avoiding self-destructive detours.

- *Self-nurturing, comfort, as a barrier against isolation.* When no one else takes care of us and heals our wounds (many of which we don't even know we have), when we feel that others have abandoned us, when our needs feel overwhelming, we have learned to turn to compulsive living patterns for the nurturing and comfort that make us feel okay. We cling to familiar habits, desperately trying to feel safe, self-sufficient, and satisfied.

All day I'm under a lot of pressure. I feel pulled in every direction by others. In contrast, evenings feel empty and forever. I've gotten in the habit of taking a drink when I'm lonely or tense, or exhausted, or bored. Or just taking a drink to take a drink. It's becoming increasingly difficult to relax or have fun without liquor.

The woman telling me this story was not by any stretch of the imagination the stereotype of an irresponsible alcoholic. Rather, she was a well respected fourth grade school teacher.

I don't want to think about the fact that my social life is pretty non-existent. In fact I've grown to look forward to being alone, so that I can indulge without comments from or excuses to others. Now I don't need anyone. I can take care of myself. Nothing and no one else seems that important. There's no risk of being hurt or let down. It's all so much easier. People say a true alcoholic drinks alone. Not me. I drink with Geronimo, my dog.

While we are indulging, the rest of the world seems less threatening, less rejecting, less immediate. Momentarily we feel independent of it, insulated from a vulnerability to its whims. A partner may have stood us up, just walked out, or hurt our feelings; at work we may have been passed over, discounted, or been underappreciated; friends or relatives may have slighted or neglected us. We have learned how to make none of this matter. We know how to detach ourselves from the excruciating pain. As an updated version of the forever dependable thumb to suck and security blanket, we have found habits that are unconditionally there for us.

• *Maintaining our identities, compensating for insecurities.* For many of us, right beneath our facade of competence lurks a scared, insecure child, quite overwhelmed by the task of trying to be an adult. And yet, every day life presents us with difficult challenges. We are supposed to be socially agile, make competent work decisions without faltering, and feel good about who we are and where we are going. In addition, everyone wants a piece of us — our family members, our friends, bosses, coworkers.

Many years ago, Henry David Thoreau wrote, "We're here to do something, not everything." We who struggle with compulsive habits have never properly learned this truth. Our lives are over-extended and over-committed. We feel responsible for everything and everyone. Our children have last minute needs and we drop all our own. Bills pile up and we fill extra time with more money-earning activities. Friends or loved ones have problems and we put aside attending to our own. We are unable to separate out what is essential to do and what to let slide. We spread ourselves too thin and have little idea how to delegate and say "no" to others. We are left feeling frazzled and fragmented.

Often, to reconstitute ourselves we retreat from the world by spacing out with familiar compulsive patterns — drinking, smoking, eating, television. We lose ourselves in such habits, and emotionally and mentally remove ourselves from all the pressures and demands of the world. Walled off into our safe fortresses, we attempt to get back on our feet. Sometimes these patterns virtually hold us together and help us maintain our sanity. Like a safety pin on a ripped shirt, they prevent us from coming apart.

When we lack confidence, our habits may serve to shore us up. Look what often happens before we meet someone new. We bolster ourselves with a drink, new clothes, or whatever will help us present a surface that doesn't give away our underlying insecurity and fears. Or we compulsively flirt in an inappropriate way. Or perhaps we become so terrified of the encounter that we stay away altogether, burying ourselves in work and rationalizing that we shouldn't be taking time off.

I remember hearing a story of what happened to F. Scott Fitzgerald when he first met Gertrude Stein. He was said to have been immensely worried that she would not take him seriously. Trying to obliterate his anxiety, he apparently stopped at every roadside tavern along the route to their meeting place. Needless to say, he was not functioning at his best when they finally met.

After many months of therapy, a middle-aged woman was finally able to understand her promiscuity:

> When I meet a new man, I get terribly scared. On the one hand, I'm afraid he won't like me for me — that he'll just walk off and leave and not care. On the other hand, I feel that if I get too close I'm going to lose me, I'll get swallowed up. I'm beginning to see what I do to try to protect myself. I transform non-sexual vulnerable feelings into sexual ones. And Lord, what embarrassments I've created for myself.

Another variation of handling vulnerable feelings and the fear of losing one's identity is to compulsively "glom" onto someone else. When we feel incomplete, this kind of attachment gives us the illusion of being whole. The problem is that such relationships pull us back into a dependency similar to what we experienced as children, which in turn makes us feel even more vulnerable.

> I miss her so much when she's not with me. We're so right together. I couldn't just be imagining it. And yet, each time she visits and leaves to stay with her girlfriend, it's like she takes part of me with her. It feels horrible when she isn't close by or in touch with me. If she doesn't phone regularly, I pace around and can't get anything done. I keep trying to reassure myself that maybe she has gotten too busy with work projects.
>
> I'm almost ashamed to say this, but a number of times I've called her, just to hear her voice, and then hung up. I've even driven by where she's staying, wondering if she is there with some other man, imagining that she is feeling close to him in a way that she can't with me. I wish she could understand how much I love her and need her, and give me another chance.

Though sounding like a teen-ager with a crush, this was actually told to me by a middle-aged, well-respected executive, speaking about his latest girlfriend.

• *Tranquilizers — lessening uncomfortable feelings.* For most of us plagued by compulsive patterns, strong feelings not only scare us, but worse yet, make us feel out of control. This devastates us. What is ironic is that we are often unaware of *which* feeling it is that is overwhelming us. We have tremendous difficulty differentiating whether we are tired, anxious, guilty, angry, frustrated, lonely, depressed, embarrassed, ashamed, jubilant — you name it.

A twenty-six-year-old woman described how she all too often handled the agony of being forever dangled by a man who was never there:

> He says he'll call — sometimes he does — usually he doesn't. Still, I count the hours and minutes in anticipation. All I can think of is the phone call. Then I can't stand the tension

and I start to overeat. Pretty soon I'm enough out of it and feel so fat and horrible that it doesn't matter that the phone never rings. But it still does matter, much too much. It's just that when I'm stuffed, the pain feels manageable.

Or think about what happens to so many of us at the end of the day. We may generally feel at lose ends and compulsively head for the liquor or drug cabinet, the refrigerator, the stores, some place to pick up a new conquest. We are not even sure *why* we are so compelled to anesthetize ourselves, much less what we are actually feeling. In fact, we may only be conscious of being drawn *toward* a particular pattern, and not that we are running *away* from something.

Regardless of what initially set off a compulsive reaction, the outcome is the same. Once engaged in a particular habit, your relationship with the rest of the world becomes diluted and your feelings and concerns become numbed.

• *Relaxation, recreation, filling time.* Compulsive patterns unfortunately offer endless possibilities for filling and killing time. You can stay busy and distracted, compulsively doing and frantically undoing the consequences of your self-destructive living style.

When there is nothing else going on or you are too lazy to find something, you easily grab your pattern of choice to unwind, space out, and occupy yourself. These diversions become full fledged recreations, occupying a treasured place in Your days, weeks, and life. You may greatly look forward to your indulgences, which can seduce you ever more powerfully from other healthier ways to relax.

I initially started smoking when I was fourteen. I felt it made me look sophisticated and "cool." But now I am completely hooked. I have no choice. It has become a part of me. I smoke to get myself going in the morning, to slow me down when I feel I am going off in all directions, to pick me up, to fill time when nothing else is going on, to relax, as part of socializing, when I'm alone, to end a meal, to end making love — in other words, practically all the time. I get a gnawing

*hunger for a cigarette when I haven't smoked for twenty
minutes or so.*

*A highlight of my day is just lighting up. It somehow makes
me feel comfortable and relaxed. I savor the whole process
— handling the cigarette, all the steps involved in lighting up,
watching the smoke as I exhale. Sometimes I've even lit up
a new cigarette without realizing I already have one in the
ashtray — or actually in my mouth.*

This was a forty-eight-year-old electrician reflecting on his habit.

You may have used your indulgences for so many years that
you have long forgotten other forms of recreation, which now feel
like they require too much precious energy.

• *Excitement, combating boredom and depression.* Those of us
who engage in compulsive patterns have a low tolerance for
boredom. If life feels too "daily," or there is too much "between"
time, we start to get fidgety. Eventually we may even begin to feel
as if we are going out of our minds, totally unraveling. From long
ago, we have learned that all of this can be handled by pushing
ourselves in a way that provides an adrenaline rush. The high drama
of compulsive patterns offers exactly that — the pressure, the
secrecy, the feeling of being "bad," the trying to avoid being
discovered or caught. But the fun costs a pretty penny.

*I've never told anyone about this before. Ever since I was
nine or ten years old, once in a while when I'm in a store, for
no apparent reason, I'll decide to pocket some small item
without paying for it. It could be a trinket from a dime store,
something from a supermarket, a small inexpensive piece of
jewelry from a department store.*

*I have no idea why I do this. I can't say I really need the
item, and if I did, I could certainly afford to buy it. There's
obviously some kind of thrill I get out of taking something that's
not mine, and getting away with it. No one knows and no one
finds out. It's just my secret — a little excitement that I guess
I don't have enough of in my day to day doings. I keep telling
myself to stop this nonsense. If anybody ever caught me I'd
be devastated. It could ruin my career. But I'm never convinced I won't do it again.*

This was related to me by a fairly depressed young woman in the course of our searching for what she did for fun in her life.

Incidentally, it is not uncommon to hear shoplifters report getting an orgasm when slipping a stolen item into a purse. This most likely comes from the high of risking being caught.

If you continually live on the edge, stay in the fast lane, move from one catastrophe to the next — hooked on and absorbed in the sensation of danger — you may, sadly, grow to need all this in order to feel alive and okay.

People seeking help sometimes have a vague sense that some of their driven habits are covering over emotional pain. Such was the case for a single executive whose life was chaotically compulsive in a number of areas.

I have gotten into an idiotic routine. I deprive myself all day, working through lunch, coffee breaks and even through dinner to log up overtime pay. Then I don't know what comes over me. I hit every department store that I can still find open, arriving home in a sort of delirium of beautiful new outfits, and a ton of guilt. Sometimes the clothes even remain in the bags unopened. What's insane is that no matter how much I look fantastic on the outside, I still feel rotten on the inside.

Living compulsively, you never find comfort and solace in peacefully smelling the flowers along life's journey. Instead, you stay frantically busy getting in and out of detours that are often disastrous.

• *A means of avoiding facing other life issues.* Though we claim to be uncomfortable with our compulsive patterns, they provide dividends that we don't like to acknowledge. As we have seen, our habits swallow up an enormous amount of time and energy and distract us from dealing with other challenges — within ourselves, our relationships, and our work.

Patients often find that even once they are progressing well in their therapy, compulsive living habits keep them immobilized. This was true for a thirty-three-year-old accountant who came to see me. He grew up poor, with an alcoholic father and a rigid, distant mother. He married early and unsuccessfully and had his own battle with the bottle. He had been sober and divorced for several years by the time he consulted me, but was puzzled as to why his life remained so stuck. In spite of earning a good salary, he had considerable debts, and in fact could never stay solvent very long. He often had to ask creditors to wait to cash his checks until he could cover them, and had even bounced checks on numerous occasions, though he eventually always made good.

> Not only is my life terribly lonely, but my finances are even more of a mess since I am single again and into the dating scene. This is embarrassing to admit, but especially with each new woman, I find myself spending far too much. I'm either going to an expensive restaurant, buying something unnecessarily fancy for her, or taking her off on an extravagant trip. What's worse, I've even given large sums of money to a couple of women. Ostensibly it was to help them out during tough times. Deep inside, I know it was because I wanted to impress them and hopefully make them take me more seriously. Not only did it not work, but on both occasions I myself had to borrow to get the money for them.
>
> It's getting predictable. The relationship invariably flops, I end up alone, and always further in the hole. I never get on to anything else in my life and I'm starting to feel like a real fool.

You may delude yourself into thinking that you indefinitely can put off participating in the rest of your life, by acting as if the future is forever. You say, "Some day when I get thin, get out of debt, get a better job, leave this terrible relationship, find the perfect mate,... I'll face other issues." But in reality, you remain dependent on the safety of your compulsive living cocoon and you never risk venturing further.

• *A form of ongoing rebellion.* In order to understand the whole picture, there is another factor that must be addressed. Compulsive habits are used as a means to rebel. Asserting our needs and appropriately expressing anger are *not* our strong suits, we are extremely uncomfortable when we do. Instead, to others we give the impression, and to ourselves the illusion, that we are doing what is expected. But at the same time, we indulge in patterns that in essence say,

"To hell with everyone."
"I don't need anyone."
"I have my own ways of taking care of myself."
"It's nobody's damn business what I do."

Part of the unfinished business of the past is that we continue to fight against what we perceive as a world full of unreachable standards, unfulfillable expectations and overwhelming pressures. Like the little children we used to be, in large part we conform. But in other ways we eternally rebel through our compulsive habits.

Let me illustrate a childhood version of this. I remember the antics of a three-year-old girl in a nursery school that I was visiting. I was told that normally this little girl was the picture of cooperation. But today, the day her mother was helping, she didn't want to put her toys away. She threw a dilly of a performance, lying on the floor and kicking and screaming at top volume. Soon she noticed that her mother was not in the same room. She quickly and coolly got up, calmly walked into the other room where her mother was standing, and without skipping a beat, immediately lay down to resume her original temper tantrum. The little girl clearly needed an audience and someone to rebel against, or to her the whole production apparently felt wasted.

Compulsive patterns are similar, sort of mini-rebellions that reveal themselves in interesting ways:

• A friend of mine in a final desperate attempt to stop smoking sought out the help of a hypnotist. Under hypnosis, when asked why he kept smoking, he answered, "To 'piss off' my Dad."

• A grown woman trying to lose weight says, "I was 'good' all day. Then I was truly 'bad' in the evening when I ate all that cake and ice cream."

• A responsible foreman by day regularly gets drunk in the evenings. He makes a fool of himself yet the next day he has no memory of it.

• A competent and well organized office manager functions

differently at home. She puts off paying bills, parking tickets and income tax until she gets second and third notices. Her procrastination screams out, "I don't want to do it. I won't do it. You can't make me do it."

• A well respected, seemingly happily married man has regular secret flings.

• The loving wife of this respected man suffers in silence and has gained sixty pounds since she got married.

• A compliant child became a chronically stoned teenager.

• A woman who works through lunch and takes on everyone else's load, drinks herself into oblivion each evening at home.

• A minister hides pornographic literature in the bottom of his closet.

And so on. And so on.

All of the above are acts of protest, done in the context of having *other people or a symbol of authority to rebel against.* Originally, this was our parents, later we use others who pass through our lives. What is especially eerie is that even when there is no one else's back to hide behind, we eventually learn to have the whole battle entirely within ourselves. We carry out both sides *a capella* — our rebellious, irresponsible self which we feel is "bad" vs. our rigid, overly conscientious self which we feel is "good." We can then be all things to everyone — seeming saints who stay alive by escaping into periodic self-destructive escapades of overindulging.

Though you may want to see your compulsive habits as being statements of independence, they are actually remnants of a childish form of getting back at your parents. In essence your habits say, "See, you did such a rotten job of raising me — I'm fat/drunk/broke/ miserable and it's all your fault!"

You have to move beyond this rebellious stage in order to give up self-destructive patterns. This is an important point to understand. If not accomplished, your reactions against authority will sabotage your recovery and inevitably undermine your attempts to gain control.

Many experts believe it is not by chance that we fall into a particular substance or life pattern to abuse. They feel that the choice of habit may be heavily influenced by our dominant emotional need. If you need a feeling of calmness, a psychic numbing and satiety, you may retreat into alcohol, food, television or some other comparable low energy activity. Your drug use may be along the line of narcotics like heroin, morphine, codeine, percodan. Or you may choose sedative hypnotics such as barbituates, and antianxiety medications like Valium, Librium, Xanax, Quaaludes.

On the other hand, if you actively seek stimulation, you may get gratification through such risk-taking activities as compulsively living dangerously, gambling, or shoplifting. Your drug of choice might be amphetamines (speed) or cocaine. All of these serve to make you feel "strong and powerful," and cover up your basic feelings of helplessness and inadequacy.

Or you may want to remove yourself from reality into fantasy and mystical experiences. Then you are more likely to gravitate towards drugs such as marijuana, mescaline, and hallucinogens like LSD.

Regardless of your compulsive route, you end up coping on the outside and hurting and rebelling on the inside. You shout your impotent rage to an ever-diminishing audience, and they don't hear you. You drivenly, and often futilely, use self-destructive patterns to try to lessen your inner pain and fill your needs. They become a familiar, habitual way of living — a refuge of privacy, sustenance and relative safety in a world that feels overwhelming and undependable. You may not know how to take care of yourself, to relax, to socialize and to have fun without them. Even when this adversely affects the rest of your life, you cannot easily stop. Your desperation is too great.

Since compulsive patterns serve such a multitude of functions, no wonder it is a Herculean task to try to give them up.

Never-Ending Cycles

"Why are you drinking?" demanded the little prince.
"So that I may forget," replied the tippler.
"Forget what?" inquired the little prince,
who already was sorry for him.
"Forget that I am ashamed," the tippler confessed,
hanging his head.
"Ashamed of what?" insisted the little prince,
who wanted to help him.
"Ashamed of drinking!"
The tippler brought his speech to an end,
and shut himself up in an impregnable silence.
                    — The Little Prince by Antoine de Saint-Exupery

Why do I do this to myself? Up until two days ago, I was going along fine. I'd really been sticking with my diet. I'd lost six pounds. I could wear some of the clothes that hadn't fit for months. I felt great. And then, as usual, things started falling apart. Everybody was loading on me at work, as if I'm sup- posed to be three people. But I kept thinking about it being Friday, and I knew I'd have two days away from the office. Besides, I was looking forward to spending the weekend with Mark. At that point, I was still keeping it together as far as my eating — I wanted to look good for Mark.

Then when I got home, there was a message on my answering machine. Mark was tied up. He had to work all weekend and couldn't see me. That was the last straw. I felt like I had been kicked in the gut — like my whole world was collapsing. It felt awful. Suddenly nothing seemed important. I just wanted to eat. I went in the kitchen, got a few crackers — then started munching on this and that — cookies I had hidden from myself on a high shelf — anything I could get my hands on, including some frozen leftover cake. And so went Saturday and Sunday. God damn you Mark.

Today I woke up feeling bloated and miserable — speak about lost weekends. And to top it off, three weeks of dieting *had gone down the tubes — or should I say sewer. This is insane. I might as well be a hamster trapped in a wheel.*

These are the words of a thirty-year-old X-ray technician.

You know through the trial-and-error of your own experience that compulsive living patterns form airtight cycles which are extremely hard to break. But you can do it if you understand the dynamics of these cycles.

Emotionallly Fueled Cycles

Let us begin by looking at daily pressures that can trigger compulsive patterns. Pressures fall into two main categories:

Intrusion and suffocation: At work, school, or home there are usually many demands and too little time. These demands could arise out of external or self-imposed duties, real or imagined. They might come from people in your life who make you feel pulled in all directions — bosses, co-workers, friends, mates, parents, children, neighbors, teachers.

Your boss asks you to work overtime when you have special evening plans. Your mother, about whom you have mixed feelings, says she is about to visit you for a month. Your children ask to be chauffeured to an event, when you are exhausted. You come home from work, and every member of your family clamors for a fragment of you.

As a result of pressures like these, you feel torn into pieces, resentful of others' impositions, drained. You may or may not be aware of feeling inundated, suffocated, and intruded upon. Most likely your "native" guilt makes it difficult for you to say "no" to anyone or anything. So you swallow your anger, and it smolders silently deep inside.

I was surprised when a well dressed, thirty-eight-year-old real estate broker, who looked calm and collected, disclosed her secret:

Nothing I do feels like it is enough. I keep running faster, yet I'm always behind. I tell myself that I have everything — a good husband, healthy children, an interesting career. I should be happy but I'm not. I'm totally overwhelmed. Xanax prevents me from coming unglued.

Similar feelings may be brought about by situations in which you feel undermined or invalidated, either at work or at home.

Rejection and abandonment: Here the situation is practically the opposite from the previous one. In this case, you don't feel connected *enough* to others. The cause may be an ongoing lonely life-style or particular predicaments that make you feel deserted — like being stood up for an appointment; a relationship not working out; not getting a promotion; unstructured free time; and so on.

Nick was having a difficult time in the five months since his marriage had broken up.

> *I hate being home in the evenings and on weekends. I rattle around my apartment and can't get interested in anything. When I was first on my own, I'd call up any woman I could reach, making dates with some and just talking to others. But none of these women really meant anything to me and I'd feel as alone when I was with one as if I were actually alone. Then I tried going to a Spanish class at the University. I even volunteered to do extra projects at the office so that I'd end up staying there later. Lately, I haven't even wanted to muster up the energy to go out. I simply put on the TV, have a few beers, and wait it out until I practically fall asleep.*

You feel a sense of loss, as if the rest of the world has walked out, and you have been left all alone. People may be physically in your life, but you feel removed from them and emotionally unfulfilled by them. This can arise from expecting too much of others, getting too little, or a combination of both. Whatever the cause, the resultant feelings are of abandonment and rejection.

* * *

Now let's see what happens in the next step of the cycle, after either of these pressures leaves you feeling overwhelmed. You are tipped back into an *unendingly lonely, helpless feeling,* very much like what is felt by small children, especially those who have been under-protected in their early years. This is frightening and you have difficulty riding it through. As a friend said to me right after her divorce, "I feel like a four-year-old-orphan suddenly plunked down in the middle of Africa, and I'll never get out or see a living soul again." A nonaddictive individual could better weather such feelings without becoming so desperate.

In this regressed state, you feel confused and uncertain. Time seems to be forever, decisions are hard to make, and you have no confidence in yourself. It's as if you are in a strange trance — at loose ends, fidgety, an outsider, terribly alone. The result is an empty, global hunger that feels paralyzing. A patient of mine felt this way after a much-looked-forward-to date that never happened. "I feel so foolish," she said:

> *He shouldn't mean this much to me. I obviously mean nothing to him — I don't matter at all to him. I feel like I'm completely vulnerable, bare. I'm not holding back anything, and he just tramples on me. I feel like I'm invisible — like I don't exist — like I don't want to exist. The pain is so great. I don't want anyone to know how bad I feel or they would lose all respect for me.*
>
> *It's just like when I was a kid — always waiting, always waiting. I never knew when anyone would be there for me. It hurt so damn much. I always had to take care of everyone else. No one took care of me. How could they do that to me — be so insensitive to my needs and feelings? They were so damn selfish. They had no capacity to care. And I kept accommodating my whole damn life trying to get a little attention from them. I always hoped it could be different.*
>
> *And now I keep getting involved with people who aren't there for me. They keep ripping into that old pain. I can't stand it. I just want to go numb.*

It is important to point out that this primitive, child-like stage may pass by you unnoticed. Later when you start to give up your compulsive habits and move into recovery, you can learn to spot, understand, ride through and effectively deal with this all-encompassing feeling of emptiness.

Any of us who has fully experienced this "generic," emotionally hungry state, is well aware of how devastating and horrible it is — practically unbearable. Hence we *unconsciously transform it into a specific "hunger,"* along the lines of whatever our particular compulsive pattern is. In other words, seemingly out of the clear blue, comes a sudden want for something to eat, a drink, a cigarette, a warm body, a poker game — whatever. This shift from a general to a specific hunger is *not* under conscious control. It automatically follows old paths that have been laid down long ago.

Such a conversion is illustrated in the words of this man as he describes what he goes through when weekend plans don't work out:

> I feel a pervasive nothingness. It's not a real depression. It's not a sadness. It's just nothing. It's not as if there is something I do want to do. It's more that I don't want to do anything. I feel frozen — like I could sit for hours staring. I have no energy to even move.

When I asked what got him out of this, he replied,

> If I have to wait it out, eventually I get my energy back. But that's not what usually happens. Instead I begin to get this unbelievable craving for a drink, and I drink until I pass out. When I wake up, guilt and my hangover are all I can think about.

Another man described what being stressed leads him to do:

> Though I'm trying to cut down on my smoking, when tension is high between my wife and me, I feel awful — right in the pit of my stomach. Before I know it, I'm out on the porch, lighting up. Not just one, but two or three. In fact, within a few hours, I've gone through a whole pack.
>
> While I'm smoking, it's like I'm in another reality. Momentarily I feel safe — complete within myself. Nothing bothers me. It feels so good not to have to care about anything else, or anyone's needs but my own. The rest of my life feels distant and less upsetting — like who cares. For a spell the inner calmness is terrific. Tomorrow I'll worry about my lungs and my health.

What happens of course depends on the *availability* of the specific substance, activity, person or escape that fits your particular style of compulsivity. For example, for a foodaholic, alcoholic, spendaholic, or sexaholic, whether or not food, alcohol, money and the places to spend it, or sex are actually accessible will determine if the impulse turns into action. *The greater the underlying emotional pain is, the more you will be driven into your compulsive* pattern *for diversional excitement.* If the urge to indulge is overwhelmingly strong, you may actively seek out a situation in which to satisfy your craving — going out for food, alcohol, purchases, or a partner.

> *Sometimes when I'm alone I can handle it. But other times I get this terrible "antsy" feeling. It's unbearable. I start thinking I've got to find some woman to be with. No matter what hour it is, if I'm desperate enough I'll cruise around until I come across an innocent, trusting woman — in the park, along the street, in the supermarket. I'm like a master fisherman. I've got my "take pity on me" sob stories so well perfected that I can always lure someone back to my apartment. After we're together, it's like I can finally relax. I try to be nice to the woman. I don't want to hurt anyone.*

This was told to me by a thirty-three-year-old divorced mailman, who was also a conscienscious father of two young sons.

You may become obsessed with the ritualization of a particular compulsive pattern — using certain utensils or tools; being in a specific room or place. While you indulge in your chosen substance or activity, momentarily you move into a sort of altered state of consciousness. At such moments, you feel comfortable, "merged," no longer vulnerable. You and your habit become inextricably bound together and you feel protected. Depending on the nature of your particular pattern, thoughts about the outside world and the consequences of your acts are more or less blocked out. Obviously, drugs can completely obliterate consciousness, whereas compulsive house cleaning still leaves you aware and, I might add, better prepared for drop-in friends than if you are drunk.

During this getting-away-from-it all stage, something or someone may interrupt your indulging — a sudden phone call, an overriding thought, an unexpected visitor. These disruptions can sometimes jolt you out of your dazed condition back into adult reality.

On the other hand, if your compulsive pattern runs its course and you indulge yourself fully, your original discomfort is temporarily lessened. You then end up feeling somewhat better with, at least, a partial distancing from the pressures and pain that triggered your indulging. Consider, though, that the original source of tension has *not* been addressed, for you have merely detoured into a "non-solution."

Depending on the specific habit, the degree of diversion it offers and the satiety that you achieve, you may move further into a disconnected, numb state, or even fall asleep. You might find that you don't even remember details about what you did.

The following stage of the cycle will be influenced by how specific patterns impact on your life. You might have a chemical hangover or emotional aftereffects — guilt, shame, embarrassment. There may be physical, social, financial and/or legal consequences that compound the general discomfort — a weight gain, increase of debts, getting further behind in work, a spouse walking out. If all of this contributes to feeling too distressed, it can re-trigger further compulsive indulging.

> After I go on one of my many spending sprees, the reality of what I've just done hits me and I feel horrible. It's so stupid the way I've spent money on clothes, jewelry and stuff I don't need. Here I am, a grown up woman, practically OD-ing in the stores. If anyone knew the way I buy things, they'd think I was loony. I keep vowing to myself that I'll never do it again. I feel so guilty that I usually get motivated to do something that needs doing — write a letter, clean up or do a chore that I normally put off. For a short time I miraculously feel better — but it doesn't last.
>
> The next day I feel rotten and I worry about how to pay off the mounting bills. It's hard to get out of bed, hard to get going into the day. All too often, I feel so terrible about myself that — this sounds insane — I go buy something else to take my mind off my worries.

This was told to me through tears by a bright young office manager.

The degree to which you are locked into emotionally fueled cycles is determined by how much perspective you have and whether you can interrupt the process and cut your losses. Otherwise, if more situations come your way that make you feel suffocated and intruded upon or rejected and abandoned, you will be even more vulnerable and likely to compulsively escape. And the cycles roll on endlessly.

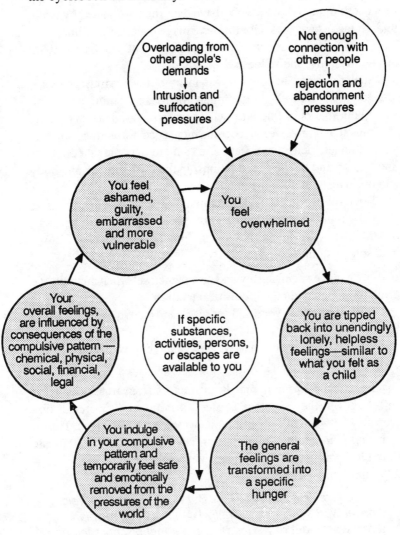

How Emotions Fuel Compulsive Cycles

Mentally Fueled Cycles

What we think about ourselves and how we view life also propels damaging cycles of dependence.

Those of us who use compulsive patterns are plagued by many underlying insecurities. Our thinking may go along these lines: "At base I am nobody. I am inadequate, incompetent, and bad. My life has no meaning, and it doesn't feel good."

Such thoughts are coupled with ideas of how we must compensate for the perceived shortcomings, that is, becoming or having something that is in line with whatever family and society value. We think that if only we can become more successful, more socially agile, thinner, richer, more attractive, more accomplished, better dressed, or find the perfect relationship then we will be somebody and our lives will have meaning.

What follows is a terrible dilemma. While we chase this elusive state of happiness to compensate for our insecurities, we bury our frustrations in the precise habits that impede our progress. Let me give some examples:

• We crave social agility and acceptance yet when anxious, we drink too much and make fools of ourselves.

• We long to be svelte and sophisticated but we overeat and get fatter.

• We want to appear like we have it all, but we overspend and end up sweating our debts.

The escapes *do* temporarily distract us from frustrations and suffering. But they sabotage success, leaving an ever greater discrepancy between our goals and the way we see ourselves. This in turn causes more emotional discomfort which we try to eradicate through more compulsive escapes. We are then caught in a "Catch-22" situation.

I'd give anything to be thin. But when I try to lose weight, it never works out. Occasionally I can stick with my plans for a few weeks but never longer. I either get discouraged and furious at myself for not losing more, or I feel deprived. One way or another, I'm soon back to my old "pigging out." No matter what I do, it doesn't work.

So complained a sad looking college student.

> *I have never been grossly overweight — no more than a maximum of twenty or so pounds. But during waking hours, it's rarely out of my mind. I always compare myself to everyone else. When I walk into a room, in an instant I size up who is fatter or thinner than me. This sounds dumb, but I feel superior to the former and very much inferior to the latter. Especially when I'm at my heaviest, I feel ugly and that everyone is looking at me and feeling sorry for me. Once in awhile, I almost weigh what I want to and I feel so good about myself. But it doesn't last. I envy people who are able to stay thin.*

It is a pathetic struggle — to indulge or not to indulge. We seek nirvana, fail to find it, and attempt to obliterate our pain with further indulgences. But our indulging actually undermines the possibility of our ever reaching nirvana. So we wall ourselves into no-win situations that are difficult to reverse.

Behavioral Cycles

When discomfort arises, without thinking, we automatically return to familiar methods of alleviating it. Here are some specific triggers that frequently set off compulsive patterns:

People — urging you to indulge or indulging around you. For instance, when you are at your parents' house and are pushed to have seconds, in spite of wanting to lose weight, you dutifully keep eating. Displeasing others makes you uneasy. So, you try not to make waves.

Situations — deadlines, vacations, holidays, parties, particular sights or smells, Friday or Saturday evenings, weekends. As an example, though you may be in debt, at Christmas you buy gifts you can't afford "because it is Christmas."

Times of day — after work, evenings, before bedtime. At the end of the day you may head for the bar without giving it a second thought.

Feelings — tired, happy, sad, lonely, bored, upset, angry, rushed, discouraged. After a frustrating week at work, you rush up to the mountains to go to the casinos, because, "How else can you unwind?"

Activities — socializing, relaxing, celebrating, traveling, visiting, entertaining. Whenever you get together with friends, you invariably smoke because for you it goes hand-in-hand with socializing.

You may not be consciously aware how these kinds of triggers lead you to your vices. But they do.

Defensive Cycles

One habit can serve as a means of avoiding another. You might try to offset a particular pattern by indulging in what seems like a less objectionable one. For example, compulsive infidelity may function as a way to not become too dependent on any one person; alcohol may be consumed in an attempt to avoid over-eating; compululsive exercising may be used to try to control drinking.

One woman who worked for years to get her life in control recalled her adolescent struggles.

> In high school, an occasional drink blocked out some of the pain that was always with me. It also blocked out how ashamed I felt about all the escapades I was starting to have with boys. In addition, I began to overeat. But it so scared me to get fat, that the risk of drinking seemed the lesser of two evils.

A real estate broker described the progression of his compulsive patterns:

> I used to drink and smoke heavily and tried to cut down for years. Then all this fitness craze came in and I became obsessed with getting into better shape. First it was just jogging and aerobics. During this time, without thinking about it, my drinking and smoking lessened considerably, which felt great. But then running started to take over my life. The 10-K (ten kilometer race) has hooked me completely.
>
> Sometimes I've run in spite of injuries and my doctor's advice to take time off. I am not only addicted to running more and more 10-Ks, but to basking in all the excitement that

> surrounds them — the pre-race rituals and tension, the chal-
> lenge of a new personal record, the time and effort that I take
> to buy just the right footwear and outfits, the endless post-
> mortems on the race with friends. I also find myself hungrily
> devouring the sports page and running magazines so as not
> to miss a 10-K race, which I will travel increasing distances
> to find. Talk of running seeps into practically all of my conver-
> sations.
>
> The rest of my life is slowly going to the back burner. In
> spite of needing the money, lately I've even turned down a
> few jobs because they interfered with my training schedule.

Compulsive cycles can run on endlessly, gathering speed and intensity, unless something jolts their courses. Each stage feeds into the next in predictable ways. The situation is serious and needs attention. To eventually make changes, you must attack all parts of the cycles.

A Well Defended Status Quo

We are never deceived; we deceive ourselves.
— Goethe

A woman called me late one evening, alarmed about her husband. He was forty-nine years old, regularly worked long hours, rarely took time off, and when he did, he was never without a drink and a cigarette in hand. They had three sons. He spent little time with the family unless she pushed him to take a vacation. Two months before, he had had a heart attack. He was now home and medically doing well, but she felt he wasn't his usual self. When they came into my office, she was notably anxious and he was indeed quite depressed. He told me he had always worked hard and long hours, felt lost since his heart attack, and frightened that he would never be able to get back to work again.

I saw him alone for two more visits. He spoke of a legacy of sadness from a barren childhood of loneliness. He had left home at age sixteen and worked himself up the corporate ladder. He went on at length about the pain of the past and his fears of the present. The more he talked, the more he disclosed a vulnerable sensitive side of himself. He told of having heard "Cats in the Cradle," Harry Chapin's song about a father who loved his son but never took time to be with him, and the son grows up just like the father. He listened and wept. He never had time with his own father and wasn't able now to give time to his three sons. As scared as he was to open up and reveal himself, I hoped he had gotten sufficiently comfortable with me to be ready to work in therapy.

I was disappointed and saddened when his wife called a few days later to cancel his next appointment. She told me that he was feeling much better, that he didn't think he needed any additional help, but that he wanted to thank me for all I had done for him. I knew better. I had obviously not been able to do enough. I asked her to have him phone me, but subsequently heard nothing.

The following week I called him to talk about setting up another appointment. I ended up speaking to his wife again. She reiterated that things were better. Her husband was back to work and his depression appeared to have lifted. I shared with her my fears that returning to a heavy work schedule without having further therapy could be dangerous to his health. She thought my concerns were unfounded, but agreed to convey them to her husband. No more came out of the matter. I hoped that she was right.

Two years later, I received a short note from her, again thanking me for my kindness. She also informed me that her husband had died nine months before — from a second heart attack.

I always think of him when I hear "Cat's in the Cradle."

* * *

It is not only the compulsive patterns themselves that play havoc in our lives, but the impenetrable defenses that encase them. These defenses are made up of all the methods we use to blind ourselves to the effect that the habits have on us. Consciously or unconsciously, we are terrified of letting go of patterns that have served since childhood, even if they served in painful ways. In other words, as much as you may be bothered by compulsive habits and want to change them, at the same time you are probably petrified of the idea of living without them. So you remain in thinking patterns and situations that support leaving things as they are.

Most of us can be surprisingly creative in the *rationalizations we find to continue our compulsive patterns and to keep ourselves immobilized.* And we're remarkably proficient. Our rationalizations are numerous, colorful, illogical, pathetic and sometimes even humorous. We use them to:

• help minimize and deny the extent of compulsive patterns, what they are doing to our lives, and how out of control the whole situation is;

• defend our behavior and release us from responsibility for it; to put the blame elsewhere and erroneously explain why we indulge;

• justify not attempting to change;

• excuse abandonment any self-improvement program.

The following examples will probably feel all too familiar, no matter what kind of compulsive habit you have:

To minimize the patterns and deny their effects, you say:
"It's not that bad."
"I've done this since I was a kid and nothing awful has happened yet."
"Other habits are worse."
"I don't believe all the scare stuff regarding my health."
"If it really harmed people, it would be prohibited."
"I'm not hurting anyone else."
"I can control it, so I know I'm not hooked."
"This isn't irresponsible. I'm doing it for someone else."
"I can quit anytime I want to."
"I'm still a good provider/mate/parent/student."
"Everyone else does it."
"I'm using it for medicinal purposes."
"Of course I indulge while I watch TV or the movies. It wouldn't be fun if I didn't."

To defend the patterns by putting the blame elsewhere, you say:
"It's not my fault."
"I had a dreadful childhood."
"No one ever helps me."
"Nobody understands me."
"Life is tough/boring/overwhelming."
"I have a terrible job/spouse/social life."
"I didn't get a raise/promotion/date."
"My husband/wife is no good in bed/the kitchen/at work."
"All the rest of my life is occupied with taking care of others."
"Pressures are crushing down on me: My children are in trouble; my parents are moving in; my dog is sick; the maid quit; taxes are due; I'm pregnant; I'm out of work; the cold/heat wave is getting to me."
"It's a weekend/week day/holiday/family reunion/special occasion."
"My husband/wife drinks/is fat/smokes/gambles/talks too much/doesn't talk enough/is sloppy/is compulsively neat/is always late/doesn't understand me/is too intrusive/has just left."

> I've always held down a good job. I take care of family responsibilities. I never drink during work. So what if I have a few drinks every evening! Why not? I work hard and I need to unwind. I've never had an accident. I'm not hurting anyone else. I quit for three weeks last summer, so I'm sure I'm not an alcoholic.
>
> In the last few months, my wife is forever nagging me to cut down or stop drinking. I personally feel she is overreacting because her dad was an alcoholic. If I'm late, she throws a terrible scene when I get home. My drinking is none of her business. I don't complain about all the bills she runs up at the department store, nor the amount of time she spends on the phone with her mother. She should stop bugging me.

So spoke the husband of a couple who consulted me.

At this point, his wife couldn't restrain herself, and cut in:

> That's nonsense about me always shopping or talking to my mother. What am I supposed to do? He's never at home when he says he'll be. When he is, all he does is drink and

fall asleep. We never do anything together. And he lies about who he's been with. If he'd just stop drinking, maybe we could work things out.

They hurled jabs at each other, and soon were off and running. I could barely get in a word edgewise, and felt exhausted by the end of the session.

The two of them clearly had no intentions of changing. Both were attached to their styles of handling life — he to alcohol and other relationships, she to shopping and an overinvolvement with her mother. Neither wanted to take responsibility for his or her own behavior, and instead chose to see the other as the one causing the difficulties. I'm sure they are still fighting off into the sunset, pasted together by bad habits and blame.

To justify not attempting to change, you say:
"What's the use."
"It's part of me — I can't imagine my life without it."
"I'm too old to change/too young to worry."
"It's too much work to change."
"Other things are more pressing in my life."
"Some day when I'm ready, I'll work on it."
"If I quit, I'll just take up some other bad habit. So I might as well stick with what is familiar."
"Trying to change has never worked in the past."
"I'm just the kind of person who can never stay with a program."
"Statistics prove that few can permanently change anyway."
"I've got to die of something, I might as well die happy."

I know I've got to write a report by a certain deadline, but it feels like sheer agony to push myself to do it. I literally keep putting it off for weeks. Now it's almost the date that it's due. I start the morning telling myself, "This is the day." Then I find myself doing anything else — wandering around the house, doing some chore, cleaning the kitchen, making a phone call, getting a bite to eat, pacing, smoking yet another cigarette — things that I don't need to do.

As the day moves on, I not only end up pushing the paper-work out of sight into a drawer, but trying to put thoughts of it as far back out of my mind as I can. But I can't stop thinking about it. I'm always left with this gnawing feeling that I should get to it, I should be more organized, more disciplined. I'm just lazy, inadequate. I get so I totally run myself down.

I know my material. I'm a pretty good writer. If I got to work on projects on time, I could probably put out a top rate paper, and I do enjoy getting positive feedback from coworkers. I guess what's remarkable is that I can do reasonably well in spite of doing it all at the last minute.

I've read a couple of articles and books on time manage-ment. I keep starting plans with good intentions, but I soon fall back into the same rut. I invariably end up writing things at the last moment — frequently staying up most of the night. All too often I even need to ask for an extension of the deadline. I'm sure my lateness has cost me a promotion, but even that doesn't motivate me to change. Putting things off must be in my chromosomes.

So pondered a close friend of mine, struggling in a half-hearted way to figure out why he was in such a rut.

To excuse abandoning self-improvement programs, you say:
"I'm too uncomfortable/nervous/depressed without my habit."
"Keeping track and staying aware is no way to live."
"There's just too much work for too little progress."
"I'm left at loose ends — life feels too empty."
"I'll never make it anyway."
"I no longer fit in with my friends."
"I slipped, so I might as well give up."
"Even though I'm not indulging, I'm still unhappy."

Regarding his attempts to quit smoking, a patient told me:

I know it's a filthy habit — stained teeth, stained fingers, cigarette smell all over the place. And more important, I cough a lot and get short of breath. My wife and children hate to see me smoke and are always wanting me to quit. Eight years ago, after my brother-in-law got emphysema, I did quit for a few years. But then five years ago, things were overwhelming

*at work. Wouldn't you know it, I started all over again, thinking
I could stop in a few months when I wasn't so upset. Not so.
I'm back to smoking two to three packs a day, and more
hooked than ever.*

The list of rationalizations for continuing compulsive patterns
is endless. We may think they are valid reasons for indulging. They
are not. They are excuses — and often rather lame ones. We indulge
because we are unwilling to do what we have to do to *stop*
indulging.

We further fix these self-destructive habits in place by living in
if only's — "If only my parents had been different;" "If only I had
a better love life;" "If only my boss would appreciate what I do;"
"If only my children weren't so demanding." We have used this
style of thinking for so long that we've grown to believe its logic
is rational. Unfortunately it fits an unhealthy need to keep our eyes
closed, and to continue on our merry self-destructive course.

In one way or another all these rationalizations say: "Poor me.
Life is hard. Indulging is the only way I can take care of myself and
feel all right. I can't do any better. There's no use my even trying
to change." In all fairness, this may have been the reality when you
were growing up. As a child or teenager, compulsive patterns may
have been the best you could do. But that was then and this is now.
You must start to see how outdated and absurd your thinking has
become.

Games We Play

Another area in which most of us are extremely clever is
tempting fate and setting up "games" that push our limits. We are
sporting people, so we test ourselves by taking just one drink; eating
only the broken cookies; "window shopping" at an "end-of-the-
season sale"; phoning a not-good-for-us old beau "only to wish him
a happy birthday." Or we just *happen to* drive near a gambling area
or bar, or to stand near the food table at a party. Whatever our
particular weakness is, *there we are,* right in the middle of an
opportunity to indulge in it.

We put one toe into dangerous waters and try not to fall in, but continue to live on the edge of disaster. We hang around cohorts who share our habits, seeing how long we can resist joining them. And when we succumb, no one is more surprised than we are. We innocently say that "it was bad luck" and not our fault that we got out of control, as the following story of one of my patients illustrates:

> I pride myself in never being late — lateness makes me feel out of control. I also try not to arrive too early. Being too early makes me feel I haven't timed things well and I've wasted time I could be using for something else. So the result is that I try to time it so as to arrive on the button. Of course, I go crazy if traffic or anything else unexpected interferes with my plan — especially when it involves waiting, getting through any kind of red tape, or putting up with what appears to me to be other people's inefficiency. It feels as if I'm having a panic attack, like I'm caught. Things won't move, I'm stuck, there's no way out, I feel like I'm suffocating.
>
> My last minute dashes are going to give me ulcers, but I can't seem to change.

We also keep ourselves frozen by *remaining* in circumstances that feed our compulsive cycles.

We stay in pressures that overwhelm us and make us feel powerless — physically, socially and emotionally. This includes frustrating, unfulfilling or dead-end relationships and jobs. We know that these trigger our compulsive patterns. But we never lessen the pressures by directly confronting what is happening, altering the situation, or finding new ways to deal with it. Instead, we simply feel victimized, and mend our wounds with compulsive habits.

Roles We Pretend Not To Play

Most detrimental to our chances of altering compulsive scenarios are the unhealthy roles we assume in relationships that discourage our changing. In fact we may actively set them up.

• We may surround ourselves with out-and-out *seducers* and *saboteurs* who regularly push the very substances, activities, and escapes that hook us, or who in some other way undermine us. These people may actually give "presents" of addictive material or excuses to quit self-improvement programs. They sometimes say, "Just this once won't hurt you," or "Party pooper!" Or they tell horror stories — "People who try to change end up nervous. If you quit you'll probably get fat."

Seducers and saboteurs can be peers, parents, dates, mates, children, bosses, so called "friends," or even incompetent professionals. It fits their agenda not to see the part they are playing in your difficulties. They might be uncomfortable with the supposed stigma put on *them* by seeing you as having a compulsive problem. Or they may be jealous of or threatened by your self-improvement plans and recovery. Or perhaps your facing problems may make them aware of their own compulsive habits. Regardless what *their* motives are, it is *you* who continue to be influenced by their behaviors and reactions.

• There are *rescuers* who bail us out of irresponsibility. They may cover up and lie for you — tell a boss that you are sick when you're hung over. They may give you extra money when you irresponsibly spend it. These rescuers, come between your self-destructive habits and your having to face the consequences. So you never break through your denial and take responsibility for your own life. Sometimes those who mean to hold out their hands from a lifeboat actually force your head under water — in the long run.

At her parents' insistence, I saw a nineteen-year-old college student, an only child, who had been the apple of her parents' eye. "In the past, she has always been so good and has never given us any trouble," they said. Times had changed. She wasn't being "so good" any more. They were at their wits end.

She dated her problems back to age fourteen, though as I saw it, they had started long before.

> I had been going with this really fine guy — I was the envy of all my friends. Then without any warning he wanted to break up. He had met someone else. I was crushed.
> I knew it was wrong, but I went into my mother's purse, "borrowed" her Visa credit card, and charged up about $200

*on clothes and cosmetics at one of the stores. Though my
family is fairly well off, my parents were furious. Finally they
simmered down because they realized how depressed I was
about my boyfriend and I breaking up.*

*I wish I could say this was the only time, but that's not
true. It keeps happening. I honestly think my parents are
ready to disown me. I can't seem to stop doing this. I don't
understand it.*

At this point her voice trailed off and could barely be heard through
her tears.

*When I feel down, I start to feel terrible and empty. Then
I get the credit card in my hand and before I know it, I'm in the
store picking out nice clothes or makeup. Suddenly nothing
else counts. I look at myself in the mirror, trying on something
new, and I feel strong and beautiful. When I'm paying for
things, part of me knows I should just return them. But I want
them too much. No matter what the consequences with my
parents will be, at that moment it doesn't matter. It's as if I
need to buy the things, I deserve them. For awhile I feel like
I'm flying, I'm a queen.*

*Then at home the same thing always happens. I try to
cover things up. Of course my parents eventually find out. All
hell breaks lose. They get mad at me. They get mad at each
other. I promise never to do it again, and at the time, I mean
it. I really think I'll be able to control myself. But I can't, and I
don't.*

In spite of recognizing that she had a problem, this young
woman unfortunately refused to get into a support group to help her
control her compulsive spending. Nor did she stay in therapy long
enough to gain an understanding of her behavior, or to work through
underlying problems related to self-confidence and separation from
her parents. Since she had a new boyfriend, she gradually found
excuses to come less and less often to therapy, and eventually went
to another college out of state.

A later visit with her parents gave me the impression that as
loudly as they proclaimed their anger at their daughter's irresponsible behavior, they also thought it was "cute" and that she would

outgrow it. I came to see that this was an air-tight family system. Members were more content with it than they acknowledged. Nobody really wanted to change. The majority of the time this young lady remained the good, obedient daughter. Then she made an occasional rebellion through her spending sprees. Everyone was temporarily upset, but soon life returned to what is "normal" for this family. And so the cycle went. Had the daughter become more responsible and independent, her parents' shaky marriage would probably have come apart at the seams. At some level, all three of them knew this, and instead chose to endlessly play out the same story.

An important part of recovery will hinge on changing interactions with seducers, saboteurs and rescuers. And when it is not possible to alter the dialogue, there is the need for a whole new scene.

Though you would like to think of yourself as being a passive victim of the circumstances of life and of your uncontrollable drives, you are *not* an innocent bystander. You generate your own Waterloos, and design and execute your own disastrous defeats.

THE SOURCE OF COMPULSIVE LIVING

Origins And Precursors

"I can't remember a good deal of my childhood, or more correctly, I don't want to remember it. I spent those years not thinking and not feeling."
— A former patient

*A*re compulsive patterns lodged in the chromosomes? Dependent on temperament? Controlled by early family conditioning? A product of our social environment? Is their development predetermined or just chance? The jury is still out. It may always be. Experts are not in agreement. Most likely all of these factors contribute to the problem.

From my own experience and my work with patients, I feel strongly that compulsive patterns arise out of an interplay of two primary variables:

• *The texture of who we are.* This is determined by our genetically inherited strengths and vulnerabilities, and our capacity to relate to and to utilize our human and physical environment for support.

• *The human and physical environment we are born into,* and how it satisfies or frustrates our basic needs.

If the match of these two variables is a good one, we thrive. If it is not, there are any number of possible outcomes, one being the development of compulsive living patterns. It is important to see that in any given family, the relationship between these variables is different for each child. For instance, in a family where both parents are busy with their own activities, one child may be peaceful, make few demands and end up moving into a healthy life style. Another child, however, may be restless, have different needs and eventually fall into self-destructive habits.

In order to get past compulsive living and to stop being a prisoner of your childhood, you must honestly look at these early years. Otherwise you will forever be condemned to repeat the coping patterns that you developed as a child.

Family Myths and Family Realities

Growing up, in the "ideal of all worlds" in the "ideal of all families" you would have felt loved and validated just because you existed. You would have had parents that were "whole" and satisfied with their own lives, who loved and complemented each other. They would have brought you into the world as part of that love, and out of their desire to enjoy and raise the next generation. They would have had time and physical and emotional energy to really be there for you, and to meet your needs. There would have been tremendous respect for and clarity about the separateness and uniqueness of each family member. In sum, you would have been given solid "roots" and "wings" to launch you into your own independent life.

In this ideal scenario, your parents *would not* have been plagued by fear, anger, anxiety, immaturity, unresolved pain from their own pasts, irresponsibility, coldness, selfishness, depression, addictions, mental or physical illness, divorce or death.

In the real world, unfortunately, most of us have experienced only pieces of the "ideal." In fact, many of us with compulsive patterns have a hard time imagining anything remotely resembling the ideal family described above.

Instead, you might have come from a family where parents

were unavailable (emotionally, chemically [alcohol or other drugs] or physically), overwhelmed, impoverished, or actually absent. Or your parents might have been preoccupied with a sibling's or relative's difficulties, or with other pressing issues — health, financial, political. Perhaps your parents were sick, depressed, alcoholic, workaholic, mentally ill, or just tired. Any of these may have led to general turmoil — ongoing friction, broken promises, even volatile behavior. The bottom line was that the family focus was somewhere else, not on you. As valid as the problems may have been, however, the loss was yours. You have only one childhood.

Your parents might have pushed you to fill in for what *they* needed or what *they* weren't, instead of tuning into what *you* needed and who *you* were. For example, if your parents needed space when you needed hugging, you may not have received it. Or your parents may have kept you too close, reacting to their own fears and insecurities, rather than responding to your need for separation. All of this made you feel that your needs were unimportant and your feelings were invalid.

It's popular these days to refer to families with these kinds of problems as "dysfunctional." That term has been used so widely and applied so generally, however, that it has lost any precise meaning. I believe such family systems are rightfully referred to as "enmeshed." Boundaries between individuals and generations are blurred. There is tremendous confusion regarding who owns and who is responsible for whose feelings, needs and problems. This can even lead to being unsure about one's own body perimeters. Differences between family members are neither faced nor accepted. It's extremely difficult for anyone to become a separate individual, owning his or her own life.

As the family constellation grew and developed, one parent may have inappropriately formed too close an alliance with you, leaving out or actually siding against your other parent. You might have had to hear confidences from a parent regarding personal matters that were none of your business. This closeness could have involved emotional and/or physical invasion of your privacy, possibly going into varying degrees of abuse or incest. Hence parental nurturing may have come with a high price tag.

People with eating disorders frequently come from childhoods where personal boundaries were not adequately respected. Those with anorexia often come from especially "enmeshed" families. The background of Karen Carpenter, the gifted singer, sadly illustrates this. Even after she was well-established it was reported that following television interviews, her mother still called to tell her what she could have or should have or should not have said. Karen's difficulty separating herself from ostensibly well-meaning — but overly controlling and intrusive — parents undoubtedly contributed heavily to the development of her anorexia. This affected her heart which eventually led to her death. A golden voice was lost to the world, a casualty of a loving family that couldn't let go.

In families that have these sorts of dysfunctions, tremendous energy is invested in keeping up appearances and *not* acknowledging what is really going on. An "elephant in the living room" is the image coined by adult children of alcoholics to describe this family conspiracy. I believe it is an apt way to refer to all "dysfunctional family" situations. Growing up in such a family was like having an enormous elephant in your living room who left messes everywhere. In an unspoken agreement, family members went to great lengths to walk around the elephant and to not step in its messes. But *nobody* ever mentioned that the elephant even existed, nor that it affected you and your entire life style. As a child, in no way could you understand what was happening. Your observations about the situation may have been frankly denied by parents or other family members.

The end result was a crazy-making situation — the messages were contradictory, but no one questioned them:

• There is no problem.
• The "problem that doesn't exist" is caused by pressures at work, the neighbors, the high cost of living, and so on.
• It is not all right to talk about the "problem that doesn't exist."

But even if no one spoke of it, at some conscious or unconscious level you may have sensed that something *was* wrong, and that it needed correcting. If you could just be different in some way, this would "fix up" the family and allow your parents to be the strong, good, loving people that you needed. No matter what you actually observed your parents do or say, you wanted to believe that at base they were all right and would protect you. This was the only family you had, and you were too young to see how alone and frightened you really were, and that there was actually no one to shield you from the "slings and arrows" of life. So you hung on to the illusion that it was within your power to make life fair and predictable.

I want to stress two things here. First, when a family is enmeshed, or alcoholic, or otherwise "dysfunctional," *there is no single villain,* only a collection of victims all desperately locked into each other's frustrations; growing up in such a situation, children sadly become unwilling casualties of circumstances far beyond their control. Second, *nearly all parents are doing the very best they can* to make the family healthy. They may lack skills, awareness, education, money, environment — but it's a rare mother or father who lacks the *will* to be a good and loving parent.

Nevertheless, if your parents were too unavailable for consistent caretaking — to give you security, respect for your feelings, and acceptance of your separateness — you were left feeling emotionally dangled. Being little and dependent with few options for coping, you had no choice but to take any crumbs of nurturing you could get. Much of your energy would have then centered on figuring out what your family expected and would allow. Even if you had to forgo your own goals and achievements, you dared not risk being further ostracized within the family.

So you attemped to be perfect and never to fail, which may have meant that you didn't even venture into endeavors where guaranteed success wasn't built in. When projects required persistence, you had little idea of how to stick with them and follow through. You had insufficient early experience being guided to do so, or seeing adequate examples.

As a result, from early childhood you relied heavily on external cues for direction and validation — your grades, the mirror, the scale. And later — and still now — the size of your pay check and your house. No matter what you did, you never felt it was good enough. Your yearning for continued recognition was like a bottomless pit. You defined yourself primarily by what you produced and accomplished, and how others received it — frequently using unreachable standards as guidelines. Your thinking became pervaded by words like "should have," "could have," and "ought to," based on a rigid all-or-none, good-bad rating system. No room was left for human frailty and your own uniqueness.

* * *

The oldest of three, a patient I worked with remembered a lonely childhood. Not that his parents weren't good people who cared deeply about their children. It was just that at one level or another, they weren't there. He tells it this way:

> My Dad was a salesman, always on the road. I know he loved us, but when he came home he had trouble expressing it. Instead, he just dwelled on our grades — I usually got A's — and cross examined my mother as to how we kids had behaved. Mom was not an emotional person. She buried herself in her own work. She was a nurse — probably an excellent one. I only wish she had done more caretaking of us.
>
> From as far back as I can remember, I always acted grown up. Since I was the oldest and Dad was gone so much, I took over and became kind of a strict top sergeant to the younger kids. I took pride in being able to get them to clean up the house quickly and generally stay in line. My parents gave me lots of praise for doing things well and keeping everything in control. And when I kept busy I didn't feel so lonely.
>
> The difficulty is that nowadays I always need to have everything under control and I can't stand not being busy. But it's driving my girlfriend nuts because I'm always tense.

Because of having to fend for yourself at such a young age, you grew up too quickly. You sensed your parents' fragility and vulnerabilities, and learned to shore up their shaky defenses. Hyper-alert to family members' needs, you couldn't fully attend to your own. And since communication was confusing and rules were unpredictable, you became agile at living each day as if you were tiptoeing on eggshells — always second guessing what others meant and felt and wanted. As the years went by, you tolerated so much inappropriateness, and got so bogged down carefully tiptoeing, that you had little idea what normal was in yourself, much less in anyone else.

Furthermore, when you stayed busy taking care of others, you could close your eyes to your own pain and unmet needs. So you appeared to cope well. You convinced yourself that you needed no one, and no one need worry about you. You hadn't even had your first paid job, and already you were fast burning out. Robbed of a real childhood, you carried on like a trooper.

Let me add a thought. I know a few people with compulsive living patterns who feel that their childhoods did *not* in any way contribute to the development of their habits. Perhaps these people are the exception. More likely they have not delved deeply enough into the past to understand the dynamics of their families.

My thinking is that just as compulsive patterns can be blatant or subtle, the same is true for family backgrounds. An alcoholic parent who mistreats and dominates the family is obvious. More hidden is the self-absorbed parent who is physically present but never emotionally there — or not there in ways that fill a particular child's needs.

Double Lives

But there is another part of the story. Growing up, the burdens that you and your environment imposed on yourself were indeed overwhelming and at times, more than you could tolerate. But undoubtedly you were leery of showing your feelings and needs, lest you be open to further hurt. So you turned to your own means of numbing the pain and not feeling so vulnerable to the inconsistent whims of others. Gradually you found ways to get respite and to insulate yourself by becoming physically and/or emotionally distant.

You learned to protect yourself, to *seemingly* be in control, and to comfort yourself with a substance, an obsession, a compulsive activity, a direct avoidance behavior, or a state of mind. Or you might have become preoccupied with your looks, pleasing everyone, getting good grades, making trouble. It was like a secret, desperate attempt to belong to yourself, a futile rebellion to be separate from your family, a retreat into a place where you could truly indulge your needs and feelings. Only here could you feel free to be someone, to have power, and to have refuge from the "shoulds" and "have-tos" of your life.

A recovered alcoholic remembers:

> *The first time I got drunk, I was eleven. I felt on top of the world — confident, no longer shy, alive and free. In hindsight, the fact that alcohol could make that much difference in how I felt should have been a warning. But I wouldn't have paid heed. I was so tired of hurting and feeling like I was nothing.*

While growing up, these distancing patterns gave you a *temporary* semblance of relief and autonomy and made your life bearable. You could count on them. They wouldn't abandon you. Unfortunately, they also set the stage for the later development of a compulsive style of life that avoided dealing with what was too painful to handle. In addition, there was a hidden agenda — an unvoiced hope that your patterns would get you the attention that was otherwise not forthcoming. If you could just get enough A's or have enough problems, maybe someone would finally notice you and hear your cry for help. But it was all for nought. Your parents were either unaware of what you were doing, chose not to see it, or at minimum, did nothing about it.

This was the beginning of your double life — trying to show others what you thought was expected vs. hiding your inner feelings, needs, protest and shame. The ever-widening gap between the two areas grew. As you got older, these means of self-comfort, escape and rebelling became more and more important parts of your life-style.

When taken to an extreme, if your external world felt too terrifying and your inner coping resources were too meager, you may have developed separation phobias or school phobias that kept you bound to home and caretakers. Or you might have increasingly retreated into a fantasy life.

Influential Variables

Whatever pattern you fell into was not just by chance, but rather determined by a number of factors:

• *Your particular genetic sensitivities.* There is good evidence that some people are genetically predisposed to such conditions as depression and alcoholism. But are spending and compulsive womanizing also genetically pre-determined? So far there is no data to substantiate the latter hypothesis.

• *Your chronologic place in the family* and sibling order; your "assigned role" in the family drama. One child may be seen as the "trouble maker", the "crazy one," the "serious one," the "cry baby," the "lazy one," the "flirtateous one," the "irresponsible one," the "fat one," and so on. Furthermore, the impact of particular family problems on you was dependent on your temperament, your developmental age and your capacity to understand what was going on.

• *The family atmosphere* — its preoccupations and what was tolerated. When you were upset you may have been given food, drink, money, a credit card, a push to work harder, an urge to get in a relationship, or such — these then became powerful suggestions as ways to handle tension. Wherever the focus of the family was, this was the issue around which you learned to center your energy and anxiety. Sexually obsessed adults invariably were sexually overstimulated children. Adults with money problems come from families where money issues were center stage. Individuals with food-weight preoccupations grew up in food-weight conscious families.

A middle aged woman, constantly battling her weight, described her mother as being obsessed with everyone's health and figure.

> *She served all of our portions at the table, constantly advised us as to what we should eat and wear and weigh. It was as if I didn't belong to myself. I felt I had no privacy.*
>
> *From way early in my life I started sneaking food — cookies, peanut butter — and stowing it away so that I could*

indulge whenever I wanted, without her comments, criticism, and control. And I can't break the pattern.

Notice that this woman's habit stays directly in the rut that her mother set for her.

• *Examples of handling stress that surrounded you.* If a parent or other relative abused a particular substance or activity, this became a powerful suggestion to you — an "acceptable" way of managing discomfort. How other family members reacted to, compensated for, or closed their eyes to this individual's problems also became important role models.

> *Growing up was such a nightmare. All too often I remember my mother drinking herself into oblivion. I never knew whether I'd come home from school to find her in a rage at me for something I didn't even know I had done. Or maybe she'd have burnt the dinner, or simply have passed out cold on the couch. I recall too many horrible evenings hiding under the blankets, trying to block out the sounds of my parents fighting, obviously inflamed by my mother's drinking. But nobody ever talked openly about her alcohol consumption.*
>
> *Then in high school I started drinking. It helped me not think about all the unpleasantness at home. The irony is that instead of having to hear the problems between my parents, trying to control my own drinking eventually became my problem.*

An alcoholic businessman in recovery pondered on the origins of his difficulties.

This story illustrates how our patterns often reflect the family struggles themselves, a blend of the out-of-control parent and the controlling parent.

• *The part that significant others played in your life.* For some, the influence of a relative, a teacher, a neighbor, or a family friend presented another representation of reality, partially counterbalancing the impact of your immediate family.

• *Available "substances," activities, and beliefs* that existed in your environment. Where money, food, alcohol, drugs, cigarettes were readily accessible, these easily became the currency of your compulsive patterns.

> *My father was a doctor. My mother was always on a diet. Dexedrine (speed) was part of our medicine cabinet. I started using it when I was a kid, first to drop a few pounds, but eventually because it felt good and I was depressed without it. By the time I was in high school I was taking it several times a week, never big doses but very regularly. I could study longer, always feel up, and keep my weight controllable. I "dealt" dexedrine to friends long before I ever knew what a dealer was. I was aware that it probably wasn't good for me, but it had become part of my life. I felt terribly down and overwhelmed when I would stop taking it for a few days.*

A twenty-five-year-old woman described how her drug use evolved.

• *Prevailing social, community, and peer pressures,* that seduced or sanctioned your patterns. For example, if long work hours or being heavy is admired in a given culture, a sixty-hour work week or overindulging in food and being heavy may be seen as normal. This will be discussed in greater detail in the next section of the chapter.

* * *

It is important not to lose sight of the whole picture. In spite of your developing some type of "avoiding pattern," early precursors of what would later become full-blown compulsive patterns, on the surface you continued to function in terms of family expectations — to cope and to try to be "good."

Bona Fide Compulsive Living Patterns

There is a significant issue that often is overlooked. For *true* compulsive patterns to evolve, an initial good-enough relationship to a parent or parent figure had to have existed. In the first few years of your life, you must have experienced at least minimal loving care from someone. But later on, caretaking may have fallen short or been so inconsistent that your efforts to get adequate nurturing eventually became too frustrating and unfulfilling. Then in your search to find satisfaction you developed compulsive patterns so you could take care of yourself and *not* risk being let down by others.

These patterns in essence became your all purpose "security blanket" or "transitional object." They served as a desperate attempt to recapture the earliest emotional satisfactions that became too elusive as your childhood progressed.

A compulsive "saver" told me,

> *I can't bear to let go of tons of knicknacks handed down to me from my family, even though I never use any of them and I don't even like them. I guess hanging onto them is some kind of attempt to make up for the love I never got enough of.*

What is critical to see is that in those of us with genuine compulsive habits, there originally had been someone with whom we could identify and bond. This is a prerequisite for the development of a conscience which plays a leading part in the compulsive drama. In other words, we *are* able to feel guilt — in fact, often far too much of it.

Because of the early nurturing that you got, there *is* a core of health within you. It is buried, though, underneath layers of faulty thinking and self-destructive living. When you move into recovery, this healthy core can emerge and flourish.

Sociopathic Look-Alikes

I want to describe people who may *look* like you but are *not* like you — people who had devastating relationships with caretakers; people who received early nurturing that was too sparse. No deep bonding took place, nor did a conscience emerge. These people may have habits comparable to yours — overdrinking, overeating, overspending, procrastinating — but the habits of such individuals are the least of their problems.

At best, these kinds of individuals are sociopaths. At worst they are psychopaths, predators who actively seek out their victims. Sociopaths, unlike those of us with true compulsive patterns, sleep well with no self-recriminations to haunt their nights. They are *not* genuinely bothered by their habits nor how others may be victimized or affected by them.

An example of this group would be "con artists." These are individuals who enjoy setting others up or conning people out of money. Con artists feel no guilt, remorse, or sadness about hurting others, though they may fake it and pass themselves off as compulsive spenders to gain sympathy or avoid the law. The threat of a prison term is the only factor that motivates them to change.

The dishonesty of sociopaths and psychopaths is an *inextricable* part of their core character, *independent* of the habits they use. For those of us who suffer from true compulsive habits dishonesty is secondary, used to cover up the damage and guilt resulting from our patterns.

Adolescent Magnifications Of Your Patterns

But back to your history. If you're like a lot of folks, the seeds of a compulsive life style were already sown by late childhood and served

• To lessen your loneliness and vulnerability;

• To self-medicate feelings that were too uncomfortabe, anxiety provoking or guilt producing;

• To fill time, combat boredom, provide recreation, and offer excitement;

• To make you feel more actively in control of your environment;

• To rebel against people and pressures in your life.

The added stresses of adolescence — separating from family; moving out into the community; being accepted by your peers; becoming your own person — contributed to the escalation of these self-destructive habits or pushed you into new ones. Attempting to stay in control often became an all-consuming concern.

A woman with multiple addictions described her past:

Adolescence was a nightmare of trying to stay away from food. I often overate and then starved myself for days to be thin enough to be popular. I had to have a constant string of boyfriends to make me feel okay. When I was thin I bought

tons of clothes and looked great. Whenever I put on extra
pounds I felt ugly, like no one would want to be with me. So I
drank a lot and used whatever drugs I could get my hands on
to avoid overeating. But no matter what I did, I always felt out
of control.

Rather than doing full battle with the challenges of growing up, you retreated into familiar patterns of avoidance, attempting to compensate for feeling that at base you were not good enough: You drank or used drugs to feel better. You smoked to look "cool." You over-ate to feel less empty inside. You continuously bought new clothes or other items to gain approval from peers. You incessantly studied to obliterate your insecurities. You escaped into extra-curricular activities or religion for a sense of belonging. You flirted and clung to relationships to combat your lack of confidence.

One way or another you tried to drive away the pain.

But what began as a safety valve gradually pervaded your time and energy and started to take over your life. Slowly you lost touch with your own authentic sense of how you felt, what you needed, and who you were. You may not have seen it as a problem if no one else knew about your habits and you didn't get into too much trouble with them. However, there were insidious side effects of your increasing preoccupation with compulsive patterns and their cover-up. You not only denied how frighteningly out of control you were, but also how guilty, embarrassed, and ashamed you felt about these patterns and yourself. And to make matters worse, you were missing out on learning essential developmental and social skills necessary for moving out from family to community.

Always Struggling — Never Free

On the surface you may have separated from your family in adolescence and early adulthood: You lived away at school, joined the service, married, or simply moved out. You had grown tired of staying at home and parenting your parents. But even if you declared your independence and lived on your own, you were not free. Guilt and a feeling that you had betrayed and abandoned your parents were your constant companions. And underneath your fragile separateness was the terror of giving up the illusion of belonging.

No matter what physical or emotional distance you appeared to have, you remained an extension of your parents, using them as constant yardsticks for how you thought, how you behaved and how you felt. You had so internalized their preoccupations and conflicts that all of your actions were influenced by their values. You kept on trying to meet family expectations and be "good," or you avoided meeting them by acting rebellious and felt that you were "bad." You couldn't act in terms of your own needs and feelings. You hadn't learned to be comfortable with them.

Most likely you also became a master at setting up your parents to worry about you, to monitor you, and to bail you out of the consequences of your irresponsibility — even as ironically you continued to feel responsible for them. You never truly moved toward a healthy, mature separation from your family. You grew older, but you weren't growing up.

Hence, if you're among those who are trapped in compulsive patterns, your transition into adulthood in part remains unfinished. You haven't appropriately moved away from relationships that were never adequately there for you in the first place — it is too painful to leave them when they are so incomplete. At some level, you keep hoping that if you hang in long enough, you can make it all come out right and get the love and acceptance for which you still hunger.

A thirty-eight-year-old married man, still waiting, told me,

> I am grown, but I feel guilty for days if I ever say "no" to a request of my mother or engage in activities that I think she would disapprove of, even when this interferes with plans of my wife and me. So I end up tolerating a lot that I wish I wouldn't — inappropriately intrusive phone calls at all hours, questions about my personal life that are none of her business, demands and inconvenient visits. I constantly think about whether I am living up to her expectations, forever trying to please her.
>
> I wish she had more of a life of her own. She seems to live through me and expect me to live my life for her. I've been

*married for thirteen years and have three children of my own.
Still I'm being the good child and not making waves because
I'm so afraid of hurting my mother or making her mad. What
makes it truly ridiculous is that she's back on the East Coast
and I've been living out on the West Coast for over ten years.*

You not only hang onto unhealthy relationships with your
parents, but in addition, you transfer these same unhealthy patterns
onto everyone else who crosses your life — teachers, bosses, coworkers, friends, and most damaging of all, eventually onto a mate
and your own children, if you have them.

My family's cats provide a perfect example of the way unresolved childhood needs are transferred onto adult relationships.
Michaelangelo had been our pet and part of the family for some
time. Sasha joined us later. Upon her arrival, she was clearly not
accepted by Michaelangelo. The two cats hissed and avoided each
other for some time. Finally Sasha found a way to relate to
Michaelangelo which ended up being satisfactory to both of them.
Apparently weaned too early, she began a pattern of compulsively
"nursing" on his belly fur, producing what one of my daughters
calls "dreadlocks." He in turn dutifully licks her and seems to
thoroughly enjoy surrogate motherhood — some would call him
co-dependent. Friends at last, they make an odd couple. Only their
psychiatrists will know the details of their childhood fixations and
unmet adult needs.

Unconsciously you set up situations that replicate your
childhood, like picking an emotionally "damaged" partner. You
become involved with someone who is "broken" and then vainly
try to fix him or her up, to help that person in ways that no one ever
helped you. Or you select a partner who has a need to be a
"caretaker," wanting this person to save and protect you. You may
become stuck in such a relationship — forever hoping, never
receiving and always hurting. But you pay a price for submerging
your own identity and needs. As you stuff down your feelings, the
compulsive merry-go-round goes faster.

It is also important to point out that as you move along in life,
a hodgepodge of pressures, losses and successes are dealt to
everyone. If you are already on the compulsive track, these easily

become excuses to act out your preoccupations or to further indulge in familiar habits. You may *claim* that your drinking, drugging, affairs, driven work, overeating, over-exercising started when fate hit you. Nonsense. A particular event simply gave you an excuse to increase the pace of your irresponsibility.

Society's Pressures And Seductions

> *Fanaticism consists in redoubling your efforts when you have forgotten your aim.*
>
> — George Santayana

They often see each other at the local bar. They live in the same neighborhood, in comparable run-down hotels. The life of each has become a shambles because of alcohol. Family and work are long forgotten.

Sitting on bar stools beside each other, they cling tightly to glasses that make little wet circles on the counter. Time hangs heavy in their wasted lives. They speak together of this and that and have a seeming conversation. But neither can break the loneliness of the other.

Vulnerable People Face To Face With Life

Just as many of us grow up in less-than-perfect families, all of us live in environments that may be comparably imperfect and which can contribute significantly to our problems. But we cannot blame society solely for our personal habits — not everyone in any given culture develops compulsive patterns.

If family life (which was really your initial society) has not adequately helped you develop inner resources to cope with the world at large, you are left merely masquerading as an adult. Underneath your facade of apparent competence is a fear of being your own person, an insatiable need for social approval, and a rigid impractical overdeveloped conscience. This makes you especially vulnerable to contradictory messages that come into your life from the environment: To excel but not to stand out; to be unique and yet be a good team player; to follow the beat of your own "drummer" while conforming to everyone else's; to take "the road less traveled" but not a socially unapproved one; and so on.

Your sense of reality is further undermined by the fact that we all arrive at adulthood having been told that everyone is equal, life is fair, and opportunities are justly available for all. Doesn't it then follow that if you're not getting what you deserve the fault must lie within you? The world is supposed to be your oyster isn't it? Why aren't you finding the pearls? Once again you're confronted with a social ideal that discounts the inequalities that you have grown up with, as well as your awareness of what actually exists in the workplace and elsewhere.

And, as in childhood, you continue to get few clear guidelines, a lack of helpful traditions, and too little support. You may, like many of us, live far from where you were born, away from your family of origin, and in impersonal circumstances of minimal, if any, feeling of neighborhood or community belonging. There are no wise elders or religious figures to guide you.

When times are hard, tragedy hits, or life overwhelms you, all too often you're alone with your anguish. In spite of efforts to destigmatize the situation, it is seen as weak to ask for help — especially from a therapist — no matter how lost or despondent you become. In fact, emotional pain is sometimes so frowned upon that the only way to show your needs is by becoming physically ill, getting into an accident, or being in some other kind of trouble.

Irreconcilable Dilemmas Of Women

Everyone must find meaningful ways to survive and enjoy life. But men and women each feel caught by additional social expectations, as well as falling prey to their own unreachable internalized standards.

As women, we feel that we must be competent workers but no threat to men; that we alone are responsible for maintaining relationships; that we should be all-giving mothers; and no matter what, that we ought to be slim, attractive and calm. As an unwritten rule, we seem to have appointed ourselves keepers of the emotional well-being of everyone — we try to please all and ruffle none. We believe we must be super-beings, filling never-ending expectations, society's and our own.

I used to stay at home with my kids and I felt I should work. Now I have a job and I feel guilty that I'm not home more for my kids. My husband and kids are fine. It's me that is so hard on myself.

A friend told me this during lunch several years ago. It is a variation on a theme I've heard many times over the years.

Women are often raised differently from men. We may be discouraged from becoming too independent from our families of origin, and in fact encouraged to stay closely connected to them. As a result, without ever learning to attend to our own needs, we can slip right into the role of nurturing others — mates, children, parents, coworkers, bosses, and everyone else. We take insufficient time for ourselves, and feel uneasy and guilty about the little time we do take.

It's a vicious cycle. In trying to be everything to everyone, we end up feeling resentful, trapped, and underappreciated. And if we abuse alcohol and get drunk, or overeat and get fat to numb our frustrations, we feel ashamed for being out of control. So we desperately hide our "bad" habits and try to stay chic and unruffled.

To make matters worse, if we should happen to go to a doctor for help, he may prescribe drugs that start us on the road to other addictions.

I thought I was okay, though in hindsight I was sleepwalking through life. I had been overwhelmed by the household juggle, trying to be everything to everyone and do it all perfectly. My doctor kept saying Valium was not addicting. Pretty soon I was regularly supplementing it with alcohol. Eventually my doctor retired. I couldn't find a new one to write more Valium prescriptions. So I went cold turkey, nearly died and ended up being hospitalized. Medically I came out all right. But I can barely remember my children growing up.

A survivor of a twelve-year Valium habit shared this with me.

Unreachable Standards For Men

Men as well as women face daily demands and tasks that require superhuman effort. From early childhood on you are expected to be the eternally strong, ever-capable protector and provider. You must stand up to all foes — human, financial and emotional — never waver in your competency, always know the answers, never be scared, and never need assistance. You feel you must be like steel, invulnerable and unfailing.

A classic example is of a man who makes no mention to others around him of his marriage falling apart. He doesn't breathe a word of it to colleagues at the office nor to friends he plays tennis with every week. His intentions are to look strong and in control at all costs. The show must go on.

Because of your fear of peoples' image of you, you keep your personal life and feelings to yourself. You worry that if you are emotionally too close to other men, people may suspect you of being gay. And, if you confide in women as friends, they'll assume you are having an affair. So you keep calm and reach for a drink, drugs, a cigarette, more busyness or whatever it takes to get you through, rather than deal directly with your problems.

A man who consulted me because of marital difficulties said:

I used to be involved in local politics. Now I'm immersed in issues related to saving the environment. I believe in what I'm doing, but I'm overextended. There's always one damn meeting or another.

I'm envious of people who are less "public minded" and who have time for other parts of their lives. But I look down on them too — their days seem so superficial and full of trivia.

I know these meetings and my concerns about the world completely take over and eclipse everything else — time with my wife, time with my friends, even time with my little girl. It's like I've put my personal life in storage.

Too many men attempt to do, to win, to work until they drop, even if it drives away their families, gives them ulcers, or causes a heart attack.

Dysfunctional Work Environments

Work pressures further feed compulsive living patterns for both women and men. Countless studies have shown that stress becomes overwhelming when demands overshadow ways to be in control. An important determinant becomes how chronic and continuous is the onslaught of everyday life hassles. Whether the tension becomes unmanageable depends on the inner and outer resources and coping skills that we each bring with us.

Even when there is not a single precipitating trauma, it's not hard to get "ground down" with trivial chores, frustrating daily red tape, paper pushing, undermining by bosses and colleagues, inadequate acknowledgement of accomplishments, loss of goals, meaningless work, and a feeling that participation in life is inconsequential. In too many jobs, the crazy messages we grew up hearing are again echoed loud and clear.

A Set-up For Disaster

With so many impossible demands and pressures, something has to go. But we have learned our childhood lessons well: "At all costs put up a good front." Never mind what is going on underneath.

Unfortunately for too many of us, self-destructive coping skills seep through the cracks in subtle or not so subtle ways. The façade can last only so long before you're burned out, tired, or sick. At work it can show up as the three classic A's: Alcoholism, Absenteeism, and Accidents. Or you go off into one of the tried and true methods of running away, especially the peer sanctioned ones — wine, women/men, drugs, food, cigarettes, spending, obsessive busyness, more work, and so on. Though exhausted and worn down, the drinking or drugging workaholic who is caught up in the everyday treadmill of survival is not seen as being in trouble.

Here again society gives muddled messages. On the one hand we are supposed to be single-minded, serious, and stick to business — "Keep up with the Joneses," "Always do your best," advance, succeed, do it all. On the other hand, we are invited to handle tension through avoidance, escape and indulgence — "Eat, drink, and be merry." Or, as the bumper stickers tell us, "When the going gets tough, the tough go shopping." Commercial pressures can be quite blatant, assuring that the right clothes, cosmetics, cars, jewelry, houses, computers, or whatever, will provide the inner security and happiness for which we so desperately search. If we can just find the proper indulgence, pain and anxiety need no longer be part of our lives.

Tremendous amounts of money are at stake in encouraging us to drink, smoke and spend. As an example, in spite of all the research tying cigarette smoking to cancer, heart disease and other illnesses, advertisements and commercials continue to link cigarette smoking with being sophisticated. The macho man is still depicted balancing a cigarette, a drink, and a beautiful woman. The stereotype *femme fatale* is shown to be emaciated, smoking and spending money.

Pharmaceutical companies promote medications as a solution to stress, and downplay the side effects and addictive potentials. Eager to keep their patients happy, many physicians become part of the problem. Cocaine is easily available in towns, small, large and in-between. Because of underworld pressures, ever-increasing amounts of money ride on getting and keeping us hooked on it.

People not only get addicted to illegal substances, but to greed itself. The arrest of a drug dealer is a common subject of current newspaper articles. Often when friends and neighbors of the dealer are questioned, they say, "He was such a nice guy, but he was in too much of a hurry to succeed. He wanted the good life instantly and got in with the wrong people."

Gambling establishments of all kinds proliferate across the country. From Native American bingo parlors and casinos to the tables of Las Vegas and Atlantic City to state-sponsored lotteries, there are plenty of readily-available places to lose money at "games of chance."

In spite of an increasing awareness of the toll paid by the use of alcohol, drugs, and other self-destructive habits, on the whole, society closes its eyes to what it publicly doesn't want to see. This unfortunately encourages what each of us privately wants to deny.

Lost In The Shuffle

Gifted young people often fall prey to the pressures and temptations that surround us:

A professional athlete is constantly under scrutiny and criticism from the public, though that disadvantage seems slight in a person who has everything — fame and fortune. So why is he self-destructive — misusing alcohol, drugs, food and relationships?

More often than not an athlete is young and naive as to how to handle being a national celebrity. He is worshipped by the public such that it is easy for him to develop an inflated self-image. There are extreme pressures for him to excel, to win no matter what — even if he's exhausted, depressed, ill, or injured. These unfair expectations come not only from fans, teammates and management, but family, community and the media. Not to be forgotten are his own inner drives for perfection. There his self-image is dangerously tied to performing flawlessly.

He may enter his professional career while still immature, with a paucity of inner resources and socializing skills. He is often on the road, separated from family and friends, in strange settings, lonely and bored. In addition, he is expected to keep up a macho image as a hard drinking, carousing, life of the party. Given the availability of immense quantities of cash, plus unlimited access to alcohol, drugs and adoring women, it's no wonder that he gets into trouble. Perhaps the only surprise is that so many athletes are able to withstand these pressures as well as they do.

From the day she starts to train, a female ballet dancer is taught that there is a right and wrong way to do everything. She must use perfect technique in her movements and sustain absolute balance and control. Self-discipline is valued above all. In essence she must be the model child who always pleases and depends on her teacher-parents. She may also have the added burden of trying to fulfill a parent's or teacher's ambitions more than her own.

Her profession demands that she maintain a certain look. So, her dilemma is complicated by pressures to be as thin as possible — no fat, no hips, no bust. She must not overeat, overdrink or indulge in any other way. In fact, it is difficult for her to find an acceptable outlet to release tension or take her mind away from her work. For many, some form of rebellion happens as an almost inevitable (non)solution. This is the perfect setup to create a bulimic condition: a woman obsessed about her weight who intermittently binges on food and then vomits, uses laxatives or diuretics. And if she basically feels inadequate and has a distorted image of her body, she could slip into a full blown anorexic trap — dying to be thin enough.

Different Strokes For Different Folks

Societies around the world have their own particular dysfunctional communications with differing pressures and seductions. For example, emphasis varies as to whether being heavy, drinking, using drugs, working long hours, being successful, having possessions, or some other habit is praised or scorned. One culture may regard being fat as a mark of status, and overeating as a sign of wealth. In a prosperous country, quite the opposite may be true — being thin will have status and constant overeating is seen as undesirable.

In the United States, we expect products to quickly wear out, trendiness is more important than durability, and we keep trying to buy the newest and latest. We don't look down upon those who live on credit or are chronically in debt. This makes it easier and easier to buy impulsively. Furthermore, we can watch the home shopping channels on television and shop on the phone right from our living rooms. Heaven forbid they figure out how to pipe alcohol and drugs directly into our homes!

Obviously, in developing countries this kind of material over-indulgence will not be the compulsive escape of choice.

In some regions of the world, specific drugs are more readily available and their use is not frowned upon — for example, peyote in parts of Mexico; opium in Manchuria. France has gained the dubious distinction of having become the world's heaviest per capita consumer of anti-anxiety pills. General practitioners freely prescribe them. It is said that in some circles pill popping is a national pastime, side by side with "raising a glass or two." In most countries cigarette advertising continues to be agressive and information about nicotine dangers is suppressed, so smoking is widespread in spite of known health hazards.

In Great Britain self-control is highly valued. Under all circumstances one should "keep a stiff upper lip." Hence it is not surprising to learn that British physicians, as contrasted with those on the continent, frequently prescribe drugs that have a sedative effect to help people feel calm and fit into society. It is also an acceptable practice in Great Britain to maintain addicts on heroin. So an oversedated patient, or one who is strung out on street drugs, may be overlooked.

In cultures where substance abuse is less socially acceptable, people shift the focus of their compulsive living onto activities — work, exercise, obsessions with wealth or youth, and so on. Recent studies from Japan reveal a startling national emphasis on expecting the average citizen to put work above everything else in life. Even free time is supposed to revolve around company approved activities that do *not* include wives and children.

The American obsession with looking young at all costs leads to far more face-lifts being done in the United States compared to countries such as France or Italy, where aging is accepted and respected.

The character of the society in which we live strongly influences our habits. We shape our style of compulsive living according to its dictates of what is and what is not permissable.

A Multifaceted Problem

It's evident that our social environments reinforce the same confusing standards and messages that many of us grew up with. We are trapped into continuing to live by irreconcilable written and unwritten rules: no one validates our awareness of the impossibility of meeting the overwhelming pressures of our lives nor helps us face them directly; we are enticed by opportunities to escape from these pressures yet told that such escapes are a sign of weakness; and all too frequently, society labels us as being irresponsible and yet covers up and rescues us from the consequences of our actions.

And of course we use the identical compulsive means that we developed as children to deal with these contradictions — coping and conforming on the outside while simultaneously rebelling on the inside, in our own particular self-destructive style of avoidance.

Compulsive living is indeed a complex enemy — a wrong direction from long ago that is fueled by the environments we live in today. We cannot radically alter the pressures and temptations of society, but there are many areas keeping us stuck that we *can* change.

4 | SETTING THE STAGE FOR RECOVERY

To err is human, but when the eraser wears out ahead of the pencil, you are overdoing it.

— J. Jenkins

A recovering alcoholic told me about the turning point of his life:

> I'm not sure why that particular morning was any different than thousands of others. The hangover was par for me, as were vague memories of the fool I'd made of myself the night before. But somehow, something clicked and got through my thick skull. I was going down in an elevator, straight down underground. If I didn't get out quick, it'd be too late. It was time to stop moving on a collision course.

Regardless which compulsive patterns you are engaged in, basic principles for gaining control are the same, and must rest on firm ground of sincerely *wanting* to change. Your motivation to alter the present status quo will depend upon your being honest with yourself about what is happening right now. See the truth, the whole truth and nothing but the truth:

- The habits you are compulsively locked into.
- Their consequences to your life.

- Your concerns about the situation.
- Other problems that you're avoiding.
- The choices you continue to make that keep you stuck.

You must consider all the implications for the years to come. In every way it is important to stop kidding yourself. Otherwise, you will end up staying in predictable self-destructive cycles that continue to go nowhere.

If you haven't already "hit bottom," hopefully this chapter can shake you up before you do. I hope it will help you shatter any remnants of denial that prevent you from seeing how compulsive patterns waste your time, drain your energy and gobble up your money.

As you have seen, in one form or another your compulsive patterns have been with you since childhood. They have been your "security blanket," your instant gratification, and your escape from having to worry about other areas of your life. Hence it will be difficult to leave them without the needed determination to carry you through feelings of being lost, at loose ends, and sometimes quite uncomfortable. Intellectual understanding and analyzing are in the long run helpful, but of little use in the nitty-gritty of getting through this painful time of withdrawal.

The courage to start and stay with a recovery program begins with *truly seeing that the price you pay for your compulsive life-style is too high.* You've been well aware of your need to indulge, it is time to get in touch with your need *not* to.

If you skip this step, your whole recovery program will be based on a weak foundation, because deep down you will doubt the necessity to change.

A Seven-Day Program

Combining what I have learned from working with patients and suggestions from other therapists, I offer the following seven-day program to help you take stock of your life-style and self-destructive patterns. Tackle one specific compulsive habit only, be it an escape into a substance, an activity or a preoccupation. Each day focuses on a particular issue:

Day 1. The details of your present predicament.

Day 2. The ways in which you keep yourself stuck in the self-destructive pattern.

Day 3. The triggers that set off the pattern.

Day 4. The payoffs of the pattern.

Day 5. The future *vis-à-vis* your compulsive life-style.

Day 6. Visualizing your life in control.

Day 7. Examining life changes necessary for recovery.

I suggest that you do all the exercises consecutively, without missing a day. But you can also do it in some other way — all in one sitting or over a different time period.

Whatever method you choose to do the program, give serious thought to each of the seven issues which are highlighted. This will help you step back and take a cool, objective look at your whole life situation as it relates to your compulsive living. You must get it all on the table, "for your eyes only," not for anyone else's.

So you can consider the issues openly and with as much detail as possible:

Don't judge what you've done.

Don't try to make sense out of it.

Don't screen out facts or figures as unimportant or ridiculous.

The following exercises should give you insight into how *you* have actively kept your compulsive pattern going. Write in a notebook or journal for five or ten minutes each morning. This is extremely helpful for enabling you to take the battle out of your head and put it in front of you on paper.

Whatever the day's subject is, stay with it by deliberately keeping it in your mind *all day*. Look at your notes whenever you get a chance and add to them at any point during the day. Then take a few minutes each evening to review what you have learned from your efforts. Again, don't battle all your bad habits at once. You're more likely to become a martyr than get beyond compulsive living.

At the end of each day's exercise I have included notes from an actual journal. It records the thoughts of an extremely successful woman with a compulsive need to be perfect.

* * *

Day 1. *Write out the details of your plight — the thorns you have created in your life. Assess the damage that has ensued from a physical, social, financial and legal viewpoint.* Look at all the worries, the emotional and perhaps monetary debts that you have created. Look at the quantity of time, energy and guilt that's locked into your habit. Look at the amount of sleep that you've lost as you obsessed on your habit and its consequences. Look at ways you're keeping your life on hold. Listen to yourself as you rationalize that "some day when I'm thin," "some day when I'm 'on the wagon,' " "some day when I'm out of debt," "some day when I'm all caught up, I'll get on to other areas of my life."

Look at how the self-destructive pattern affects your relationships to parents, mate, friends, children. Think about how often you have used poor judgment so that you could continue to indulge, or ways you have been dishonest in order to hide your habit from others. Look at its impact upon your work, your capacity to concentrate, and your ability to live in the moment and enjoy life. *Write it all down.*

When you open your eyes to what is happening, you will realize that in one way or another, you are marking time. Though your style of stagnating may be unique, the way in which it has derailed your life is not. Up until this point, your one-and-only life has not been lived in your own best interests.

Journal: *"My feeling that I always have to be perfect is like an albatross around my neck. It's gotten worse and worse. I can't let myself feel good about anything. If it's not perfect, it feels like it's worthless. No matter what I wear, it doesn't seem attractive enough. I beat myself for not being a better wife and mother. At work, I never feel I have presented things well enough at meetings. I always feel I could and should do more. I don't attempt many activities if I feel I won't be able to do them perfectly. When we have friends over, I feel that what I've prepared isn't adequate and guests won't be satisfied. Often I can't get to sleep because I'm still rehashing how the day could have been done differently. Many times I can't shift gears and feel like making love. My husband thinks I'm foolish to worry so much, but I can't stop. The lightness and fun have gone out of my life."*

* * *

Day 2. *Today is an opportunity for you to see how clever you are at keeping your pattern alive.* All day long, stay aware of the choices that you make, whether they are made actively or passively. For example, you just *happened* to walk into the liquor store; you just *happened* once again to take a new date to an expensive restaurant that you really can't afford; you just *happened* to have a gallon of your favorite ice cream at home on the exact day that you started your diet; you just *happened* to buy three cartons of cigarettes, though you are intending to cut down smoking — well, they were on sale; you just *happened* to call up the "love of your life" whom you're trying to forget; you just *happened* to work through lunch every day, do everybody else's job, and then go bananas, O.D.ing on shopping in the evening; you just *happened* to do nothing to climb out of your depression; you just *happened* to hang around with friends who are losers and who never make any changes in their lives. I think you get the picture.

Again, *do not judge yourself* — just be a curious detective and look at all the devious ways you use to keep your compulsive pattern in place.

Journal: *"It's almost as if I purposefully go back over something I've done just so I can criticize it. And I know I actually set up negative comments from others. When I ask for feedback and people give me praise, I push them until they point out a fault, and then I dwell on my shortcomings until they obscure everything else. I never look back on my many accomplishments. This sounds nonsensical, but it's almost as if I can't let myself feel good about anything."*

* * *

Day 3. *Write about the kinds of situations, feelings, and people that send you out of control.* Does it occur after pay day, on Monday, on Friday? Is it after a call from your father, a fight with your spouse, a new relationship that didn't turn out well, a job interview that went nowhere? Do you engage in your compulsive habit when you are angry, lonely, bored, happy, anxious, tired — or maybe all of the above?

As you go through the day, see exactly what your habit is used for. When does it help get you going? Calm you down? Fill time? Provide recreation? Handle uncomfortable feelings? Automatically accompany other activities such as driving, watching television, socializing? Focus on the *predictable scenarios*. Write them all out. The key is to see exactly which comfort functions your habit is bonded to.

Journal: *"When I'm tired, which is more often than not, I'm extra hard on myself. Also, any contact with my parents sets me into feeling terribly critical of myself. Or when my husband speaks highly of someone in his office — especially if it is a woman — I always feel he is seeing me as being less. I'm particularly competitive with other women. I feel I have to be better — forever the best. I'm sure this relates to the lifelong conflict I've had with my younger sister. If I don't get a constant fix of praise, I start to sink into a chasm of self-doubt."*

* * *

Day 4. *Think of the payoffs that come from your compulsive pattern and its consequences.* At some level you are enjoying letting your habit pervade your life. You spend your days engrossed in your pattern, and gamble on how well you can put up a good front — never a dull moment! Your habit is a terrific weapon to get back at people who make too many demands on you, or who you feel let you down — a spouse, your parents, intrusive or unavailable friends, a pushy boss, society, the world.

Furthermore, you are so guilty about your compulsive pattern that you feel you have no right to make demands on anyone else, much less get angry. When things get to be too much of a mess, "rescuers" bail you out. In addition, you are so entrenched in obsessing about your pattern that you don't have to deal with other areas of your life — social, love, work, health, taking risks. Take a good look. You are getting a lot of "goodies" out of your habit. Again, don't criticize yourself — simply open your eyes to what's happening and *write it all down.*

Journal: *"This is hard for me to admit. I guess my needing to be so perfect has led me to tackle superhuman tasks. That's the good part. But it has also fed my hanging on to the illusion that if I can do things perfectly enough, that will make me okay inside. My accomplishments make me appear to be superior to others, but underneath I feel inferior to everyone. I also know that since I'm so critical of myself, other people end up trying to reassure me that everything is all right. What a nutty way to get attention. Sometimes I don't know how my husband puts up with me. Looking at my basic insecurities scares the hell out of me."*

* * *

Day 5. *Picture what your life will be like one year, five years, ten years, twenty years from now if your compulsive pattern continues unchecked.* This will be a bit like the nightmare vision of the future that Scrooge had in Dickens' "A Christmas Carol." Visualize yourself incessantly struggling with food-weight preoccupations and possibly getting fatter and fatter; continuing to gamble or otherwise live beyond your means, and maybe getting further into debt; forever procrastinating; burying yourself in work; staying in the same self-destructive relationship and getting older and not wiser; running from what makes you anxious; continuing to abuse alcohol, drugs or cigarettes and jeopardizing your health; forever feeling bad about yourself as a human being. Think about how it will impact on your pocketbook, soak up your time and energy, and where it will eventually lead — all the embarrassment, shame, and guilt.

Visualize it and write it all out. That's the way it will be, unless *you* choose to make changes. Today is the day to go hog wild with your *fantasies* of indulging in your self-destructive pattern to your heart's content, staying with it "until death do you part." But keep it mental. There is no need to actually O.D. and do yourself in before the week is even over.

Journal: *"Envisioning the future makes me sad. Like I'll keep wasting my days chasing perfection and I'll miss all the beauty and joy of being human. This is very painful for me to step back and really think about how meaningless my life has become. I have a fine husband and three lovely children and I don't even savor the daily gift of having them near me. Ten or twenty years from now, reflecting back, I am going to have too many regrets if I don't change."*

* * *

Day 6. *Now visualize your life with your compulsive pattern in control* — confident about your body, your looks; unafraid of creditors, an angry spouse, a law suit against you, making a drunken fool of yourself. Think about what it would be like to live each day in control:

• Your life could become less dramatic and more predictable, but possibly feel boring.

• You could become more emotionally vulnerable, perhaps overwhelmingly so, because you'd be left with raw feelings and no comforting escape into compulsive patterns.

• You could become freer, but maybe you'd feel frighteningly alone and empty.

Let your imagination go. Get a clear image of your life uncluttered by compulsive, out-of-control habits and all the messy but exciting consequences.

Journal: *"Not being obsessed with being perfect sounds like a dream — but I have trouble imagining it. Since I was a child, I have so measured my worth by external praise and trying to be perfect, that it's hard to picture what it would be like without this. I'm sure I'd have much more energy free. I wouldn't be driving my husband crazy asking for reassurance. Wow! But I'd also feel like a little ball bouncing around in an empty room with no direction or purpose.*

"This is difficult to think about. I guess I'd have time to find out who I am and what I really want to do with my life. I can't believe I just wrote this."

* * *

Day 7. *Look specifically at what you need to change in your life in order to let go of your compulsive patterns.* Your life could no longer center around the next hit of a substance, an activity, or a preoccupation. This might entail not associating with certain people. This could mean avoiding situations where indulging regularly takes place. You would have to face uncomfortable feelings without numbing or distorting them with your habit. In addition, you would need to find new ways to use your time and energy, new activities, and perhaps new friends.

Think about the realities of what you would have to let go of or alter in your life if you are truly going to stop being run by compulsive living patterns. *Write out all of the details of these monumental sacrifices and changes.* You must not trick yourself into believing that you can get something for nothing. There is no magic pill or quick fix for your dilemma.

Journal: *"If I'm going to change — and I've got to for* me *— I will practically have to bite my tongue so that I stop hounding people to reassure me. I will have to stop working on projects when they are already good enough, and stay with my anxiety. I'll have to remind myself that my friends don't value me for being so perfect — in fact, they are probably put off by it. Certainly my husband and children are sick of it. What's clear is that I'll have to do some heavy duty soul searching that I've been putting off for my entire life."*

* * *

Repeat this week as often as necessary to facilitate your seeing it "as it is." I want to caution you about a potential blind spot. If your health and wealth have not markedly deteriorated, you may underestimate the seriousness of your plight. Watch out. Don't take lightly the tragedy of a life that has remained largely unlived, especially when it is *your* life.

A Weighty Decision

You have time to carefully *weigh the pros and cons of the whole situation.* No one is pushing you to make a decision. It is your habit, it is your life. Let all the facts start to sink in. From the ponderings of the last seven days you have some raw data to examine. In fact, if you have been open with yourself, the data may be a bit more raw than you had expected.

Balance the known comfort, the predictable fun, the guaranteed excitement, and the convenient escape of continuing your compulsive pattern against entering the unknown world of not having an emotionally, physically, socially and/or financially messy life. Contrast the driven, out of control chaos of today against the possibility of having a clean future that you can be proud of. A compulsive pattern is like an old, warm, cozy, but outgrown coat. It doesn't fit well, but it is familiar and extremely comfortable. Are you willing to take it off and temporarily go bare?

Soberly and seriously mull over the possibility of putting compulsive living into the background of your life. Bring all the pros and cons into sharp focus and try to envision how you would feel if you were free, as opposed to the way you are feeling now.

Figure out what will be in your own best interests, *not* the interests of your parents, spouse, or creditors. Your reasons for wanting to change must be *intensely personal*, or they will not be powerful enough to motivate you. Remember, being obsessed with pleasing others has gotten you into your present predicament. Don't again fall into this rut.

Recovery cannot be effective until you are able to make a genuine commitment to change. If you are in therapy, don't hide your compulsive habits from your therapist, or he or she will be struggling in the dark to appropriately help you. You earn no "brownie points" in deceiving your therapist. Only you will be the loser.

Though you had hoped for a miracle or at minimum, a parental rescue, it hasn't arrived. Your future rests entirely in your own hands. It is up to you whether you decide to change your patterns. Unless you take full responsibility for this decision it will be unusually difficult to weather the "withdrawal" period from your particular self-destructive habit, and to stay with a program that will allow you to get into new more satisfying life patterns. This conscious decision will be the cornerstone of your recovery. It is the first step toward taking charge. Make the decision for yourself. Don't set up anyone else to make it for you.

Hopefully you are sick and tired of being sick and tired. You have spent enough time rebelling and withdrawing from life. Are you ready to put more energy into riding with and enjoying it?

It's your move.

Overall Perspective — Getting Into Gear

*Things could be worse. Suppose your errors were
published every day like those of a baseball player.*

— Anonymous

Listeners of my weekly San Francisco Bay Area radio talk-show
often send me nice letters, sharing their triumph over problems.

*Looking back, I remember some soul searching I did in
my mid-twenties that changed everything for me. Up until
then, rejection seemed to be the story of my life. My mother
died when I was little. My father didn't want me. I was raised
by a loving aunt. But still I always felt rejected.*

*I spent high school asking out girls who weren't interested
in me or who were in love with someone else. More rejections.
Then I started gambling a lot and regularly buying lottery
tickets. I never won, which depressed me. Even the lottery
rejected me.*

*One day it dawned on me that it was stupid to keep
fighting the odds and getting hurt. I stopped buying lottery
tickets. That was the beginning of taking hold of my life.*

Maybe this knowledge can help someone else.

Now that you're seeing your life more clearly "as it is," you
may be wishing you weren't. But stay with me. It's time to get a
realistic overview and properly assess the damages. How far you
have sunk will depend on the interplay of a number of variables:

1. The inner strengths you have been able to mobilize to
compensate for and to fight against your compulsive habits.

2. How extreme and central to your life certain patterns have
become. Patterns may remain contained, or they may intrude into
every nook and cranny of your existence.

3. Whether your work and your relationships have also become
contaminated by your compulsive living. The more these are intact,
the more they can sustain you through a lot of thick and thin.

4. In addition, if you are abusing substances, the overall picture

may be further distorted depending on the nature of the drugs involved:

- Your judgment may be chemically impaired.
- You may have varying degrees of chemically caused depression and anxiety.
- Symptoms related to physical craving and withdrawal could be complicating how you feel, as well as your physical health.

Once you move into abstinence and these chemical factors are no longer throwing up a smoke screen, you may be pleasantly surprised to find that many situations are not as bad as you had feared. On the other hand, when denial plays a less prominent part in your life, neglected areas may look worse.

Sizing It All Up

Possibly, you are beating yourself for your stupidity at getting into this predicament. What you actually have created is a golden opportunity, a potential for a guaranteed growth experience, although you may not recognize it as such.

Of course you can put your head back into the sand, grab all your old defenses and compulsive patterns, and deny and avoid right into the grave. You can close your eyes to the fact that you have been playing out self-destructive scenes to an empty house. You can continue to kick and wallow along the way about how unfair everyone and everything has been to you, and "What's the use anyway." Or you can sit up straight and simply say, "Damn, damn, damn. How cleverly I have deceived myself. But my life is not yet over, and I want a hell of a lot more out of it."

If you choose this latter course, read on. Yes, you have been bogged down with self-destructive and often pathetically ridiculous compulsive patterns. So what? What gives you the idea that everyone else has it easy — that their lives always skip along smoothly and effortlessly?

Like many before you, in one way or another you have valiantly struggled to keep up a good front and to appear all right to those around you. In actuality the cover-up has been as much for your own benefit as for others. You haven't wanted to face how bad you were feeling about yourself. Finally, though, you have had the courage to take off your rose-colored glasses and look — really look. And the view is stark, but not yet beyond repair.

> *I went to a slide show of the Cancer Society that was set up to help people stop smoking. Seeing slides of blackened lungs, people with cancer or people who had heart attacks was pretty grisly, but somehow it felt distant and too abstract. After all, I thought, it doesn't happen to everyone. But I couldn't tune out the dry coughs all over the room, including mine, practically every few seconds. And one fact that the Cancer Society presented I was unable to get out of my mind: They said that if you smoked two packs a day, at age fifty-five physiologically you'd be sixty-five or seventy-five. That shook the hell out of me and eventually got me going.*

A thirty-one-year-old woman explained what finally pushed her to quit smoking. After countless false starts and lots of helpful tips from friends, she eventually succeeded.

Don't Confuse What You've Done With Who You Are

You may indeed be *doing* "bad" things and making poor choices, but that does not make *you* a "bad" person. It is essential that you begin to separate out *who* you are from *how* you behave so as to avoid needless despair.

It may be helpful to stop reading for a moment and reflect on some of your strengths. You genuinely care for others. You are conscientious, have a sense of humor, are enthusiastic, supportive, practical, understanding, and so on. Step back and think about yourself as others see you. Though you may have used poor judgment and even victimized others, underneath it all you are aware of right and wrong. A friend of mine said that "the bottom line is you are okay if you are not robbing the poor or doing people in for fun." A bit extreme, but you get the point.

As previously stated, a big part of your total difficulty is that you have always been *too* good and *too* responsible. You have not adequately taken care of yourself in healthy ways nor allowed yourself to have enough legitimate fun. That empty place in your life has become filled with compulsive patterns. When you feel frustrated, you use them. When you feel down, you use them. Situations that make you feel rejected or trapped set off really frantic behavior. These habits may have run your life for so long that you have lost track of who you are and where you are going.

Clearly you are caught in nonsolutions that create far more problems than they solve. These seriously get in the way of your fully experiencing life. The world of compulsive living is lined by too much shame and guilt and loneliness.

No matter what form your compulsive living takes, *you have ended up not playing one hundred percent at the game of life.* This is a tough game to play even if you have a full deck of cards, which at present, you don't. Many of yours got stuck in your past. While you were busy going around in circles, life marched on without you.

"It Isn't Over Until The Fat Lady Sings"

Have no illusions. Getting off the compulsive merry-go-round entails much more than merely controlling "bad" habits. It implies nothing short of giving up a self-destructive life-style and moving on. But as is true for any illness, first monitor the symptoms. Otherwise you will be destroyed long before you actually recover.

To start, all effort must be put on stopping the downward spiral. You cannot use *not having* your act together as an excuse to continue your irresponsible ways. Later, when you are in control of the habits themselves, you can heal yourself on a deeper level.

A crucial part of recovery is learning to like and to take better care of yourself. Your life is just as important as anyone else's. As a matter of fact, to you it is a lot more important. For it is the only life you have. If you don't begin to value it, enjoy it, and get it straightened out, who else will? Rabbi Hillel said, "If I am only for myself, who am I? If I am not for myself, who will be for me? And if not now, when?"

Yes, perhaps your parents could have and should have given you a better start. But they weren't able to, or didn't know how to, or didn't want to put the necessary effort forward. In sum, they didn't. That is water under the bridge.

At this point circumstances are different. You are no longer a helpless child. You no longer need to wait for other people's attention and nurturing and approval. There are many more options. You can make your own decisions. For you to continue to use outdated survival means is unnecessarily self-destructive.

If you think I am trying to give you a pep talk, you are right. You have gotten waylaid into self-defeating habits. But hopefully what separates you from the herd is that you are wrestling with doing something about it. This will require reaching into yourself for strengths that you didn't know you had.

Where Do You Go From Here?

In order to travel from a place where you're run by compulsive patterns to a healthy, fulfilling involvement in life, serious work must be done. Just as would be true for any journey, you need to know exactly what is happening now; you must stay clear about where you want to go; and you have to maintain confidence that you *can* get there.

There are three basic phases to recovery which will be covered in the rest of the book. Though all of these go on simultaneously, your goal is for Phase III to dominate.

Phase I: Let go of the compulsive habits themselves. Correct any resultant problems — particularly serious ones relating to your health and to your pocket book.

Phase II: Develop new positive habits.

Phase III: Get preoccupations about your unhealthy patterns into the background of your life.

To prepare for the trip into recovery you need to have the right image and attitude and pack all the appropriate tools for change. Too many good intentions fall by the wayside because people get lazy about this essential preparation stage — not at all a place to cut corners.

A number of distinct areas must be targeted to get you "unstuck." I am speaking both of the process of moving into what alcoholics classically call "abstinence," as well as entering into full recovery. All of these subjects will be greatly expanded upon in subsequent parts of the book. Here is a preview:

• Adequate support will be invaluable. You need to establish both an informal and formal emotional refueling system, and become appropriately interdependent with it. Unhealthy people in your life who undermine your growth must be spotted and weeded out.

• Tangible behavior changes can be planned. This includes modifying coping patterns, and rehearsing alternate behaviors and reactions to potentially difficult situations. "Emergency urgency," the temptation to fall back into old compulsive patterns, will be a foe for which you have to stay on guard and be extremely well prepared.

• The way you think about yourself and about your life needs renovating. This involves letting go of feeling that deep down you are not good enough. It means discarding outdated beliefs leftover from your childhood that interfere with change. You will also need skills for staying with your program even when progress is slow or discouraging.

• Troublesome rationalizations and excuses must be systematically combatted.

• Means can be found to avoid sabotaging yourself. When you do slip, you can learn how to get back on course, so as to prevent a full blown relapse. You also must become comfortable with success and genuinely feel you deserve it. Unless this is properly done, you will keep "shooting yourself in the foot" — hauling in old familiar self-destructive patterns that forever derail your life.

• Strategies for changing specific compulsive patterns need to be planned in detail.

• In order to emotionally heal, you have to truly move beyond compulsive living. You must accept your past for what it was, your parents for who they were and who they are, and yourself for being human. Only then can you utilize the opportunity that now exists — to grow and to dream and to be fully alive.

Special Considerations

Before we go to material applicable to *all* forms of compulsive living, I want to mention special factors pertinent to particular habits. In planning your recovery program, notice which of the following three groups your habit(s) fall into:

1. *Patterns in which total abstinence is necessary.*
   - Substance abuse — alcohol, drugs, cigarettes
   - High risk activities — gambling, shoplifting, sexual promiscuity
   - Leading a life ruled by phobias

The guidelines for recovery, though hard to swallow, in these cases are painfully black and white. Eventually you need to completely desist from such forms of escape.

2. *Patterns in which you must abstain from the unhealthy part, but continue with the healthy part of your involvement.*
   - Compulsive eating, loving, spending, working

In other words, because these areas cannot be eliminated from a normal life, recovery programs must include re-education as to how you appropriately relate to food, family, friends, lovers, money, and work.

3. *Patterns in which the consequences of indulging must be addressed.*
   - Weight deviations brought on by compulsive eating
   - Debts caused by compulsive spending or gambling

In these cases, it is imperative that recovery programs include means to correct the "damage" — to lose or to gain weight; to financially get in the black.

Methods for tackling the issues raised in (2) and (3) can be found in Part III.

Onward

Gaining control of compulsive patterns may sound like an impossible road to navigate. But not for you. You have always been a fighter, a survivor. In difficult circumstances, you have consistently done the best you could for who you were and what you had. With greater maturity, perspective, and choice of coping skills, you can now do far better. Deep down you want much more out of your life than you have been getting. Your determination will help you develop an appropriate living style, infinitely more fulfilling to your needs. And you don't have to get there alone.

Adequate Support — Informal And Formal

A friend is one before whom I may think aloud.
— Ralph Waldo Emerson

I wanted to call him. God how I wanted to call him. My whole body just ached to hear his voice, to again have some connection to him. Just thinking about him made me dissolve inside.

I forced myself to remember all the awful times — when he would be distant and never available, or the multitude of times he'd cancel out at the last minute. It didn't work. I kept struggling with myself to try to get him out of my mind. Then I decided to call Jane — she said I could call at any hour, though I was sure she wouldn't be crazy about being woken up at 2:00 a.m.

When she answered the phone, she couldn't have been kinder. We talked and talked, and she helped me weigh all the positives and negatives of getting back in touch with him, of which there were far more negatives. Within fifteen minutes we were both laughing, and somehow I knew I'd be okay. And I was. After I said good-bye to her, I got busy with some things around my apartment and I didn't call him.

Thank you, Jane.

Informal as well as formal resources can provide crucial emotional and practical support. Without these, too many recovery programs stumble along or self-destruct. Let us look at kinds of support networks that are available, and how to become appropriately involved with each.

Informal Support

Informal resources are caring friends and family members who stand at your back and listen when you need to talk. You should not underestimate what they can offer. They can fire you up when your commitments to yourself falter. They can give you perspective and infuse humor into situations when you slip on your plans. They can cheer you on when you stick with your resolutions. They can celebrate your successes with you.

The challenge for you will be to decide which people in your life to count on. Then let these people know exactly how they can help you. Be specific about what you need. For example, you might tell a friend or family member, "When I am feeling weak, remind me not to overeat/drink/phone that jerk/cop out on my exercise program/escape into work or the stores." It is critical that you utilize your "on call" support system *before* you succumb to your weakness and pass the point of no return.

In enlisting others' help, be aware of which friends and relatives contribute to the solution of your problems, as opposed to those who may only add to your difficulties. Do not allow someone to play a parent role to you — knowing your every wish without your even asking, over-directing your life, or bailing you out of your irresponsibility. Nor should you use anyone who seductively leads you into indulging. As previously mentioned in "A Well-Defended Status Quo," many of us have dragged around an entourage of people who regularly undermine our efforts to change.

Some saboteurs are educable and can be taught to stop working against you. Others, for whatever reason, have much too much at stake in keeping you in your present predicament. You may not be able to sway them off their course. Often these are people who think they have *no* "bad" habits themselves. They have a holier-than-thou mentality and severe emotional limits. Since they are unable to fully lead their own lives, they try to lead yours. They are full of advice, liberally peppered with "shoulds": "You should just straighten yourself out"; "You should just stick to a diet"; "You should stay within your budget"; "You shouldn't drink so much"; "You should spend more time with your family"; "You should not be so lazy and self-indulgent"; "You should grow up"; One can find so-called friends, family, and even therapists in this group.

These kinds of self-rightious people are rarely of any help. They will only make you feel guilty, miserable, and even more rebellious. Try and figure out how to gracefully eliminate them from your recovery program. You might say, "I know you love me, but your advice is driving me nuts."

Use discretion regarding what you share with friends and relatives about your self-destructive habits. People close to you do *not* need to know — and may not even understand — all the intimate aspects of your life. Such personal details can make friends and relatives unnecessarily uncomfortable. Consequently it is often better to get support from individuals who are not part of your everyday life.

Formal Support Programs

If trying to change on your own has not worked out, have the courage to get some kind of formal support. Don't become immobilized by false pride and the idea that it is weak to ask for assistance.

Letting go of a compulsive life-style is like moving to another country where you must shift into a foreign language. It helps to get pointers from other expatriates — empathetic people who have themselves made the transition:

• They can share practical strategies from their own experiences for getting through painful withdrawal periods;

• They can help you feel all right about leaving unhealthy relationships that pull for your particular compulsive pattern;

• They can share your triumphs and reinforce your new identity.

In short, formal support can provide nurturing and companionship while you plod along — a sort of extended family, sheltering you from being so alone in this time of distress. Here you can instantly belong and feel totally accepted.

Some women prefer to be in all-women groups and some men in all-men groups — and some women in all-men groups, and some men in all-women groups, but that is another story. As was stated in the section on "Society's Pressures and Seductions," women and men tend to feel caught up in different expectations, coming both from society and from within themselves. There are also differences between women's and men's groups in what they talk about and the way members interrelate.

In all-women groups, members *let down their hair.* They respond to each other in a more personal and nurturing fashion, and frequently give hugs and other signs of comforting support. They are likely to share and compare information about their families — mates, children, parents. They often talk about feeling that they have no identity and are just "Jim's wife" or "Margy's mother." They speak of using their compulsive habits to compensate for feeling inadequate; to numb their feelings of powerlessness and helplessness; to dilute their unending guilt; and just to get through the day and cope *in spite of* feeling overwhelmed and depressed.

In all-men groups, members *let it all hang out.* Interaction is inclined to be more openly confronting. There is less fear of direct expression of anger. Talk is more likely to center on work and accomplishment issues. "Drunkalogs" and other war stories of misadventures abound, sometimes embellished in an unspoken can-you-top-this macho competition. Issues may revolve around the challenge of acknowledging and showing feelings, being emotional and vulnerable. Furthermore, men's compulsive habits, more than women's, may be tied into trying to improve performance and to compensate for anxieties in social situations.

In mixed groups, I have found that the focus and interactions of participants have their own distinctive nature. Members of each sex sometimes try to impress those of the opposite sex. The women may become caretakers of men. The men may attempt to be strong for particular women. Whatever happens, there is a definite quality that can add to or detract from the effectiveness of the group process.

One type of group is no better than another; go with the environment in which you feel most comfortable. Shop around until you find one that suits you. A healthy support group should complement, but *not* replace, any therapy or medical treatment that you're receiving.

A Wide Variety Of Formal Support Programs Is Available

Support systems can range from peer groups to professionally run outpatient and inpatient programs. Let me give you an overview here; details related to specific habits come up in Part III.

Twelve-Step Programs

The Twelve-Step Programs, originally started for alcoholics, now exist for many other compulsive patterns — drug users, smokers, overeaters, co-dependents, debtors, gamblers, and so on. Groups differ widely as to size — several people to hundreds, — constituency, life-styles and backgrounds of members. The philosophy of Twelve-Step Programs is sound and embodies much wisdom, especially if you follow the program fully and utilize the help of a sponsor. There is no charge, only a nominal donation to cover costs if you so choose.

Each of the twelve steps has much to offer. The steps that I find especially valuable are

Step 1 "We admitted we were powerless over alcohol/drugs/food/etc. . . . that our lives had become unmanageable." This means acknowledging that your life is out of control.

Step 4 "(We) Made a searching and fearless moral inventory of ourselves."

This involves seeing your strengths and weaknesses, and starting to reclaim responsibility for your own life.

Step 8 "(We) Made a list of all persons we had harmed, and became willing to make amends to them all."

Step 9 "(We) Made direct amends to such people wherever possible except when to do so would injure them or others."

This shifts you from good intentions into tangible actions.

In Twelve-Step programs participants recount their struggles with and triumphs over a particular compulsive pattern. They openly discuss their experiences, painful tales that keep fresh in your mind the realities of addiction, horrors you never again want to experience. Heavy secrets are shared with perfect strangers who feel like intimate friends. There is little small talk. As a result, you can know someone's horrible childhood and never know that he or she likes Beethoven.

Due to the nature of Twelve-Step interactions, you benefit from a collective strength and wisdom when you identity with the group — a group that respects and values you for who you are, no matter what you do or have done. Where else can you find a club where eligibility comes from being in pain and having skeletons in the closet? While abstinence is the goal, it is *not* the most important first step. The only requirement for membership is a sincere desire to gain control of your life and a willingness to keep coming back to meetings. In Twelve-Step and other self-help groups, helping others with similar problems can further cement your recovery.

Status comes from gradually facing your troubles and not running away. There is no formal hierarchy. In fact the speaker of the day is probably an individual who felt too guilty to turn down an invitation to help out.

Let me bring up a few criticisms that are often made about Twelve-Step Meetings:

• Some people are put off by the focus on a higher power. This can be interpreted in a personally relevant way. As someone once told me, "You don't have to believe in a higher power, you just have to realize that you're *not* it." But you *are* somebody. And the universal values of honesty and humility are valid for all of us whether you are religious or not; however, it is up to you to face your feelings and make responsible choices.

• Some people are annoyed by the quantity of smoking in meetings. In some communities, consequently, you can now find meetings that are non-smoking.

• Still others may be bothered by the fact that groups are impersonal and deemphasize group discussions, except that directed to the speaker of the moment. This can also be a plus, especially if you are in an initial stage of recovery and do not want to be too visible. Later in recovery, you may want to supplement the help you are getting from a Twelve-Step Program with participation in a therapy group, where cross-talk is encouraged.

• Twelve-Step members tend to attribute life problems primarily to a specific addiction and fail to see other causes of difficulties, such as unresolved childhood pain, low self-esteem or mental illness, which must be addressed.

• In addition, members may see the addictive problem as an *excuse* for irresponsible behavior, instead of as an *explanation* for it. For example, "It's not my fault I ran over the man. I was drunk because I'm an alcoholic." You are responsible for your actions whether an addiction waters down your judgement or not.

As they say, "Take what you can and leave the rest." I suggest that you try a number of meetings to see if this kind of program is right for you. Don't make up your mind on the basis of attending only once or twice. Being a newcomer is always awkward. Furthermore, the first time you gather up your courage to go, anxiety will most likely prevent you from being objective.

* * *

An acquaintance, now many years in recovery, recalled his first Alcoholics Anonymous meeting:

Entering the meeting hall of the neighborhood church, I was terrified. I felt sick to my stomach and thought my legs would buckle underneath me. I was convinced that my history was tragically unique and would horrify anyone who heard it. So I took a seat at the rear of the room, as far as possible away from the center of attention. I sat on my hands to keep them from shaking and refused the offer of coffee as I knew I would spill it.

The room slowly filled with people who appeared content and confident — I was surprised how many there were. Suddenly I got totally paranoid because I thought everyone would spot that I was the outsider, and they'd expect me to stand up and recite my entire past. The only thing that kept me from getting up and leaving was my embarrassment that people would stare at me — which I assumed they would do.

What actually happened and what was said at the meeting to this day remains a blank. I was too anxious to focus on anything but "me." I just remember feeling like a cat in a dog kennel and having a desperate craving for a drink. This sounds ludicrous as I think about it now.

When the meeting was over, I bolted for the door. An elderly woman must have noticed me in the crowd and sensed my discomfort. She spoke to me with compassion, urging me to please return to the next meeting on the following night. I nodded "yes," nervously smiled and then quickly left. I would have agreed to anything so as not to get caught in conversation.

On the way home, I was in a daze. But something in me felt a sense of safety that hadn't been there for a long time. I made a decision to give this group a try. I had nowhere else to turn. It was my only hope.

In my estimation, for initially gaining control in alcohol, drug, and gambling addictions, nothing surpasses Twelve-Step Programs or groups with comparable basic principles. For other compulsive patterns — around food, money, relationships, sex, codependency — Twelve-Step programs can provide an important part, but *not* the totality of what is needed. Since you cannot go on the wagon for these habits, educational and other supplementary support are also necessary.

Let me also add that if you struggle with many compulsive habits, you can get help from a group that addresses even *one* of your problems. For as you will see, the whole recovery process is basically the same, regardless which specific habit plagues you. Furthermore, though at first you may have to tackle the habit that is most destructive to your life, in order to get off the compulsive merry-go-round you must confront other patterns and difficulties as well. For example, you might first be in Alcoholics Anonymous to gain control of your drinking; then be in Alanon or another codependency group to deal with why you wrap your life around partners who drink or who are otherwise unavailable; and finally be in an Adult Children of Alcoholics group to better see the dynamics of your family of origin.

Other kinds of peer support groups

These may be at the homes of individuals in your community or meet in public facilities such as hospitals, schools, and churches.

Some groups are modeled after Twelve-Step programs but have less emphasis on a higher power and/or less emphasis on humility. Women for Sobriety is an example of such a group.

Private educational support groups

There are also groups for stopping smoking, monitoring spending and weight control. Examples are Weight Watchers and SmokEnders. These charge specific fees, usually have professional consultants, and are of varying degrees of competence. Most such groups meet once a week for a set period of time, six to twelve weeks, or function on an ongoing open-ended basis.

Professionally supervised outpatient programs

Such programs often operate in association with a hospital. Or occasionally a physician might work with you while you are in a Twelve-Step program or in a group that does not have medical supervision.

Inpatient hospital treatment programs

These programs are available for drug and alcohol detoxification, eating-weight problems, codependency and gambling addictions. They may be indicated if your daily functioning has been severely incapacitated by your habit and/or when outpatient programs have failed. Thanks to Betty Ford and other celebrities, entering an inpatient treatment program has been somewhat destigmatized. A number of insurance companies and employers are willing to finance employees in such recovery programs, even providing leaves of absence.

Inpatient programs can offer the following:

• An opportunity to interrupt a self-destructive downward cycle;

• Nutritional, medical, and psychological supervision, especially important if serious health and emotional problems are present;

• A safe opportunity to sample life without your addiction within a highly structured environment;

• Starting you in Twelve-Step Programs that can carry over after you leave the hospital;

- Education to help rectify the ravages of your pattern as well as to prepare you for a future without your habit;
- Relapse prevention training;
- A chance to begin to look at other issues in your life which may have been obscured by compulsive living patterns;
- A program involving significant family members. In all compulsive patterns — especially those involving alcohol, drugs, and gambling — relatives can participate in their own groups such as Alanon, Narcanon, Gam-Anon. Here family members can learn to support your recovery without undermining it, to stay out of enabling, nagging, and/or rescuing roles. Positive shifts of family dynamics will both ease your recovery and make relapses less likely to occur. Keep in mind, however, that if family members refuse to be part of the recovery process you can still do it yourself.

If you take an inpatient route, a reasonably good program in your home community is preferable to a high prestige one outside of it. There are several reasons for this:

- There is a greater possibility of integrating family members into treatment, when this is indicated.
- The transition to outpatient treatment resources can be arranged while you are still in the inpatient facility.
- High-prestige programs don't necessarily yield more successful long-term outcomes.

People tend to think that inpatient treatment is always superior to outpatient treatment, but the research does not support this. Yes, inpatient treatment can be an excellent launching pad to recovery. But it is *not* a magical solution. There certainly are individuals who are best off in inpatient programs, but that is not necessarily the case for everyone. Furthermore, many insurance companies will not fund inpatient stays.

Most programs, in general, work if *you* make good use of them. Solid recovery depends much more on your motivation and willingness to make changes than on any particular group or facility.

Note: Detoxification from heavy and/or long-term use of alcohol and certain drugs can be hazardous. For example, withdrawal from even low doses of benzodiazepines (e.g. Librium, Valium, Xanax) that have been used for more than six months can be extremely risky if not controlled by a physician. Be sure physicians involved in your recovery are savvy about addiction, or you may end up getting incompetent and sometimes dangerous advice.

Psychotherapy

It is also wise to entertain the possibility of getting into individual or group psychotherapy. This can greatly enhance your recovery. I strongly advise that you pick a therapist who (1) understands the problems of addictions and family systems, (2) is able to be a "real person" in addition to being a caring and competent professional, — and (3) is firm and confronting as well as warm and supportive. In other words, at base, you're looking for the "good" parent that you never had. Trust your gut reaction when making a choice. Therapists familiar with addictive and compulsive problems are aware that they may need to be more available to you in times of crisis, by phone or by extra appointment.

Psychiatrists, psychologists, social workers, and those trained in specific addictive fields can all be excellent therapists. The capability of the therapist is far more important than the specific training background. However, at the risk of antagonizing my colleagues, let me suggest some therapists that you may want to avoid:

• Do not pick an "emotionally absent" therapist — this includes those that are too formal and/or stuffy — or you will again experience the frustration that you had with your original emotionally absent parent(s).

• Beware of a therapist who inappropriately shares too much of his/her own personal material, or uses you as an arena to solve his/her problems — this also can replicate your childhood.

• Don't link up with a therapist who may mean well but lacks skills to examine the transference issues that occur in the therapist-patient, or therapist-client, relationship. Transference refers to inappropriately transferring unfinished feelings from past relationships onto current relationships. An exploration of this area is vital to your working out problems of intimacy, vulnerability and trust.

• Be leery of a therapist who is antagonistic toward or threatened by your attendance in a Twelve-Step program or other peer support group.

If you prefer group to individual treatment, there are an increasing number of legitimate, professionally run groups for specific addictive patterns, for adult children of alcoholics, and for adult children of other kinds of dysfunctional families. I recommend that you find a group led by a professional who knows your particular addiction from the inside-out, not just from training.

Therapy for many is a new arena. It can provide a supportive neutral zone where you can venture into an unfamiliar but healthier new life-style. Therapy can help you examine what function compulsive living serves in your life, what triggers your indulgences, and — most importantly — how to live your life without engaging in self-destructive patterns. Exploring why you initially fell into a particular kind of habit is academically interesting, but doesn't necessarily help you move into recovery. In fact it all too readily can become an end in itself and yet another excuse for staying stuck.

As you work together with your therapist, the closeness inherent in the therapy process might feel uncomfortable. Your past experience with closeness may have been hazardous. This can be worked through. It will be an important component of your total recovery.

A competent therapist will help you listen to your own inner wisdom, and sort out healthy as opposed to unhealthy responses to situations — figuring out what is age- or stage-appropriate as opposed to what is something to be concerned about. Good therapy will not only keep you honest with yourself, but can also provide a nurturing environment in which you can try out your new "wings" towards personal growth. Your therapist won't know all the answers, but can stand by while you discover them for yourself.

You may be asking yourself, "Why does anyone need a professional therapist — can't friends do the same thing?" The answer is yes and no. Yes, friends can stand by, giving you love and support and suggestions. *But* there is a limit to how much friends can help, and how much you can use them as you bail yourself out of your pain because:

- You'll wear them out.
- You have to reciprocate.
- They aren't trained to "teach you how to fish," though intuitively they sometimes can. If they are close friends, occasionally they'll feed you a fish when you are starving — but this may postpone your learning how to make it without them.

When you are in good therapy, on the other hand, the focus is on *your* needs and *your* feelings and *your* becoming responsible for yourself. During your work in therapy, sometimes your needs will be self-centered, your feelings will be negative, and your "becoming responsible" will have setbacks. That's par for the course. But you are paying good money to your therapist to keep being there and *not* to take any of this personally.

Putting It All Together

In most instances, a combination of different kinds of support is the key to solving the compulsive riddle: You can use *peer support* to get control of specific patterns and catch up on necessary social skills. *Educational groups* can help correct any damage brought on by your indulgences, and can teach you to relate in a healthy way to substances and activities that you formerly abused. *Therapy* can help you start to feel more confident and better about yourself, so that you no longer need to use compulsive living as a feeble compensation.

The support groups that are most helpful will address the *process* of forming new behaviors and attitudes, not just the desired end result. And they will keep *you* in charge and not play into your self-defeating, perfectionist thinking nor your need to rebel.

Here's a report from a woman I worked with, describing two different weight-loss groups she had been in:

> *The first one focused so much on sticking with their particular diet plan — which was supposed to bring a steady weight loss each week — that I never felt comfortable talking*

about all the difficulties I was having. I didn't want to be "bawled-out," so I just didn't tell them about the ways I kept cheating on their program. I finally did lose weight. But I didn't lose my bad habits. I was still struggling each day.

In the second group, we would all discuss places we were having trouble, and some of the unwise and often ridiculous overeating we kept falling back into. We had a lot of laughs and a few tears. This group turned out to be much more valuable. It enabled me to make major changes in my whole relationship to food, rather than me just being a good little obedient dieter.

Remember, no matter what support system you use, informal or formal, do not delegate away your life. It is *your* recovery.

It is important to point out that not all emotional problems are secondary to compulsive living patterns. As mentioned previously, many such difficulties are quite independent of your habits and in fact may have been camouflaged by them. These problems can better (sometimes *only*) be addressed when the compulsive patterns are in control. Any depression, fear or anxiety that is immobilizing should be taken seriously and handled professionally. Occasionally, supplemental medication may be indicated as part of your treatment.

* * *

In selecting a support system, whether it be friends or relatives, self-help or education groups, outpatient or inpatient programs, individual or group psychotherapy, keep the following in mind:

Find people with whom you can share your feelings and thoughts. It must feel like a safe place to be *you*, where your needs won't be discounted and you won't feel demeaned.

Find people whom you can count on for support, without risking their taking over and attempting to rescue you. You want to feel connected but not smothered.

It should be a situation that not only gives "roots" and refueling, but also gives "wings" to move on and become your own person, without fear of being abandoned. The people there should not be threatened by your progress.

Last but not least, *there should be complete confidentiality* so that information shared is never disclosed in other places.

I had an experience some years ago that showed me how private and safe Twelve-Step Anonymous programs truly are. A friend in much distress called me early one evening; he had lapsed into heavy drinking following a year of abstinence. He was very apologetic for bothering me, but obviously distraught. I urged him to come to my house immediately, and he did. After we talked for some time I got him to go with me to a local Alcoholics Anonymous meeting.

We entered the room and, as we sat, my friend was obviously very drunk, clinging to me and draped over my shoulder. At this particular meeting there were not one, not two, but three people familiar to me from other parts of my life, none of whom I expected to see there. They clearly knew this was not my husband, but their kind glances toward me showed no trace of suspicion or judgment.

When I subsequently ran into each of them in the ensuing months, nothing was said of the incident. They asked no questions. I offered no explanations. Sometimes I think it spices up life to remain a woman of mystery.

A Cushion Of Caution

I must give a word of warning. Unfortunately there are a number of treasure hunters and charismatic charlatans about — con artists who are eager to prey on those desperately wanting to stop abusing drugs or alcohol, quit smoking, lose weight, get out of debt, solve life with one quick fix. These types are far more interested in your money than in your well-being. Keep in mind that greedy individuals sometimes have degrees behind their names — M.D., Ph.D., M.S.W. Education does *not* give a person a conscience.

Furthermore, just because someone has written a book or been on radio or television talk shows, don't assume that he or she is legitimate. Publishers accept books on the basis of what they feel will sell well — they don't give lie detector tests to authors. It's only fair to tell you that the publisher of this book is a psychologist as well, so I think that the ideas you're reading here have met a higher standard than most! Media select guests because of their entertainment value, not for their level of integrity.

There are also groups which have included "anonymous" in their names, that are not genuine Twelve-Step Anonymous programs. *Beware.* Use caution in getting support and advice. In your time of vulnerability, do not be tempted by these sorts of people. Stick with recognized and well-established support groups; self-help groups with minimal or no fee; groups led by responsible professionals who have had their own first-hand experience with your particular situations; or therapists who neither offer an instant cure nor tell you that years of therapy are necessary.

Be highly suspicious of overly expensive programs or mail-order plans promising miraculous results. If in doubt, triple check the resource for references.

Reading

Last, I want to mention the vast amount of available literature that relates to compulsive patterns. Books can offer a great deal but *never* the whole deal. Reading can clarify your predicament and help you pierce through your denial, leading to an "aha" feeling of insight. Reading can be a source of perspective, understanding, inspiration, and practical suggestions. However, just as love is not enough, neither are books — including this one. They cannot substitute for human support, nor the concrete game plans and hard work necessary for strong recovery.

Different Needs At Different Stages

The kind of support system that is appropriate will depend not only on who you are and which compulsive pattern you are battling, but also on what stage of recovery you are in.

During the *preparation stage,* as covered in the last two sections of this chapter, utilize anything or anyone that helps you "see it as it is'" and get perspective. This is the time to break through denial and rationalizations. A firm, no-nonsense relative, friend or therapist can give important feedback, if you are brave enough to hear it. If you are in therapy, your therapist can be a supportive ally as you begin to excavate the roots of your compulsive habit:

• Seeing how specific patterns are interwoven into the fabric of your life;
• Helping you acknowledge that continuing to indulge keeps you stuck — secure but stuck;
• Exploring your reluctance to change and your fears about relinquishing the status quo.

At the *stage where you get into abstinence and develop new healthy habits*, group support plays a critical part. For alcohol, drug or gambling addictions, consider regular Twelve-Step program attendance — staying mindful of the recommendation of "ninety meetings in ninety days" — or entering an outpatient or inpatient rehabilitation program. For those caught up in smoking, food, or spending addictions, support-educational programs may be essential for change: Smoke cessation groups can help smokers map out day-by-day weaning strategies; groups for overeaters and over-spenders can offer practical food and money plans. For compulsive patterns around work or relationships, try to find comparable support groups. There are an increasing number of available mini-classes associated with colleges and universities that focus on getting control of your life and relationships.

The main function therapy can serve at this getting-abstinent level is to keep you motivated and honest about how your self-destructive patterns impact on your life. This will reinforce your commitment and remind you that recovery will be in your own best interests. Therapy can also help you deal with newly liberated feelings that emerge when you no longer drown them out with compulsive busyness.

In the *maintenance stage of recovery,* continue to use whatever helps keep you away from old self-destructive patterns. For those struggling with alcohol and drug dependencies, the first "clean" year or two may be pure hell — overwhelmingly painful. Do not underestimate the necessity of staying in regular Twelve-Step or other group support programs. For those pulling out of food-weight addictions, you may want to dip in and out of a variety of "attack" programs. Compulsive spenders might need ongoing financial counseling. Each type of habit will have its own treacherous and seductive pitfalls. Enlist any support that can help you stay out of them.

Once you are beyond the throes of the initial abstinence period from compulsive living, unresolved areas of your life may come crashing down on you. If this happens, intensive psychotherapy can be invaluable for dealing with them. Your recovery will rest on far firmer ground the more you can make sense out of your past:

• Reconstructing and understanding the family atmosphere that you grew up in;

• Seeing how your compulsive patterns evolved in response to your family's interactions;

• Leaving the past in the past.

In sum, use whatever support you need to get off the compulsive merry-go-round. And keep using it as long as you need it.

TOOLS TO GET IN CONTROL

5

New Ways To Cope

If you don't run your own life, somebody else will.
— John Atkinson

Once your support system is in place, what next? It is time to find new ways to cope so that you can begin to gain control. In this chapter, you will become familiar with a game plan and tools of recovery that are applicable to all forms of compulsive patterns, whether they involve substances, activities or preoccupations. You can refer to these tools frequently along your journey of transformation; they are an integral part of any good recovery program.

Let us begin by examining the following crucial areas:

- Setting *goals* for yourself.
- Handling potential *pitfalls*.
- Breaking emotionally fueled *cycles* by learning to appropriately deal with strong feelings.
- Weathering *overwhelming urges* to indulge — "Emergency Urgency."
- Incorporating *exercise* into your life.

Particularly in the early phases of habit changing, writing can be a tremendous aid. A daily journal — keep it private — will enable you to both look at problem areas and to appreciate successes, small and large. If you are like most of us, you will fight writing things down and probably inconsistently do it . This is to be expected. But every little bit will help and can facilitate your moving toward success. Keep central in your mind that since you are changing for *you,* you are also writing things down for *you* — not for your parents, spouse, doctor, boss, or anyone else.

Setting Goals For Yourself

To properly "dress for success," you need to *delineate a tangible goal for yourself.* You have to know where you intend to go if you truly hope to get there. There must be conviction regarding what you want and what you do not want. The goal must be extremely relevant to your needs.

Setting goals affirms that you are starting actively to direct your life, rather than staying in the passive, reactive, victim role. By having goals, you are saying that your needs are important and that you are going to focus energy toward meeting them. Many people are hesitant to set goals, feeling that

- Goals are pointless. What's the use anyway?
- You'll become obsessed with a goal and it will run your life.
- If you don't reach your goal, you will be even more of a failure.

This kind of thinking misses the point. Goals are simply guidelines that *you* create. They can always be revised as you travel along.

When you are changing patterns of any kind, several factors will help in setting goals:

Be realistic as to what you can accomplish in a given time. It is important to get success under your belt. Compulsive patterns are big-league contenders and cannot be conquered overnight. For example, if you are moving out of a couch potato, pot belly stance, do not plan a six-hour-a-day exercise regime, expecting to change instantly into world class shape. A regular hour of bicycling twice a week, with the enjoyment of feeling more active, may be a good place to start.

It also helps to have definite criteria by which you can measure progress. For example, "I will lose ten pounds in six months." Or for a compulsive spender, "I will save $50.00 a month."

Formulate a workable day-by-day, or hour-by-hour plan, which includes lots of tangible mini-tasks. For a procrastinator, on the first day you could clear the desk, on the next day you could get out the bills and sort them, and so on.

Write out your goal, pertinent action steps, and target dates. Frame your statements in a *positive* light. "Each day I will stick with my spending plan," is far more useful than "I will never again spend impulsively." Treat this as a sacred document. Put it in a prominent place and look at it daily. Keep reminding yourself *why* you want to reach your goal by thinking about what your compulsive patterns are keeping you from being, feeling, and doing. Use a calendar to count off days that you stay with your program. Update and revise your goal sheet whenever necessary.

Frequently visualize yourself at your goal. You are no longer overindulging and out of control. You are staying sober, thin, caught up, out of debt, and sane. Picture in detail how you look and feel, what you are wearing and doing, who you are with, and how you are relating to them. See yourself being calm, relaxed and fulfilled, completely at peace. Think of all the new avenues of life that will be open to you. If it helps, use an actual photo of yourself, or of some movie star or other hero or heroine.

Some people prefer to imagine the opposite — being demolished by the consequences of a continued indulgence in a self-destructive pattern. This is a form of aversion therapy. To make it effective, be sure to tie the specific bad habit to the awful consequence. For example, see the piece of cake stuck right on your hips.

Handling Potential Pitfalls

Another critical area is to anticipate troublesome pitfalls, so as to avoid falling into them — especially into the same ones again and again and again. "To fail to plan is to plan to fail" — an old maxim guaranteed to be true. I want to point out that while you are in the midst of wrestling with each compulsive habit, you will need to be intimately involved with all aspects of it. Stay aware of everything related to your pattern.

Quitting smoking was one of the toughest things I've ever done. I had no idea how much I could work against myself. First I thought I'd just stop buying cigarettes. I'm the kind of person that is embarrassed to ask for things from other people. So I figured if I didn't buy cigarettes, I wouldn't be able to smoke.

But the urge was too great. I'd bum cigarettes off of friends or colleagues at work, and then feel so guilty about it that I'd buy a whole pack to give back to the person — and of course buy a pack for myself. So not only had I accomplished nothing, but I was paying twice as much for cigarettes. I eventually abandoned that plan.

Then I thought I'd go ahead and buy my own cigarettes, but only by the pack rather than the carton. My idea was that whenever I felt strong, I'd break the cigarettes in two and throw them out. That plan didn't work either because there I was in the wee hours of the morning, picking the cigarette pieces out of the wastebasket, taping them together, and then smoking them.

Finally I got a little wiser. I not only broke the cigarettes in half but I then flushed them down the toilet. I still had to work hard not to traipse out to the store at all hours of the night to buy more. Well, I would go two or three days and then succumb. But there came a time when I was busy with an art project that intrigued me and I suddenly realized that I had gone seven days without a cigarette. So I really pushed myself and that did it.

From when I first tried, the whole quitting process took about two years, because one time I reverted back to smoking for nine months and another time for a month. But now I feel pretty secure. I haven't smoked for eight years.

Though the fifty-four-year-old man was smiling as he told me of his past struggles, weaning off cigarettes had clearly been a difficult task.

Pre-plan all of your time during early days of habit breaking, even if such planning seems excessive.

Being at loose ends leaves you too vulnerable for retreating into old habits. For instance, decide exactly what you will do in the transitions of the day — getting going in the morning, shifting gears after work, moving into evening relaxation, and so on. Figure out how to fortify and take care of yourself in non-addictive ways. Have specific details in your plans.

If you are battling compulsive eating you might say to yourself, "When I get home from work I will pick up the mail and take it directly to the living room to read without entering the kitchen. Then I'll go change, lie down a few minutes, and only when I'm relaxed will I let myself go into the kitchen to get something to eat."

Carefully rehearse how to handle particular rough spots — potential Waterloos.

You might want to zero in on one specific hurdle each week. You can choose a difficult time of day, a place, or a situation that normally does you in. Visualize it in all its gory details, and the horrible scenario that all too often unfolds: where you are, when and with whom it happens, associated activities. Remember the "hangover" feelings and aftermath.

Then think through possible response options and exactly how you would *like* to handle the situation: a play-by-play plan of specific steps necessary to avert disaster. The whole idea is to move from passive to active, so as to eliminate the horrible helpless feelings that set you up for backsliding.

For example, if you want to avoid alcohol at social situations, here is the way your thinking might go in regards to a party: "I don't know many people there and usually feel awkward making conversation, particularly if there is a potential romantic interest present. How can I get through this anxious time without drinking?"

Then you might visualize yourself getting ready to go to the party, all dressed up, looking splendid and feeling confident. This image could be followed by seeing yourself arriving at the party, walking calmly around the room, and starting to feel centered. You could then move on to finding non-threatening people to chat with.

During this time you would take a glass of ginger ale and then stay far away from the bar, firmly refusing any other offered drinks. Eventually you envision yourself feeling relaxed and starting to converse with an attractive person.

Be ready to manage "trigger" situations that may fall into your lap.

- You can literally leave.
- You can react in a non-self-destructive way.
- You can have an "emotional first-aid plan" on hand.

A woman who had struggled against being so driven and "Type A" came to my office in triumph one day. During the previous week, the computer at work was down as she approached the deadline for an important project. In former times she would have panicked and blown up at everyone in earshot. But this time, due to our having discussed alternative reactions, she left the office early, called a friend, and they went out and enjoyed a matinee movie. She also said that she now carried some of her favorite tapes in the car. Whenever there was a traffic jam rather than steam and rant, she used the extra time to enjoy opera.

Plan exactly what to say to those who push.
Let's look at an example — how will you react when someone says, "It's a special occasion. One drink won't hurt. Don't be a wet blanket."

Think about situations where you have given in to such pressures. Remember the disastrous results? It is high time you stop pleasing everyone by taking everything offered to you or always following *their* wishes, just so you won't make waves or offend someone. You have a right to do what you want. Risk being rude. Stay aware of your needs and learn to communicate them effectively to others. "No thank you," will suffice. You needn't defend nor explain further. It is up to you if you share any more. Some people prefer to add a pat statement relating to their particular habit:

"I'm allergic to liquor."

"I'm a non-smoker."

"I want to stick to my food plan. Please don't tempt me." Actual role playing with someone else can be an excellent preparation for these situations.

Stay aware of your level of control at any given time and place. Don't set traps for yourself. Steer clear of substances and activities that you can't resist. Keep them locked up or under wraps. Also, be alert to conditions such as being tired or intoxicated which can lower your resistance and make it difficult for you to maintain control.

Carefully monitor or even avoid seductive situations that you associate with your habit. If there are people or circumstances that absolutely draw you in like a magnet, stay away from them altogether. Examples: If you always smoke when you drink coffee, only drink coffee when you have no cigarettes available. If overeating is a problem, don't have guests in the kitchen.

If you should slip back into old patterns, forgive yourself and get right back "on course."
See the slip as something you chose, a poor choice perhaps, but not a sign of failure or moral degeneration. We'll deal more with this later.

Breaking Emotionally Fueled Cycles

Next, it is imperative to examine specific feelings and uncomfortable areas that formerly triggered compulsive patterns. These cause you to feel overwhelmed, caught, pulled in many directions, drained, at the mercy of others, rejected, invalidated, and so on. When the feelings occur, you invariably walk right into the "opportunity" to indulge compulsively and immediately succumb to your particular pattern — the instant gratification, convenient escape, and quick "non-solution."

The following emotional areas discussed in Chapter 2 must be handled in new healthy ways:

Refueling and self-nurturing.
You are important, and it is essential to become comfortable taking care of yourself. Get back in touch with your own history, continuity, and life direction. Look at old photos, papers you've written,

letters from friends, books you've enjoyed, art that is meaningful. Listen to music that moves you. You might rekindle neglected friendships from the past or better reach out to present ones. Take a walk in the park, a drive in the country. Reacquaint yourself with nature, things eternal and inspirational — the ocean, mountains, camp fires, flowers, animals, natural beauty. Sit and take in the splendor of what is there. Feeding ducks always serves me well.

Resurrect or develop restorative activities that are simple and calm and to you nonaddictive — a good (or bad) movie, a special treat, a browse in the book store, a call or visit with a supportive friend, a laid-back non-productive couple of hours, a distracting outing or exercise. Be kind to yourself. Engage in something you truly enjoy.

When you need time away from others to change pace or get space, ask for it in direct ways that people understand. Take an hour, a day, a weekend for yourself. Even short respites can be refreshing. Some people benefit by regularly getting to appointments fifteen minutes early in order to take a few moments for themselves. You are less vital to the running of the world than you think.

Providing enough excitement to keep life interesting and challenging.
The place in your life that has been stuffed with high drama followed by all sorts of hangovers needs to be filled in more healthy and satisfying ways.

The problem at hand is how to find natural highs that you feel good about. Participate in what to you are nonaddictive activities, work or sports that truly keep you on your toes. You might set up projects for yourself that stretch you to your limits. You may want to travel and have other adventures to keep life interesting. You could make spur-of-the-moment social plans. Try a variety of directions. Remember, you don't need your parents' permission to do any of these.

But stay cognizant of the danger of setting up excitement as an escape. For it would then simply become a new variant of compulsive living, detouring you from facing what needs facing in your life.

Having fun, relaxing and handling in-between times.
Most of us who have wrestled with "bad" habits have had great difficulty giving ourselves permission to slow down and relax. We feel guilty when we do, for we are exceedingly uncomfortable with nonproductive time, often going out of our way to avoid it. The little voices in our heads forever haunt us with all we "could" and "should" be doing. We have not been able to kick back unless we are spaced out, and have watered down our consciences with our particular habits. In other words, we at base are so driven by responsibility that we can only allow ourselves to be irresponsible when we use self-destructive patterns as vehicles. We have inextricably tied relaxation with indulging in our pattern of choice.

> *Since I stopped smoking four months ago, I've put on seven pounds. Evenings are my downfall. All day I'm busy. But after I come home, make dinner, clean up a bit, I feel lost and disconnected. I don't know what to do with myself. If I don't have specific plans, I wander around my apartment, indiscriminately watching TV and munching my way from dinner to bedtime. I push myself to slow down, relax, and just savor the evening. It's not easy but I'm getting better at it.*

That was a thirty-three-year-old lawyer who was actively attacking one of her problem areas.

You need to practice being comfortable with doing nothing, partaking in whatever suits your fancy that is not self-destructive. One fear will be that you will turn into a total vegetable. Have faith that eventually you will find your own energy from within yourself — an energy that is exhilarating rather than driven. The trick is to intersperse controlled "doing" with planned "not doing," so that there is flexibility in your life. This shift of gears can begin with consciously and regularly setting aside one half hour a day, at minimum, to slow down and to ponder what you really feel and want — to find new interests or to reinvest in old ones.

Self-medicating feelings that seem overwhelming.
In facing life without the insulation of compulsive patterns, you must ride through many painful times. The anxiety and tension that formerly kicked off self-destructive habits will pull for old deeply

buried, raw intense misery from your childhood — feeling worthless, abandoned, helpless, and not knowing when the agony would end.

This pain can be so overwhelming that it leaves you feeling frighteningly out of control — a terrifying emotional state that you have spent your life time trying to avoid. There was no help then. There is now. With patience and support, you will be able to build up your toleration for such feelings and delay your need to escape. Even strong feelings won't last forever. They will eventually dissipate on their own. Meditation, contemplation, long walks, journal writing, or contact with a good friend can help give perspective and enable you to regain your inner sense of balance. There are specific relaxation techniques that you can master to help you along.

I want to highlight *anger,* as it is a complex feeling that needs sorting out. When you are aware of being angry, be especially careful so that you understand what it stands for:

- It may be a justified reaction to a present circumstance.
- It may be the result of a small current injustice having opened up a whole gunnysack of stored up anger.
- It may be a cover-up, masking uncomfortable feelings of sadness, vulnerability, and a reluctance to face life as it is.

In sum, as you begin to spot particular emotional triggers that precipitate crises, you can learn to interrupt the compulsive cycles that up to now have been out of your control. The first step will be to stay with feelings long enough to identify them. This will enable you to think of alternative ways to handle these feelings:

- To simply weather them through;
- To actively let go of them;
- To express them to other people;
- Or to act on them in appropriate ways.

Unfortunately, while these pockets of tenderness are being explored, it can feel as if you are at the dentist, having a tooth drilled without anesthesia. As you get more experience using new coping skills, this degree of horror *will* pass. Remember, what happens to you in life is often out of your control. But you have choices regarding how you *feel* about what happens.

There is a point that needs emphasis. As you move along, recognize current feelings that seem inappropriately magnified, way out of proportion to what a present situation warrants. Such feelings have dipped into past unfinished business. Therapy may be indicated if you feel too uncomfortable or become immobilized.

Weathering "Emergency Urgency"

Be mentally prepared to ride through feelings of "emergency urgency." In those of us plagued by compulsive patterns, the overwhelming urge to indulge can take over like an unexpected storm. *You must do everything in your power to prevent yourself from fading into an altered, "mindless" ego state, where automatic indulging follows.* Here are some suggestions that can fortify you when seductive urges beckon unmercifully:

Get in the present. Remind yourself that you are in charge, you are not helpless, you have choices. Look in the mirror if that helps.

Delay and distract yourself. You are biding for time. Each second and minute can make a difference. Push yourself to wait ten to twenty minutes. Horrible feelings and urges won't go on forever. Start writing. If you can write two pages on what you feel, you will probably travel from feeling like an overwhelmed child back to feeling like an "I can hang in there" adult. Hopefully a small light of perspective will shine through at the end of the tunnel.

Physically move out of the potential scene of the crime — far away if necessary.

Take care of yourself in a nonself-destructive way that requires minimal thinking and energy — *not* figuring out taxes or some other chore you hate. Thumb through a magazine, take a nap, laze around, make a phone call, take a bubble bath, take a walk. Permit yourself to relax without using your compulsive pattern.

Visualize the full-blown scenario of going out of control, and realize you don't have to do it.

Take out your goal sheet and look at it. See yourself at your goal, and then the whole thing dissolving before your eyes. Then reconstruct your goal sheet.

Stay extra alert to all decisions that could set up disaster. Watch the "I just happened to walk into the store" kind of nondecisions.

Try to figure out what your basic hunger is really for — love, nurturing, support, validation? If you weren't so busy obsessing about whether to indulge or not to indulge, what would you be thinking about?

If you can, get in touch with what you are feeling — tired, anxious, tense, overwhelmed, angry, lonely, bored? Then do something appropriate for the particular feeling. If it is impossible to figure out specifically what is bugging you, stay with the nonspecific generic discomfort and simply move on to a pleasant distraction or diversion. Don't use your habit as self-medication, a time filler, or a source of excitement.

What are you not doing for yourself that you would like to be doing? Don't use your habit as compensation.

What are you doing that you don't want to be doing, and are feeling resentful about? Are you taking care of everyone else's needs but your own? Are you being a martyr to avoid hurting other people or disappointing them? What are you running away from? Don't use your habit as an ineffective revenge.

What are you putting off that is a necessity to do — work projects, letters to write, phone calls to make, and so on? Don't use your habit as an escape gratification.

What undelivered messages to others are you stuffing down inside yourself? Are you angry because people aren't reading your mind? Don't use your habit as a fruitless rebellion.

Use your "on-call" support system. If you can, tell other people exactly what you want — tea, sympathy, love, whatever. If you can't be specific about what you want, just tell someone that you need to touch base with another human being.

If you do start to indulge, cut your losses as soon as you can. Stop mid-binge. Spit out the alcohol or food. Put out the cigarette. Hang up the phone or say good-bye to the "not-good-for-you" partner. Run out of the store. Switch your mind back to the business at hand. Force yourself to break the pattern with some other activity.

Get right back with your program. What is done five minutes ago is done. Don't beat yourself to a pulp. You are fallible like everyone else. Get back on the horse — but not on a compulsive one.

Incorporating Exercise Into Your Life*

The word "exercise" scares a lot of people. It does not have to be of monumental magnitude. Exercise simply means becoming physically more active. Try out different activities to find what fits you, your life-style, and your schedule. Build the activity into your daily and weekly routine. Find a friend to do it with so that you don't cop out on yourself.

Exercise can serve a number of functions:

• As part of new healthy life patterns, it can encourage you to let go of old self-destructive ones.

• It provides time just for you which can start to be fun.

• It gets you back in touch with using and being comfortable with your body.

• It helps burn off calories by increasing your metabolic rate. This is obviously important if you are fighting the battle of the bulge.

Some years ago, Sister Marion Irvine, a San Francisco nun and grammar school principal, was a guest on my radio show. She shared with us how she had started running. When she was in her late forties, she was bothered by a constant weight struggle and a two-and-a-half-pack-a-day cigarette habit. A niece suggested she take up jogging to improve her health. Having never liked exercise, Sister Marion resisted but finally started to jog so as to avoid being nagged by her niece. Slowly she found herself loving to run and going out into the park whenever she could. Her weight problem and cigarette habit gradually fell by the wayside as she enjoyed having greater stamina.

Often she encountered a race in progress and asked to join. To her and everyone else's amazement, she consistently started to win. One thing led to another and to make a long story short, at age

*This part should be disregarded by readers for whom *compulsive* exercise is a problem!

fifty-four years, in 1984, Sister Marion became the oldest woman ever to qualify for the Olympic marathon trials.

Taking up exercise will most likely not lead you to such glory, but who knows? At minimum, you will win a better shape.

Begin to walk greater distances; this can get you going. Regularly go by foot rather than drive or take a bus. When you do drive, park three or four blocks from where you are going so that you get an extra walk. Take the steps instead of the elevator. Begin to walk a little faster and longer.

I only caution you to be careful that an activity doesn't become yet another driven pattern. According to my jogging friends, the paths are riddled with recovering alcoholics, smokers, and over-eaters. These people compulsively jog with the same obsessiveness that they formerly focused on substances. They are not yet off the merry-go-round.

The Old And The New

In order to pull together how you might use these new behavior skills, let us look at three sample scenarios. First I will spell out probable old patterns like:

• The spendaholic who is also a latent relationship junkie: You were supposed to meet a new date downtown. You wait for an hour. The other person never shows up. You feel devastated and abandoned. On the way home, you pass a store where there is a sale. You walk in to browse. Some $250 later you leave, arms loaded with unneeded items. You guiltily enter your house, stuff your purchases in a closet, flake out, and feel like a total failure.

• The compulsive eater who is also a latent compulsive perfectionist: The day has been full of disasters. There is too much work and too little time. You feel totally over-stretched and under-appreciated. After dinner, you remember that you need to make cookies for your daughter's class. As you are baking, you taste a little dough. You are tired. Why not? However, this leads to eating the broken cookies, the slightly burnt cookies, and eventually close to half the cookies. You start to feel sick, probably more from guilt than from what you have actually eaten.

• The compulsive gambler who is also a latent excitement junkie: You haven't gambled lately, nor even been near the action. Your wife wants to get away for the weekend. You remember how beautiful Lake Tahoe is — you haven't been there in years. Why not go to South Lake Tahoe, such a nice little town. The closer you get, the hungrier you get to look in on the casinos. It wouldn't hurt to watch for a half an hour. But as you go through the doors, you already know that you have gone too far, well beyond the point of having any control.

Though stories for your habit may differ, the plot undoubtedly unfolds in a comparable way. Particular situations precipitate feelings that make you uncomfortable. These trigger you into an automatic response; you underestimate your powers of control; and you walk right into the opportunity to partake in your compulsive pattern of choice. Your indulging is predictable, followed by a hangover of guilt and remorse, and endless promises to yourself to abstain in the future.

As you learn to get in the behavioral driver's seat, you will recognize forks in the road leading to potential disaster, at some level each being a decision *not* to take responsibility. With self-honesty and preplanning you can make clear alternate responses:

• Arrange your life so that it feels more manageable.
• Directly address unavoidably stressful situations.
• Weather out uncomfortable feelings.
• Stay away from opportunities to indulge.
• Move into non-addictive activities.
• Choose to sometimes indulge *but* not run yourself down for it.

Incidently, do *not* indulge in a substance or in a risk-taking activity if recovery for you mandates total abstinence. In these cases, occasional indulgences *cannot* be a viable option.

* * *

Let us revisit our three compulsive people, now in recovery:

The spendaholic: You have planned exactly what to do after a disappointment. You call a friend, arrange to meet at a restaurant, spend ten minutes kvetching and complaining, and then go on to make some fun plans.

The compulsive eater: On "one of those awful days" you announce to your family that you need time alone. First you glance through the newspaper. Then you run a hot bubble bath. While you are luxuriating in it, you ponder how much simpler but lonelier single life used to be. You also think about ways you have become everyone's servant, and that you best have a family meeting to discuss a better distribution of the work load. Since you had already promised to bring a snack to school, instead of baking you decide to buy some cookies from the store.

The compulsive gambler: When your wife wants to get away for the weekend, you think of Lake Tahoe and the beauty of the mountains. It is very, very tempting. But you quickly remember the proximity of the casinos, and realize that you are feeling too vulnerable. You know you will be drawn in, so you go to Monterey instead.

A lot of practice and a number of setbacks will most likely occur as you move along the road to recovery. There are no right or wrong ways to get there. Averting relapses will be explored in greater detail in Chapter 7. The important thing is to use what works, and take responsibility for doing it. You must keep refocusing on your goal, stay honest with yourself about any difficulties you are having, and keep plugging away. An anonymous note sent to me during a rough time of my life said, "A person doesn't fail, he just gives up trying."

An Updated Mental Outlook

My life has been filled with terrible misfortunes, most of which never happened.

— Mark Twain

So far so good. It looks simple. You set a goal, make plans and alter your responses to certain situations. Compulsive patterns fade to the background of your life and, presto, you are in control. Wrong. Nine hundred and ninety-nine times out of one thousand, things do *not* go according to such a schedule. Your intentions are fine. Your plans are well rehearsed. What is holding up the show?

Combatting The Undertow

In the last section, we concentrated on basic skills for modifying self-destructive patterns. This is equivalent to stopping the symptoms, an essential and difficult preliminary step. However, while you are busy transforming your behavior patterns, you must also deal with what is underneath or you will be obstructed by it. Compulsive habits are but the tip of the iceberg, kept afloat by a faulty self-image and belief system. These thought processes are deeply embedded in your whole being and must be actively confronted.

There are many subtle and not so subtle ways in which you have been at odds with your good intentions. Your efforts to get into recovery have frequently run up against self-created "dragons": cynicism, pessimism, hopelessness, laziness, fear, impatience, and countless sneaky rationalizations and excuses.

While part of you has too weakly said, "I will try to change," consciously or unconsciously, a whole chorus of powerful voices shouted back, "I don't deserve anything better," "I'm scared to change," "I don't know how to change," "What if I can't change?" "What if I fail?" "What if I don't do it as well as I should?" "What if I do change and I don't like what I become?" "What if others don't like what I become and I end up all alone?" Bogged down with all this inner dialogue of negative self-talk, it is not surprising that your recovery program all too easily grinds to a halt.

In no way can these dragons be slain overnight. But you can start to challenge them and take away their power. As was discussed earlier in the book, worthless feelings come from not having felt sufficiently valued and supported in your family of origin. Because of the way children think, you blamed yourself for not getting what you needed. You convinced yourself that you were "no good," and that the cards of life dealt you were somehow appropriate to your "badness."

You must eventually see that what happened to you just happened. It was by chance that you were born into a particular family at a particular time of life. The events of your childhood subsequently unfolded, quite out of your control. There was nothing inherently bad or defective about you then, nor is there now.

For you to give full energy to your recovery program, the essential task at hand is to move toward adopting a whole new self-image. This is not a small task. But with time it is one that can be accomplished. Once you realize that you don't need to be defined by who you were and how you behaved in the past, there is potential for all kinds of changes. You need an updated view of yourself. You must begin to see that you are somebody who has worth.

Beliefs And Attitudes That Get In The Way

The thinking patterns of those with compulsive habits are extremely counterproductive. They have an absolute, all-or-none character where one mistake becomes an indication of a lifetime defect; you expect perfection in yourself and others; you feel that what you do equals who you are; life is a burdensome pursuit of inaccessible goals; and you believe successful people never make errors nor have to exert any effort.

You may have spent your life time dwelling on the negative, always seeing the glass as half empty instead of half full. It is important to take your self-defeating, doomsday proclamations out into the sunlight and look at them with fresh eyes. For example, you may have told yourself that you have to do things perfectly in order to be a worthwhile person and to be liked by others. Has this been true? When a project has gone perfectly, has that suddenly improved your character and made you instantly popular? And when you failed to be perfect, did you lose meaningful friends? Nonsense.

Furthermore, you are likely to be someone who loses perspective when something doesn't go one hundred percent according to plan. "I ate an extra piece of bread" equals "I blew my diet," which becomes "I can't stick with any food plan," which evolves into "I'll never be able to get control of my weight," which automatically means "I'm a failure." This makes for a tough life. One mistake and it's all over. Something indeed may not have gone according to plan. Over a lifetime, unless you attempt nothing, you will fail in countless individual endeavors. These do not make *you* a failure.

The only failure of tragic proportions is to be so afraid of making mistakes that you take no risks, and settle for a minimal life of untried dreams.

Also, you probably only respect history when it reinforces your worst fears, whether it relates to you or to someone else. You then give it unconditional power over your present life. For example, you have heard about a friend who was a smoker, an alcoholic, and a workaholic. He suffered a heart attack, was unable to change his patterns, and subsequently died. Therefore, you quickly conclude, "No one can change. What's the use of even trying." Notice that in arriving at this conclusion you fail to find, or choose to disqualify, any stories of those who have been able to modify their habits. Positive facts don't count. How come?

Another self-defeating thought pattern is the way you feel responsible for *everything*. The car breaks down; your children don't get good enough grades; your spouse flirts. Surely it is *all* your fault, an indication of your inadequacy, laziness, and poor character. Though I make this a bit extreme, most likely you are troubled by comparable pervasive guilt and a false sense of total responsibility for others. This is much too heavy a burden to carry in life. Be charitable with yourself and accept the fact that you do the best you can. Others also have choices about how they think, feel and behave. They have inner motors of their own, stop feeling you are or should be their God. Once you begin to evaluate yourself, you will find that your thinking is loaded with such distortions.

Changing The Tapes
Call to mind outdated beliefs and thinking patterns from childhood that you are still going along with or rebelling against. These may have come from your parents or they may have been dictated by your severe "three-year-old conscience," and later

reinforced by others in your life. Substitute new reasonable adult beliefs . At first the old ones will feel as if they have been laid down in cement. Not so. They can be changed, if you are willing to systematically work at them.

Here are a few examples of what I mean by replacing old thinking with new.

Old: You must always do things perfectly.
New   I'll do what I can — it doesn't have to be perfect.

Old: If you make one mistake, you might as well give up.
New: Of course I'll make mistakes, but that doesn't make me a failure. I'll just keep trying.

Old: To take care of yourself is selfish and self-indulgent.
New: I have a right to attend to my own feelings and needs.

Old: It's your responsibility not to upset others.
New: I'm not responsible for other people's feelings and reactions.

Old: If you are "good," others will love you.
New: I have got to be "me." The people that really count will love me for who I am.

* * *

I knew a man who became extremely fearful about driving alone to unfamiliar places. He was convinced he would get lost. In childhood, he had been teased for never being able to find things, an image he had taken to heart. Indeed, his anxiety would so overwhelm him that all too frequently he did lose his way.

We talked at length about putting a new "tape" in his head. Instead of telling himself, "I'm going to get lost. I'll never find the way. I'm just no good at this kind of thing," the next time he felt lost, he was to pull over to the side of the road. Then he was to take ten minutes to get himself relaxed, and start saying to himself, "I can find my way. There is no rush. If I temporarily take the wrong route, it doesn't matter. I will persist until I get there."

It worked. Though this was not the last time he had troubles, one success gave him confidence that his track record could be altered, that he could change. He gradually stopped seeing himself as someone who got lost — someone who could never get anywhere, physically and symbolically.

Affirmations

Another way actively to transform your self-image is through affirmations — positive statements that you say to yourself:

"I feel good about myself and my life."

"I am a good person."

"I like being in control."

"I like being my own person — not dependent on others for permission."

"I can survive strong feelings and don't need to run from them."

"I can take care of myself and don't need others to rescue me."

"Indulging won't solve anything."

"Only I know what I want in my life."

Affirmations can be both spoken and written. If there are negative thoughts that get in the way of the positive ones, it is important to argue them out with yourself. For example, if you find yourself obsessing that "Things will never work out," talk back and say, "Yes, they can this time." If you are stuck with "I've never succeeded in the past," answer back with "But I intend to stick to my plan now." "I've always given up before," can be knocked down with "I have no intentions of giving up now." This process is sometimes referred to as "thought stopping." As you will see in Part III, affirmations can also target specific hurdles for particular patterns.

The basic idea is to demolish all the pessimistic doubting parts of your psyche that have been given too much power in the past. After all, *you* are supposed to be in charge. How about pounding a little heavier with the gavel?

A number of years ago, I worked with a woman who was laboring to gain control of her eating patterns. She forever sabotaged herself with negative thinking. In order to help her handle an upcoming social event, together we rehearsed some affirmations: "I am not really very hungry," "I don't need to eat," "I'm here to enjoy the socializing, not the food."

After the event, she told me what had happened. As she was standing in the buffet line, apparently she got carried away with her affirmations. First reciting them to herself, she so mentally blocked out the presence of others that she started saying her affirmations out loud. Finally another guest, also in line, turned to her and asked why she was getting food at all, since she obviously wasn't hungry. She felt a bit foolish, but the affirmations did the trick. She didn't overeat.

Rationalizations And Excuses

Let us again examine another important area of potential trouble. Remember the rationalizations that we looked at in Chapter 2? These are regularly used excuses that you employ to cop out on your good intentions, or to forsake your efforts to change when the going gets tough. They relate to so-called "reasons" for abandoning your plans because of a mood, time of day or week, special occasion, et cetera, et cetera, et cetera. Even though you may sincerely want to let go of old patterns, rationalizations make it possible to cling ferociously to the status quo. They always lurk around, waiting to grab you in a moment of weakness.

When you think of past efforts that have fallen by the wayside, rationalizations have often been the culprit. For example, you made a resolution to quit smoking. You weathered through the initial withdrawal time, and stayed clean for fourteen days. Then an important meeting came up. You felt nervous. You lit up, telling yourself you "needed a lift" and would "only smoke one cigarette." Indeed, you only smoked one cigarette *at a time*.

Another story: You decided to stick with a budget. The beginning of the week went fine. You kept track of all you spent, stayed out of the stores in the evenings, forced yourself to keep busy with other activities. Then came Friday evening. It had been "such a hard week," you told yourself. You felt you deserved a "little extra something." The problem was that the "little extra something" could barely be carried home.

Rationalizations imply that there is an authority figure to whom you are accountable and must explain your behavior. Have you forgotten that you are a grown-up? It's time to renovate your thinking and climb out of the mentality of acting as if others set the rules and your only option is to obey or to rebel. You have done enough publicly pleasing others while privately filling your own needs on the Q. T.

So, as you reach for the drink, the piece of pie, your credit card; as you run to a self-destructive relationship, to unnecessary work, or just run away; as you rationalize to yourself that "it doesn't matter" — STOP. *You* know which choices are wise and which aren't. Don't try to fool the most important person in your life — you.

Staying On Course
Along the path to recovery, you will undoubtedly make mistakes. You are human, not God. In order to stay on course and not feel discouraged by plateaus or setbacks, an ongoing objective inventory will serve you well. Here are some areas to regularly ponder:

Keep acknowledging each bit of progress. All of it is significant. Be proud of the distance you have already come. Don't diminish it by dwelling on the work yet to be done. In an interview with Jackie Joyner-Kersee, the 1988 Olympic gold medal heptathalon winner, when asked the secret of her success, she answered, "Determination, dedication, and discipline."

Take stock of what went as you had hoped. Notice the pre-planning and support that helped you stay with your program; the non-addictive ways you took care of yourself; the "emergency urgency" you resisted; the issues of your life that you faced directly. Give yourself a nice big pat on the back for each triumph.

Look at any particular times, situations or feelings that gave you trouble. Perhaps there were circumstances in which you mistakenly thought you had more control than you actually did, or areas in which you mentally sabotaged yourself with old beliefs, thinking patterns or rationalizations. Where are you still living dangerously, flirting with potential disasters?

Examine your goal and see if it needs revision. Be sure it continues to be realistic and relevant to your needs, and that sticking with your plans is in line with reaching your goal. Also, stay sufficiently in touch with the discomfort of *not* changing your patterns, to properly maintain your motivation. Your goal and plans to reach it will need constant reworking.

Look at what hanging on to compulsive struggles is serving in your life. What are you avoiding feeling, facing, doing, and being? Deep down you know the answers to these questions. In sum, zero in on where you are actively resisting success. You must take full responsibility for the ongoing job of identifying hurdles that interfere with adhering to your program and moving toward your goal.

Postmortems are an important tool to help you stay in charge. Learn from your mishaps, and hopefully see the humor in the self-created consequences. Then go on to do more of what works and less of what doesn't.

You can gradually learn to distinguish appropriate as opposed to inappropriate feelings and reactions to a situation. It is normal to feel annoyed and frustrated when progress is slow. But when you feel ashamed and guilty, you are caught into useless suffering. Life is difficult enough without making yourself unnecessarily miserable.

It's Your Show

I firmly believe that the road to success is paved with action. As you zero in on your trouble spots of compulsive living, keep the following in mind:

• At all times, maintain an overall picture of the recovery process so as to be able to fit each component of it into its proper place.

• *You* stay in charge, even when you use other people, support groups or professionals for help.

• No matter how difficult the uphill climb may be, gaining

control of bad habits is possible. Other people have successfully done it. You can too.

• Whenever you run head on into a brick wall, creatively attack your dilemma from a new angle.

• If you are scared, feel the fear but walk right through it.

• Don't give up — you only have to try one more time than you fail.

It takes conscious effort to update a mental outlook. You are shifting from a passive to an active stance: "I will try," to "I will"; "I am supposed to," to "I choose to." The difference may sound inconsequential. It is not. It is the difference between being a child and being an adult.

6

A TWO-WEEK DETOX PROGRAM

We are continually faced by great opportunities brilliantly disguised as insoluble problems.

— Anonymous

*J*ust as you can't learn to swim from reading books, you can't recover from compulsive behavior by simply gathering information and thinking about recovery. If you are ever to make headway, you have to jump into the water and do something.

Prepare Yourself For Success

Look again at the recovery issues already raised:

• See your compulsive living *as it is,* without rose-colored glasses. Face how you really feel about it and what it's doing to your life. You've weighed the pros and cons of continuing to live in the fast lane, compulsively avoiding life. Though your old habits have become comfortable and familiar in rather a "sick" way, hopefully you are game to take a risk and go out into the world naked, without them.

• Recognize your compulsive pattern as being separate from you, a misdirection that you have taken. Remember, you're a "good" person with a "dumb" habit.

• Create an emotional, a physical and a social environment to give you maximum support for letting go of your self-destructive habit. It is stupidity, not strength, to avoid getting necessary support.

• Set a goal that is *for you.* You'll want to refer to this over and over again, whenever your good intentions weaken.

As mentioned previously, for some patterns — compulsive drinking, abuse of drugs, smoking, gambling, shoplifting, pursuing dead-end relationships, promiscuous sex, phobic avoidances — the goal is total abstinence.

For other patterns, your goal will be to taper off and/or abstain from the self-destructive aspects of your behavior, while developing the healthy aspects: For obsessive working, you want to sense and separate out the escapist part while learning to work in a non-driven way. In regard to out-of-control eating you need to stop overeating, binge eating and purging while learning to have an appropriate relationship with food. For compulsive spending, you must stop irresponsible spending, spending sprees and spending beyond your means while learning to responsibly manage your money. In addition, if you are overweight, your goal will include sensible eating that leads to a desired weight loss; if you are in debt, your goal is to control spending and get out of the red.

• Confront anticipated emotional, behavioral or social hurdles armed with clear plans of attack.

• Psych yourself up with a positive attitude. Do whatever you have to do to sustain it no matter what setbacks occur.

Get Set To Bite The Bullet

In order to rob rationalizations of their power, it is best to take them on directly, one at a time. The Two-Week Detox Program that I am about to explain is specifically aimed at doing this. It will give you a method to steer clear of "mind traps" that are rampant along the road to recovery. You can then choose *not* to give in to them, to walk right through them. Ultimately, to stay in charge, you must stick with your plans and not be sidetracked by mental hurdles that obstruct your journey.

Whether you're in a formal program or breaking out of compulsive living patterns on your own, this two weeks can fortify you. It will keep you cognizant of the choices that you have and get you launched in a new, controlled direction. Though it is not exactly like being in the Betty Ford Clinic, don't underestimate its potential benefits. And it will not stretch your pocketbook the way expensive outpatient and inpatient care programs can.

I want to underline in red letters that this program is NOT a magic quick fix for your habit. I know of no one who ever permanently shifted completely out of compulsive patterns in two weeks. This would be rather unlikely. If it could be done that easily, you would not have this book in your hands.

The two weeks will simply be a focused period of time to help you get a handle on your self-destructive living — into "abstinence", "on the wagon," "off the plastic," "out of the refrigerator," into forward gear, or whatever. It evolved from my own experience as well as that of patients and friends. In the past, I tried making it a three-week program, but found that it was too much — folks either got bored or burned out. Two weeks seems about right.

The more serious you are regarding your decision to stop a particular self-destructive habit, the better use you will be able to make of the program. Though willpower is helpful, it is like a fair weather friend — nice to have around but it may abandon you just when you need it. Decision, on the other hand, is a much more reliable companion. If you are not yet firm in your decision, try out the program as a test run. Hopefully it will give you enough success to kindle your motivation.

While you are doing the two weeks I strongly suggest the following:

- Pick a period in your life that is not unduly hectic.
- Get enough sleep and eat three healthy meals a day.
- Arise early enough so as not to be rushed.
- Take a brisk fifteen-minute walk once or if possible twice a day.

"D Day" — Week One

Tackle one habit at a time. Follow all the days in succession. Each day targets a specific area of faulty thinking. Don't skip anything.

Day 1. Set up a workable plan.
Day 2. Accept the nuisance of staying vigilant.
Day 3. Don't use blame as a cop-out.
Day 4. Don't use life's unfairness as a cop-out.
Day 5. Battle pessimism.
Day 6. Don't fool yourself into making exceptions.
Day 7. Recognize but don't give into discomfort.

This first week will be rough but you can do it. You will have the best results if you write about the day's topic in a journal for five to ten minutes every morning. Writing will help keep you aware and in charge. Try to fix the topic in your mind all day. Don't expect to do this week or any other week perfectly. You're a beginner on developing new life patterns. If you run afoul, simply get right back with the program.

As an example of how to do the program, at the end of each day's exercise of the first week, I will give excerpts from the journal of a compulsive eater.

* * *

Day 1. *Today is the day to set up a plan for modifying your behavior.* Be very specific about what you will do. This is an essential first step. Make something to hang your good intentions on that you can live with. If there are "command performance" matters that must be attended to immediately — emotional, physical, social, financial — include steps towards handling them. Do not try to get the rest of your life in order in this two weeks. Simply make a reasonable, workable day-by-day plan that won't allow space for playing games with your limits. This plan is not etched in stone. It's a "trial flight" for two weeks that can be revised as often as is necessary.

Journal: *"I always blow my diets when I'm at loose ends. I head into the kitchen. My plan of action will be that I won't wander into the kitchen unless I already know exactly what I intend to eat. I'm going to be particularly careful in the evenings. I'll make myself put food on a plate, take it out of the kitchen, and sit down* before *I eat. And I'll keep a diary of everything I eat on a piece of paper that I'll put up on the refrigerator."*

* * *

The following days of the program will give you an opportunity to zero in on specific rationalizations that most of us use to sabotage our programs. Go all out when you expand on these. But at the end of each daily journal entry write, "BUT NO MATTER WHAT, I WILL NOT USE MY COMPULSIVE PATTERN."

"No matter what" refers to such things as being stood up by a date, having an unexpected and upsetting visit from a relative, not getting a promotion, holidays, setbacks, bad weather. This means that *no matter what happens* to you, compulsive living can no longer be seen as an option to feel better, to celebrate, to relieve boredom, to escape.

It is important to have the argument of excuses entirely *between you and yourself.* In this way you can learn to avoid self-destructive rebelling. Gradually you will see how outdated and inappropriate your whole compulsive act has become.

If at any time during the day the going gets tough, write some more — *a lot more* if necessary. Each day's rationalization is an enemy that will do you in if not properly confronted. You will be tempted to use these as reasons to run back to your old escapist habit. Don't do it. Be strong.

* * *

Day 2. *All day focus on what a nuisance it is to stay vigilant about your compulsive pattern.* It is a royal pain in the neck to stay aware of what you are doing with your time, your energy, your feelings, and your money and not just space out. What a drag to write down every bite eaten, every quarter spent, every time you turn on the TV set or let your mind wander onto some preoccupation instead of facing something. Here you are, an important person with a sparkling personality, a responsible job, devoted friends, a promising future. Why should you struggle so hard to give up one little bad habit? You want to just relax.

Remember — it is *you* who are choosing to stop your compulsive pattern. Tune out this negative thinking. Stay conscious and don't let any of your actions go by unnoticed. Ponder and write about the bother of staying vigilant, but that you will not use this as a rationalization to forsake your plan.

Journal: *"I knew I wandered in and out of the kitchen a lot, but I had no idea how often. Yesterday I felt like I was a deprived — or depraved — person, battling not to go into a forbidden room of ecstasy. Indeed it is a damn nuisance to preplan what I'm going to eat and then write it all down. It takes all the fun out of it. It feels like prison! BUT NO MATTER WHAT, I WILL NOT USE MY COMPULSIVE PATTERN."*

* * *

Day 3. *This is the day to blame anyone or anything* you feel contributed to your compulsive pattern in the past, or continues to contribute to it in the present. *Do* make your list complete:

• *Your parents, siblings, grandparents*: "They always argued with me or each other about food/cleanliness/alcohol/work/money/sex." "They nagged/fought/complained." "I had a rotten childhood."

• *Your spouse, mate, or date*: "She/he is never there for me." "He/she always criticizes me."

• *Our society:* "There are always pressures to buy/eat/drink/smoke/be sexy/keep up with the boys/keep up with the Joneses." "They keep sending me credit cards." "The liquor store is open all night."

• *Cruelty of life:* "My social life is zero." "The furnace blew out. I just wanted someone to keep me warm."

• *Work:* "The boss asks too much." "Coworkers don't help." "It's tax season. I need the extra money."

• *Doctors:* "They didn't tell me it was addicting."

• *Strangers:* "It's not my fault if women/men keep flirting with me."

Get it all out. Make your list as long as possible. There probably was and is much to blame in your life, and now is the time to name names unmercifully. However, for your present choices, *you* must assume responsibility.

Journal: *"First off I'm going to blame my mother. When I was a kid, she was never there for me after school, and instead would leave me a plate of cookies that I regularly gobbled up. Next I'll blame all the media hype about being pencil thin. It makes me feel guilty for ever weighing extra. Next I'll blame my family. If it weren't for them, I wouldn't have so much food around to snack on. I guess my goldfish are the only blameless souls in my house. But I'm sticking with my plan. NO MATTER WHAT, I WILL NOT USE MY COMPULSIVE PATTERN."*

* * *

Day 4. *Look how unfair life is.* Other people haven't had such a terrible time growing up. Other people have better parents, spouses, children, jobs, looks. Other people can eat, drink, gamble, flirt without it getting out of control. *It's not fair.* Really wallow and feel sorry for yourself. Write it all out. Nobody else understands your burdens and the troubles you've seen. But *do not indulge in your compulsive pattern, no matter what.* Your irresponsible behavior will not right the wrongs of life.

Journal: *"It is NOT fair. My husband and kids can eat what and whenever they want, including rich desserts. They don't gain extra weight. My girlfriend easily drops five pounds if she happens to put it on. Damn it. I wish the results of my bad habit weren't so visible to the world. And I wish I didn't think so much about my weight. I hate sticking with my plan. BUT NO MATTER WHAT, I WILL NOT USE MY COMPULSIVE PATTERN."*

* * *

Day 5. *Battle pessimism* by getting into "what's the use!!"

• *Past:* Trying to get in control has never worked before — "I always fell 'off the wagon.' "

• *Present:* You're too weak/short/tall/whatever — "I can't say no to my parents."

• *Future:* The odds of really changing aren't that great — "Most people eventually go back to indulging after they quit. So what's the use of trying."

Go all out as a pessimist, but keep choosing *not* to use your compulsive pattern. "What's the use" is a sneaky, seductive rationalization. Don't use it and don't listen to others that spout it. Remember, take one day or one hour or five minutes at a time.

Journal: *"This is futile. I don't know how many diets and programs I've been on — I could get the title of 'Ms. Yo-Yo.' Maybe I'm just kidding myself. Maybe I'm born to be fat. I probably won't be able to keep the weight off, so why am I even attempting this two weeks. All right. I've promised myself that I'll at least stick it out for one week. NO MATTER WHAT, I WILL NOT USE MY COMPULSIVE PATTERN."*

* * *

Day 6. *Exception Day.* How easy it is to see each day as special and unusual — one in which to make an exception and have a "little" drink, a "little" cookie, a "little" game of poker, a "little" phone call with your ex, or some other "little" step backwards into the jaws of your old vice. Perhaps company is coming, your husband will be late, it's your birthday, your mother just called, TGIF, TGIMonday, end of the weekend, beginning of the month, you don't feel well, heavy day at work, the car broke down, you just found out your spouse is having an affair, you didn't get a raise, whatever. Look at all the ways today feels like a rational time to make an exception to your new plan, but *don't do it.* Remember, you are choosing *not* to make an exception today, *no matter what.*

Journal: *"Today is Saturday. I've worked hard all week. I want to just relax and kick back. I've always done this with food. Why am I torturing myself. It's a weekend. I ought to be able to eat what I feel like, especially since friends are going to be dropping in later. This is grizzly. BUT NO MATTER WHAT, I WILL NOT USE MY COMPULSIVE PATTERN. I've got to hang in. I better leave out some tasty nutritious snacks for myself so I don't cave in."*

* * *

Day 7. Focus on the *discomfort* that comes with not being able to take care of yourself with your compulsive pattern. You must be honest with yourself about what you are going through. This will vary according to whether or not there is a chemical withdrawal associated with the physical withdrawal. Your habit has been such a wonderful security blanket, tranquilizer, recreation, and companion that it's going to feel rotten without it. You will have a certain amount of emotional and possibly physical pain. But *you* are choosing to stop using your compulsive pattern for your own good. Write down alternative activities you might do and supportive friends you could call on in emergencies, where you can feel comfortable, accepted, and nurtured.

Journal: *"What a crutch food is for me! It's like I always want to have something in my mouth. I should try sucking my thumb. When my mouth is empty, I feel all fidgety, especially in the evening. I'm beginning to have great sympathy for drug addicts that go 'cold turkey.' I had no idea how much I was using food as a comforter. Well, most of the week is over. I think I can hold out a bit more. I'm going to buy some junky magazines to have on hand. If all else fails, I will chew on them. BUT NO MATTER WHAT, I WILL NOT USE MY COMPULSIVE PATTERN."*

* * *

Your burst of enthusiasm of feeling a bit in control, and having a glimmer of hope that you can get on top of your compulsive pattern may have made the past week a snap. On the other hand, your pervading pessimism and mixed feelings about facing life without your familiar habit may have left you open to sabotaging yourself quite regularly. So be it. What's done is done.

Week Two

Here's the scenario for the second week.

Day 8. Shift to a calmer pace in your daily life.
Day 9. Consider where potential "mess-ups" can happen.
Day 10. Beware of belittling the problem.
Day 11. Allow yourself a small "slip."
Day 12. Spell out your own favorite rationalizations.
Day 13. Mourn the passing of your habit.
Day 14. Acknowledge any progress.

Remember, set aside time each morning to focus on and write about the days preoccupation — more potential rationalizations and excuses that *you* choose not to give into. Keep with the working plan that you developed last week, unless it was too out of line with reality and needs a revision: You allowed zero money for lunch, a movie, or even a phone call; your eating plan only had all the foods that you hate; you left no space for relaxing and having fun.

This week, we will look in on the journal of a compulsive procrastinator.

* * *

Day 8. *If you don't use your compulsive pattern, life will be calmer but perhaps feel boring and too predictable.* You miss the drama of behaving impulsively and sneakily, wondering who will catch you or bail you out, whether you will gain a pound, lose a dollar. You miss the high of slipping by with your outrageous behavior, playing "brinkmanship," getting away with murder. Think and write out all the details of this new predictable, bland, noncompulsive life-style. Otherwise, you will run back to your old habit for excitement. "Boring" is not an acceptable excuse for hopping back on your compulsive horse.

Journal: *"I'm better caught up. I've paid the bills that were pressing. I wrote my father. And I've even made an outline for the report which is due at work the end of the month. I'm being so damn good that no one will have anything to nag me about — not my credit union; not my father; not my boss. I'm so used to having undone things hanging over me. I'm feeling strange as hell — sort of like I have no anchor. I thought this is what I wanted, to have everybody off my back including my own conscience. But it all seems sort of dull, like I've sold out. Maybe I'll get used to it. BUT NO MATTER WHAT, I WILL NOT USE MY COMPULSIVE PATTERN."*

* * *

Day 9. *Concentrate on ways that you could "mess-up" but won't.* No one would know that you used the rent money to cover a past debt; that you ate the whole cake and baked another one to replace it; that you sneaked out and bought some cognac; that you had a "quickie" with a neighbor; that you spent the weekend with your horrible ex; that you again put off attending to important matters. You can tell yourself that no one will know. But *you* will know, and you'll be kicking yourself and sweating it out. So choose not to play cheating games which may lead to getting out of control.

Journal: *"My plan has been to do a little on the office report each day. I sure as hell don't feel like writing today. Work was chaotic and I'm beat. I want to have a drink, put on the TV and do nothing. Hey, I deserve it. Okay, okay. That's not what I'm going to do. It'll be sheer agony, but I'm going to make myself sit at the desk and write for one hour. I've got to do it. NO MATTER WHAT, I WILL NOT USE MY COMPULSIVE PATTERN."*

* * *

Day 10. *You're getting a bit smug.* You're telling yourself that whenever you want to, you can control your habit. It's much easier than you expected. Maybe you don't really have a problem. So what's all the fuss. You're further rationalizing that it's too much bother to plan and keep track of everything. Anyway, there are worse habits. *Watch out. Stay vigilant. Pride rides before a fall.* This is classic thinking of an addictive person. Don't allow yourself to belittle your compulsive habit nor all the hard work that you are doing to control it. Write about the temptation to abandon your plan, but don't do it.

Journal: *"I am doing pretty well. I haven't been this caught up in years — nothing huge has been put off. The report is moving along well. I'm not as bad off as I had thought. It hasn't taken me long to get in gear. Maybe I can take off a few days. Seductive as hell, but I better not. NO MATTER WHAT, I WILL NOT USE MY COMPULSIVE PATTERN."*

* * *

Day 11. Today is unique. *This is the day to slip — not on a big scale, but in a little way.* Purposely slip and eat a cookie, call an ex-lover, buy an unnecessary small present for your new girlfriend. Then go into your usual thinking, "I slipped, so to hell with the whole thing." "I ate something not on my plan so I might as well clean out the refrigerator." "I bought the shoes so I might as well splurge and buy the whole damn outfit." STOP.

This is the kind of all-or-none, black-and-white thinking that's carried you into a heap of trouble in the past. So you made a slip. Get some perspective. It's not the end of the world. You're not a bad person, just a struggling human being. Though you have flirted with your compulsive pattern, you don't need to bed down with it. *Choose to get back on your plan.*

Note: DO NOT SLIP IF YOUR COMPULSIVE PATTERN RELATES TO ALCOHOL, DRUGS, SMOKING, GAMBLING, OR SOME ILLEGAL ACTIVITY SUCH AS SHOPLIFTING. In these cases, just *visualize* slipping.

Journal: *"Though it feels a little eerie, this evening I'm going to come home and do nothing — no reports, no cleanup, no opening the mail, nothing. I'm not even going to take a shower. I'm just going to grab my usual drink and couch potato it until I zonk out. I hope to God I can get back on course tomorrow."*

* * *

Day 12. Are there *other favorite rationalizations?* Write as many as you can create — excuses that you *could* use: "There's a sale at Macy's." "The bus left me off at the wrong place and it was in front of the liquor store." "My girlfriend just baked my favorite cookies." "My ex-lover happens to be going to the same party." Let yourself go, you can come up with some dillies. Focus on writing a long list and CHOOSING NOT TO USE THEM AS EXCUSES TO INDULGE IN YOUR COMPULSIVE PATTERN.

Journal: *"Whoopee. I'm back with my plan. But I'm scared to slip too much. One of the biggest ways I sabotage myself is by conveniently forgetting what I don't like doing. I shove unwanted jobs out of sight and out of mind. So if I'm going to change this pattern, I have to keep everything in plain sight on the desk, right in the living room. And I'll make reasonable mini-goals and put them on my calender — not on a stick-on note, not in pencil, but IN INK. No matter what, I WILL NOT USE MY COMPULSIVE PATTERN."*

* * *

Day 13. This is an important day. *It's the day to focus on sadness — a real mourning.* Compulsive living has been such a comfort for years. When the rest of the world walked out or overwhelmed you and no one was there for you, you always relied on running and indulging. You found yourself a pleasurable escape and compulsively avoided many of life's hardships. But you've sized it all up, and you're going to say good-bye to your compulsive habit. As familiar as it is, it makes you feel too rotten about yourself. It creates too much chaos in your life.

Especially today, however, allow yourself to feel sad as you would for the death of a friend. You may well experience an emptiness and unending aloneness by choosing not to behave compulsively as you go through the day. Be sure to take care of yourself in other ways — time alone, a call to a friend, a walk on the beach, or anything that *doesn't* touch off some form of compulsive living.

Journal: *"Being caught up feels unfamiliar and very alone. I didn't expect this. It's like I have no debts of time. I don't owe anybody anything. It feels as if something is missing. Is this what being grown up is? Though I say I hate it, I guess I also like the rush feeling when I barely get away with doing things in the nick of time and everyone hounds me. I can see how easy it would be to fall back into this. BUT NO MATTER WHAT, I WILL NOT USE MY COMPULSIVE PATTERN."*

* * *

Day 14. Last day of the program. *Acknowledge to yourself what you've accomplished, even if slips have occurred.* People with compulsive patterns tend to be so hard on themselves that anything short of earth-shaking success is a sufficient mortal blow to catapult them into giving up. Guard against this. You've begun to gain control and to take charge of your compulsive habit. It will be a slow and often bumpy process. But eventually you can create a history of living directly and fully, without ODing or avoiding life with crazy detours.

This is a good day to review what you've written down and learned in the past two weeks. Give yourself full credit. You've made changes in a difficult area. Be proud of all your hard work. A two-week program can serve as proof to you that patterns can be broken and habits can be altered. Tell yourself, "I've made a start. I can do more than I thought I could."

Journal: *"No one is more surprised than I. For two weeks I have done pretty damn well at sticking with my plans — correspondence up to date and the report is going beautifully. Not bad. I thought I was too old to change. Maybe there's hope for me. But I'm also aware of the fragility of my new approach. I feel like a toddler learning to walk. I know I'll need to put ongoing effort into staying on top of things, or I'll quickly degenerate into old habits. NO MATTER WHAT, I WILL NOT USE MY COMPULSIVE PATTERN."*

* * *

Compulsive patterns are unfortunately enemies that don't easily die. They can remain lifelong challengers. At any point along the way to recovery, if "bad" habits again start to swallow you up, jump right back into this Two-Week Detox Program to regain control. It can serve as a booster shot to strengthen your immunity against the bite of the compulsive bug.

7

NOT SHOOTING YOURSELF
IN THE FOOT —
RELAPSE PREVENTION

*The man who wins may have been counted out many
times, but he didn't hear the referee.*

— H. E. Hansen

*I*n speaking about a hoped-for-get-together, a friend recounted
what went through her mind:

> *He told me he would phone when he got to town, though
> nothing was said of which day and what time. Going into my
> typical doormat stance, I kept the whole week clear, making
> every other commitment tentative. Then it occurred to me that
> I was falling right back into codependent patterns. It was a
> struggle, but I finally went ahead with other plans. When he
> did call, without much difficulty we were able to find a mutually
> satisfying time to meet.*
> *The "old me" shows up when I least expect it.*

Through superhuman effort and gritting your teeth, you have
gotten some control of your compulsive patterns — not perfectly,
but a clear improvement. Of course you feel "clean," virtuous, and
proud. You also feel naked, frightened, and a little bored. Daily
existence might seem quite monotonous and meaningless. So you
are asking yourself, "Is this all there is to life?"

You probably hoped that banishing self-destructive habits would bring instant success and happiness: "If I stop being a workaholic or alcoholic, my marriage will be perfect." "If I get thin, surely I'll have no trouble finding Prince Charming. He'll know me by my glass slipper."

How nice it would be if everything worked this easily. It doesn't. You are putting aside well developed, time-consuming detours that have been nonsolutions for years. Many underlying problems remain. Resultant wreckage from your compulsive living may surround you. New healthy coping skills are not yet firmly in place. Right now you are in a sensitive in-between zone.

Here are some factors to consider:

• *You are a novice at walking to the beat of your own drummer.* In the past you have been so busy pleasing everyone else and rebelling behind their backs that you have insufficient experience being your own person.

• *You now have extra time on your hands,* time formerly locked into chaos — compulsively living in the fast lane; getting out of messes that you never should have gotten into in the first place. Having free time leaves you open to unfamiliar and possibly painful thoughts and feelings. Living in the slow lane provides few distractions from this reality.

• The temptation will be great to clutter up your life with unhealthy diversions and detours — anything to recapture the old tried-and-true method of feeling comfortable and "alive."

• *You are at high risk to fall prey to new compulsive patterns, as well as to grab hold of the old ones.* For example, your alcohol/eating/nail biting is under control, but you are smoking like a furnace. Or you have stopped being such a workaholic, but you are taking a different partner home with you every night and compulsively jogging each morning. Or you have given up an addictive relationship, but now stay in your apartment and get spaced out on marijuana each evening. It may look like a new horse but it is still part of the same compulsive merry-go-round.

Vigilance

You must stay mindful of situations that can propel you into downward, out-of-control spirals of shooting yourself in the foot. This means learning to weather out stressful periods and unstructured time without becoming frightened by fears of being out of control. Stay conscious of concerns you may have about being vulnerable to and dependent upon others. The Alcoholics Anonymous buzz word HALT is helpful — watch out for times when you are *H*ungry, *A*ngry, *L*onely, or *T*ired.

It is wise to continue to over-plan your time. Every day visualize your life without any compulsive escapes. Mentally walk through each hour. Plan for possible moments of weakness. Reread earlier chapters on coping strategies and mental approaches to help you deal with these circumstances. Continue to use whatever support you need to keep your spirits up, so that you don't get weak in the knees.

Unfortunately the battle with the bottle, as with every other compulsive habit, will be an ongoing one for quite some time. There is *no quick fix*. On a daily basis, you must continue to make responsible choices when cravings nag and temptations scream out to you.

Remain psychologically well centered. Remind yourself how lucky you are to have gotten control of your life before it was too late. Though you lost valuable time, you left compulsive living before it destroyed you. All of that is getting further and further behind you. How wonderful it is to be proud of yourself and to wake up each morning feeling whole and glad to be alive.

If you find yourself dwelling on fond memories of compulsive life, vividly recall horrible scenes of what follows even one indulgence — a drink becoming a pathetic debacle; a food binge moving into days of out-of-control eating; a spending spree turning into a whirlwind nightmare; returning to a bad relationship leading to a total loss of self-respect. Don't permit yourself to exaggerate any benefits of your old self-destructive life. One drink or binge, one return to the old horrible ex, one outrageously expensive purchase will *not* solve anything. It will only compound your problems, bringing shame, guilt and embarrassment. In addition you will feel sick about the time and the energy that get wasted.

It serves nothing to allow yourself to get into a "poor me" game of "Life is unfair because I have to stay vigilant." With all the potential tragedies that exist, having to abstain from compulsive patterns does not rank as one of them.

"Close Encounters Of The Worst Kind"

One of the many arts of staying in recovery is to spot places for potential relapses and nick them before they occur. These are what I refer to as "close encounters of the worst kind":

• Beginning to obsess about your old habit, "It's his birthday, maybe I could give him a call. Surely I'm now strong enough not to get hooked again."

• Starting to play with control, "Maybe I'll drop in on the poker game and watch. I haven't seen my buddies in a long time."

• Just "happening" to be in a too seductive situation, "I had a fight with my girlfriend, and took a walk to get away. I don't know how I happened to end up near the liquor store." Or having trouble controlling your eating and finding yourself going to the kitchen to fix snacks for others who could well fix them for themselves.

If you slide into any of the above predicaments, know that they are warning signals and act immediately:

• Stop kidding yourself, and *promptly move away from the opportunity to indulge or to get out of control.* Again, Alcoholics Anonymous has an apt warning: "If you don't want to slip, stay out of slippery places." It is much easier to stop *before* you step back into an old rut, than it is to climb out of it.

• *Become aware of your tension and consciously relax.* Visualize yourself in a safe place. Get some rest and do whatever works and is not addictive to refuel yourself.

• *Use any support system that you have.* I have certain "foul weather friends" that I can always count on when the chips are down.

• *Redirect your energy onto yourself.* Think of something you enjoy and start doing it right away. Act rather than agonize.

• *Search within yourself and get in touch with your feelings and needs.* It may not be easy to let yourself want or wish for anything. It might make you feel too vulnerable or weak, as if you'd be a set up for a devastating disappointment or rejection. You rather fall into the habit of blindly marching along and praying that someone will magically grant your unspoken wishes. You don't ask for anything, so you think no one will have reason to be annoyed, threatened, or put off by you. No reason at all.

People cannot read your mind. You must let them know exactly how you feel and what you need. Be clear about what you will do and what you won't, what you *can* do, and what you *can't,* even if it means leaving some projects undone or unfinished.

• *Look at other real life issues that need your attention:* Bills, your social life, intolerable working conditions, your biologic clock, intrusive parents, an overbearing spouse, children who have gotten out of hand, an overcrowded schedule, an empty nest, fears of growing older.

Your health might have been sorely neglected over the years, and doctor or dentist visits are in order. Furthermore, wallowing in self-destructive patterns may have resulted in misused or damaged relationships to parents, relatives, mates, children, or friends. You need to learn healthy skills for interacting with others — getting the space you need, as well as being appropriately intimate. Since your early life most likely left you with a defensive need to control others or be saved by them, it will take time and possibly hard work in therapy to relinquish these guarded stances.

There may be relatives and former friends who are so intertwined with your compulsive patterns that they can no longer be a viable part of your support system, or your life. In fact, many old cohorts may be hell bent on seducing you right back into dangerous waters. Drop them.

Lastly, your compulsive habits may have caused financial debts, difficulties and even disasters. You may be facing legal problems. If you are going to move into the driver's seat of your life and stop waylaying yourself with compulsive patterns, you have to honestly address all of these areas and finally, take full responsibility for real life solutions to them.

Shift whatever feels helpless in your life back into an arena where you have choices, even if the choice might be to stick out a situation that isn't ideal. When you actively make your own decisions, you will not feel that you are a powerless victim.

Some people coerce themselves into staying with recovery programs by setting up harsh consequences for backsliding. This method can be used for compulsive patterns where total abstinence is necessary.

For instance, if you are a cocaine addict in recovery and a staunch Republican, you could write out a check for $5,000 or $50,000 to the American Civil Liberties Union. Give the check to a friend with explicit instructions that it be mailed immediately if you should again start using cocaine.

Though rather a radical form of therapy, if this type of plan deters you from slipping, by all means use it. The American Civil Liberties Union will have to get by without your money.

Slips Don't Have To Turn Into Relapses

If you do slip, you have clear options. It is important to see them. You can fall back into old self-destructive cycles, or you can see the situation as a new challenge. The past is past and already gone. In the present, you are not bound by the past. There are new paths that can be followed.

Get out pencil and paper and start to write:

"I slipped on my program because . . ."

"The immediate trigger to indulge was probably . . . (feeling, place, situation?)"

"Problem areas I need to focus more attention on are . . ."

"I'm scared to let go of the compulsive living struggle because I would then have to go on to face . . ."

Be honest with yourself. You want to look at your own resistance to changing your patterns. It helps to see the whole recovery process as an interesting, complex puzzle that *can* be solved. Life offers a succession of moments, each of which holds an opportunity for choices. You are going to persist in learning to make wiser ones.

You need to view slips as part of the compulsive condition. The true test of being in control is *not* to never go off the straight and narrow. Rather, it is to be able to quickly recover when you do. Size up the situation and take full responsibility for what happened. An analogy I often present to patients is that the test of a good musician is not the playing per se, but how well you can recoup after a wrong beat. So when you slip and lose the beat, get right back with the music.

Check your emotional pulse: Are you again being "good" on the outside, stuffing your feelings on the inside, and getting even by playing in the murky waters of compulsive living?

Cutting A Relapse Cycle Short

If a slip evolves into a full-blown relapse, it is time to bring out your full artillery of recovery tools. You have sworn to yourself and to others, "I will never start back into old patterns. I feel so much better being free of them." But, lo and behold, here you are again, abusing substances, food, money or relationships, or caught into being run by work, activities, or other escapes. "How could this have happened?" The answer is, "all too easily."

Relapses don't break out like a rash. They come as the result of a series of poor choices in circumstances where you can eventually learn to intercede. Below are some common precipitants of relapses:

1. *Exhaustion.* This may be a result of running away into work, or of working too hard to make up for lost time, time formerly spent in compulsive living.

2. *Boredom* — not making enough plans for in-between times.

3. Using *rationalizations;* reverting to old self-defeating, all-or- none thinking patterns. "I smoked a cigarette. To heck with it, I'll finish the pack."

4. *Negative thinking* — "stinking thinking," as the Twelve-Step programs like to say. This all too quickly shifts to feeling sorry for yourself and "What's the use of trying?"

5. *Impatience.* Remember, this is part of your original makeup that got you into jams in the first place.

6. *Overcommitment to others.* You may have returned to old martyr patterns. Many of my patients have bigger case loads than I do as they carry on twenty-four-hour rescue missions. If your life becomes too inundated with "shoulds" and "have to's," *watch out.* Taking care of everyone *but* yourself and burying your own feelings and needs will leave you ripe for indulging in familiar self-destructive scenarios, all too reminiscent of the bad old days.

When you take charge of your own life, you will begin to see in more vivid relief the problems of others. Be careful that your awareness of their pain doesn't seduce you into becoming part of it.

A woman who formerly was the caretaker of many others, but not enough of herself, used to mend her own wounds with alcohol and obsessive work. To stay in recovery, she said she needed to continue to be watchful:

> *I so easily fall back into trying to solve everyone else's problems — partly because I feel it's my duty, but also because I don't want anyone to be upset with me. I still have to consciously catch this. It's hard for me to say "no" to anyone. But now I'm doing it more regularly — though it feels strange. When I can, it's a radical difference and I don't feel that overwhelming urge to run away.*

7. *Cockiness, overconfidence.* You might have been testing your level of control, putting yourself in increasingly tempting situations, playing games with trying controlled indulgence — deluding yourself into thinking precaution wasn't necessary.

8. *Setting yourself up for disappointment by having unrealistic expectations of yourself, of others, of the world.* You may again have gotten in the habit of relying too much on others for validation, leaving yourself wide open to be let down.

9. *Placing yourself in seductive social pressures.* Passively or actively, you may be under more pressure than you can handle by hanging around those who indulge and escape. This is especially dangerous at stressful times of your life.

10. *Letting go of disciplines necessary to stay in control.* At some level you may have lost your motivation or chosen *not* to stay vigilant. Or you may find that old risk taking patterns keep creeping into your life.

11. *Inadequate support system.* Not having it, not using it, or feeling embarrassed to go back to it.

12. *Lack of effective coping skills to deal with relationships and life.* You became overwhelmed by vulnerable and dependent feelings. Or you have stayed away from meaningful social interactions and ended up feeling too isolated.

13. *Bad luck.* This is — appropriately — number thirteen on our list of relapse causes. All may have gone well until some unexpected trauma walked over you — the loss of a job, the end of a significant relationship, the death of a loved one.

14. *Starting to obsess about your old substance or activity, and letting the obsession fester.* A former food addict told me the kind of ruminating that easily leads her into trouble:

> *I love being thin. But I truly miss not being able to "pig out" and go "mindless." If I'm not careful, I keep dwelling on it more and more. Then it's like I start testing my control. I wander into the kitchen, open the refrigerator to see what's there, nibble on a a few things, then a few more things. Only, pretty soon, I don't have any control.*

15. *Failure to intervene in a downward spiral.* You either passively or actively chose *not* to see the signs of loss of control — the "I just happened to . . ." phenomenon. Or if you did see them, you did not *do* anything about them.

16. *Not making fundamental life changes.* This means inadequately evolving a new healthy identity, and *not* filling the gaps left by the removal of compulsive patterns. Unless a sound outlook on life is cultivated, you will again feel hopeless and helpless and be at risk. (More on this in a later chapter.)

No matter how the relapse actually evolved, what finally occurred was that you allowed pressures to indulge to go up, and/or the barriers against it to go down. And as you might expect, water went over the dam.

Recovery mandates learning to anticipate and access all of the above factors, and to actively and appropriately intervene at each juncture. You *can* stop the progression of backsliding and turn it around. Think about what has helped in the past. Reread earlier chapters for specific suggestions. Stay aware of all the branching side paths leading nowhere, in order *not* to get off the main trail.

If you should go into a full blown relapse, do *not* head for the nearest bridge and jump. It may feel like you have drawn a Monopoly card that says, "Go to Jail. Do not pass go. Do not collect $200." This is not true. You are *not* a criminal and you needn't be punished. Relapses are unfortunately a common part of recovery. Simply return to the beginning of Chapter 4 and restart your recovery process.

Becoming Comfortable With Success

There is a last, but no less important, area that needs to be addressed. Regardless of how many successes exist in their lives, most people struggling with compulsive patterns feel themselves to be losers. You may be a successful doctor, lawyer, or Indian chief, but if you drink, eat, or spend too much or compulsively overindulge in any other area, deep down you feel as if you are *nothing*. As unpleasant as this image might be, in other ways it may feel extremely safe. It has meant that, as Zorba in Nikos Kazantzakis' *Zorba the Greek* said, you have never dared to "cut the rope and be free." You have never really taken ultimate responsibility for your own separate existence. You have never completely moved out from your family. You have never allowed yourself to fully compete and be proud of your own uniqueness. You probably have also consciously or unconsciously felt guilty about succeeding when many others in your life were unable to. You never felt you deserved to win.

Fears of succeeding must be effectively dealt with. You will have to stay alert to all the subtle ways that you could sabotage your success and the enjoyment of it:

• Diminishing it because it hasn't been achieved perfectly and at record speed.

- Constantly and unfavorably comparing yourself to others who you feel are more successful.
- Discounting any achievement by dwelling on all that is not yet accomplished.
- Attributing all success to good luck and negating ways that you have changed and actively contributed to it.
- Staying around those who fail and becoming uncomfortable because your success has made you different from them.
- Feeling unworthy of success.

Admire and relish each victory no matter what its magnitude. You can feel proud of accomplishments that don't necessarily move mountains, get A's or result in promotions. If others can't handle your successes, that's their problem.

A college student I worked with had always been bothered by being overweight, a problem her family harped on constantly. After a fair amount of therapy and being in a support group, Anita finally lost the weight that had plagued her, and ended up looking quite stunning. When she triumphantly returned home to visit her family, they not only made no comment about her weight loss, but added insult to injury with a remark about her dressing too provocatively. Anita was hurt and very much taken aback.

When we discussed it, she was able to see her family's emotional limits and their tremendous need to control her. Thus, when Anita did something for and by herself, even when it coincided with what they claimed they wanted for her, her success was perceived by them as abandoning the family. As distorted as this thinking may sound, many of us from dysfunctional families are all too familiar with these kinds of contradictory messages. Each of us, it seems, fills a unique place in the system that is our family. If you change yourself, you "disrupt" the balance of the family system. Although the change may be one other family members have asked for, they'll likely resist it, and try to restore the balance, however dysfunctional.

After further work in therapy, Anita came to terms with the situation, felt proud of her success and appropriately sad that her family was unable to share it with her.

It is important that you view success as being strictly for *you,* and not as part of acquiescing to others' expectations. This entails savoring your own triumphs and not being influenced by the applause, or lack of it, from other people.

Staying In Recovery

In sum, you are in the process of shedding the outgrown compulsive living style of the old you, but you have not yet found a healthy living style for the new you that fits properly. Be patient. Good friends and a sense of humor can help immensely in giving you the perspective to keep moving forward. Remind yourself that a backward step into old habits will only bring on familiar chaos again.

As is in the Serenity Prayer of Reinhold Niebuhr used by the Twelve-Step Programs, you have to accept the things you cannot change, have the courage to change the things you can, and have the wisdom to know the difference.

Hence each day, especially during difficult times, have wisdom:

Accept the things you cannot change — the reality of the past and all that is involved in being fully alive in the present. At times, external pressures will feel overwhelming and internal pressures will feel very painful, but this can't be used as an excuse for engaging in irresponsible behavior. Stay aware of your tendency to indulge when the "going gets tough," for there are sure to be moments of nostalgia for the "days of wine and roses."

You must find responsible, non-self-destructive ways to get your needs met in a not-so-perfect world that is often full of injustice. We are not equal in what we have — looks, intelligence, talents, parents — from the time we're born throughout our lives. Misfortune and illness strike many fine, decent people. Competent, hard-working people don't necessarily get appropriate raises on their jobs and may be as apt to be fired as lazy incompetents. Innocent people get preyed on by the dishonest, and sometimes crooks do get away with murder. There is a Spanish saying, that "Bad people don't die, and even if they do, no one cares."

Hanging on to the notion of how things *ought to be* interferes with putting energy into *what can be*.

Change the things you can. Choose your priorities — decide what *you* want and plan concrete steps to make it happen. Stop the game playing and rationalizing that keep you stuck in self-destructive living. Do what *you* know needs to be done to stay in control. Responsibly attend to the real issues of your life — emotional, physical, familial, social, financial, and legal.

It is difficult to navigate the stressful waters of life. Don't get careless and take your recovery program for granted or you will end up shooting yourself in the foot.

Part III: Attack Plans for Specific Patterns

*T*his section of the book is a bit different from the previous chapters. Here we will zero in on specific habits and suggest attack plans tailor-made for each.

What you've read in Part II applies to all compulsive living patterns. The following chapters are intended to supplement but *not* replace this. Each chapter gives criteria for identifying a specific category of compulsive habits and highlights relevant strategies for recovery. I was not sure what order to list various patterns, but finally decided to move from the subtle to the classic. Hence I start with types of patterns that are commonly found in all of us, but often not recognized as being compulsive, and end with addictions to alcohol and substance abuse.

I suggest that you glance over *all* the chapters of Part II, even though you think that some categories of patterns don't apply to you. You may be surprised. As I've said before, the compulsive war can take place on a variety of battle grounds. It behooves you to examine each of them. Especially look at the chapters on driven thought patterns, compulsive activities, and relationship fixations. These categories of compulsive living are heavily intertwined with other self-destructive habits. Remember, your goal is to permanently get off the compulsive merry-go-round, not just to hop onto a different horse.

Where group support is necessary and clear resources exist, such as for alcohol and drug abuse and compulsive gambling, I have given more general guidelines. However, in areas where there are either (1) inadequate resources, as is true in the case of compulsive spending; (2) a confusing array of resources, as exists for eating-weight problems; or (3) where you may well be doing it on your own — in workaholism, procrastination, smoking, and so on, I have given more explicit plans of attack.

It's All Connected

In the following chapters, you will see that each type of compulsive pattern is part of a preoccupation engaged in to offset various fears. For most people your own experiences may differ, but the oversimplified synopsis goes like this:

• Underneath driven thought patterns and phobias are basic fears: In driven thought patterns, you *mentally* avoid the feared situation by being obsessed with something else. (For example, you are obsessed with staying young to cover anxiety about growing older.) In a phobia, on the other hand, you *physically* avoid the feared situation altogether. (For example, you don't fly at all rather than endure the terror that you would feel during plane trips.

• Underneath compulsive work, activities and escapes is a fear of not being good enough.. You feel defined by what you do, and feel that you must perform flawlessly. Without enough accomplishments, in your eyes, you don't measure up. Hence you either drive yourself unmercifully, or take refuge in escapes and don't even attempt a task.

• Underneath relationship and sexual fixations is the fear that if you are alone, you are inadequate and inconsequential. As a result, you are preoccupied with being attached to, or sexually involved with, someone else as a means to feel whole.

• Underneath compulsive patterns around weight — whether you are too heavy, too thin, or average — is the fear that if you don't look impeccable, you will fall short as a human being, You are then obsessed with eating and food and being the "perfect" weight (whatever *that* is.)

• Underneath compulsive patterns around money and possessions is the fear that if you don't keep up with the Joneses or surpass them, you will not be valued by others. You are then preoccupied with accumulations so as to become powerful and invulnerable.

• Underneath various forms of substance abuse is the fear that if you feel your feelings and reveal your real self, you will be overpowered by your feelings and be seen by others as inadequate. You are then obsessed with trying to be relaxed, socially agile, and seemingly in control.

DRIVEN THOUGHT PROCESSES, PRE-OCCUPATIONS AND FEARS | 8

> *The greatest mistake you can make in this life is to be*
> *continually fearing you will make one.*
>   — Elbert Hubbard

*A*s I mentioned, countless preoccupations and fears combined with driven attempts to compensate for them are behind the scenes in all compulsive patterns. These issues eventually become so inextricably mixed that the original components are hard to identify. For example, at the bottom of many self-destructive habits is a fear of being out of control, coupled with an obsession to always be in control; a fear of being vulnerable leading to trying to be invulnerable; a fear of being imperfect causing a preoccupation with forever attempting to be perfect; a fear about growing up covered over with a rigid pseudo-maturity; and so on. And when you compulsively indulge in a substance or activity as self-medication and/or diversion, it may mask the underlying preoccupations and fears.

Identifying Driven Thought Patterns And Preoccupations

Here we direct our attention to how *a state of mind becomes a compulsive pattern.* When certain insecurities and feelings cause discomfort, consciously or unconsciously you mentally distance yourself. You shift your thoughts on to some familiar worry or obsession.

Driven thought patterns and preoccupations can center around any number of areas: Health, staying young, being thin, political and social issues, becoming rich and powerful, moods of depression and bitterness, pulling back into your own concerns, and still others. When you are preoccupied, you are not fully in the here-and-now.

It would be difficult to fit these mental patterns into any single framework. Rather than attempting that, I will merely mention a few common ones:

Fixation on a cause. This could begin during childhood; it might have come from adolescence at a time when you felt lost moving from family out into the world at large; or it may have developed later in an attempt to give your life meaning and direction.

It can look like this: Mrs. Jones is not only the backbone of the P.T.A., but she also is room mother for Larry's second grade class and a co-op mother in Ruth's nursery school. She goes to no less than four evening meetings a month in addition to holding down a full-time job. She regularly participates in both her children's school activities. She frequently heads fund-raising drives. She is constantly on the phone. The teachers and the other children love Mrs. Jones. Her family rarely sees her.

You may be heavily involved in a political or social cause, a traditional or evangelical religion, defending the underdog, saving the downtrodden. No one could argue about the meaningfulness of your chosen activity. But the activity becomes self-destructive when it so pervades your life that your most personal concerns are neglected — when your cause eclipses everything else.

An *obsession with an idea* per se can also dominate someone's life. Whether it be power, success, wealth, fame, revenge or whatever, thoughts can haunt you day and night. You feel that all would be happy if only you could achieve your goal. The tragedy is that along the way you may actually sacrifice the present — relationships, avocations, enjoyment of the moment — in pursuit of your elusive obsession. There are stories of athletes and others so obsessed with winning that they killed themselves rather than fail.

It's hard not to be influenced by the Horatio Algier dream of rising to the top, achieving monumental success and having great wealth. Unfortunately, for many, the quest for this dream overtakes their lives, they become hostage to the attainment of ever more fame and money. I once found a wise fortune in a Chinese cookie, "Money doesn't change people, it only unmasks them."

People in your life may be used and discarded in terms of their assessed worth to you. They are seen and treated as assets or liabilities in relation to your goals. The extreme of this is shown in the ancient Greek myth of King Midas. If you recall, in his obsession to accumulate gold he even transformed his daughter into it. An updated and sometimes fatal version of being addicted to wealth is seen in many who traffic in drugs for which, one way or another, they eventually pay with their lives.

Some of us run into problems because of our *addiction to taking risks and living dangerously*. There can be physical risks, such as driving at breakneck speeds; sexual risks, such as having affairs when you are married; financial risks in consistently living beyond your means; legal risks of petty dishonesty and theft; and so on. All of these behaviors are linked by an aversion to living in a calmer way. Anything less than the fast lane feels too humdrum.

Another compulsive pattern at a purely thinking level is to be *chronically entrenched in a mood* — lonely, depressed, pessimistic, angry, bitter. Like other habits, this one can consume endless quantities of energy and lead nowhere. If you have familiarity with A. A. Milne's *Winnie the Pooh*, you'll recall that Eeyore, the donkey, was the epitome of this. Eternally addicted to his misery, he always dwelled on the negative. Others cling to a sadness, usually initially well founded, but eventually outdated. They are never able or willing to let go and move on. The original loss was devastating enough. The real tragedy is the mood not only visited, it became a permanent resident in someone's life.

Some twenty years ago, a woman I knew was crestfallen when her marriage ended in divorce. Right after the breakup she was angry, bitter and overwhelmed at having to survive in the world as a single mother.

I lost track of her in the intervening years, but happened to run into her recently at a party given by some mutual friends. After exchanging the usual salutations, within five minutes she lapsed back into venom about her former husband as if it were yesterday.

He had ruined her whole life. Maybe some day he would realize that. In actuality he had long ago remarried and is reportedly extremely happy. She has never entered other relationships and obviously clings to her bitterness as if her life depends on it. And I guess at some level it does.

Compulsively pulling back into your own thoughts is a more subtle compulsive pattern than many others. It is not given away by any seeming external activity. You simply focus inward on your own thoughts and in essence shut out the world at large. You mentally leave the scene of discomfort. Everyone normally does this from time to time, but what makes it compulsive is when it is habitually and often uncontrollably used to handle life. You are physically present with others, but your mind is far away — obsessively daydreaming, on thoughts of the past or future, or just blank.

The extreme of this condition is to be so entrenched in your own inner world that it becomes your primary reality, with the world at large being merely a backdrop for your thinking — actual loss of contact with reality as in a serious mental illness.

Concerns about health issues can become a driving force of monumental proportions in a person's life, with preoccupations about illness and even death. This was true for a forty-two-year-old man who consulted me.

> *My family always worried about illness. I was sickly as a child and forever going to doctors, getting shots, taking pills, and "being careful so you don't catch a cold." My parents are no longer living, so I guess I end up doing the worrying for them. I've become obsessed with trying to stay healthy. It's always on my mind and I'm constantly thinking about eating nutritiously, taking vitamins, getting enough sleep. When I do get sick it terrifies me. I go to a number of different doctors, have innumerable tests, and spend much too much money. Thank goodness nothing serious has ever been found. But with my luck, I'll probably end up dying of worry.*

This may not exactly be your version of the preoccupation. You might be someone who with a cold you think pneumonia, a headache means brain tumor, and life feels like one long death trap.

It is hard for you to relax and feel good and free, for disaster seems only a step away — you can never be too careful. You must forever be vigilant about your health.

The irony of this kind of obsession is that your worries may actually materialize into the reality that you've dreaded. "You'll worry yourself sick" is a common expression, but constant worrying has been shown to deplete the immune system.

Obsessively trying to stay young. A woman — or man, for that matter — may be preoccupied with worries about wrinkles and other signs of time. She may spend endless time with her hair dresser, manicurist, masseuse. I knew a woman who, after a series of face lifts, could no longer smile.

The male version of the fear of aging often shows itself in his preoccupation with a receding hairline or his virility. There is sometimes a denial of the aging process that leads him to younger and younger sex partners or to obsessive exercising.

Many of us worry about getting older some of the time and that's fine, but when we do it all of the time — thinking of little else — then we have a problem.

Strategy For Recovery
Step I: Take stock of the situation.
What the particular preoccupation is matters far less than when and how you are using it, and what it is doing to the rest of your life:

• How pervasive has your preoccupation or obsession become? In what ways are you wrapping your life around it? Do you *always* think about money? About not getting old? About your health?

• How much has this become unconscious and seemingly out of your control? Do you have trouble concentrating and going to sleep because you are thinking about it?

• Have you neglected your own needs and those of your family? Are you consistently letting the necessary upkeep of life go undone?

Be careful that just because you are not abusing substances or a specific activity, you don't allow yourself to rationalize, "It's not

that bad." Yes it is. Your obsessions are ruling you and overshadow-
ing the rest of your life.

Step II: Support.
No specific support groups exist for this more subtle category of
compulsive living. You will have to do your own honest soul-
searching — in a quiet place, in a journal, with a friend, and/or with
a therapist.

Step III: Plan of action.
You need to interrupt the diversion of energy into "mental es-
capism."

• Become aware when your mind is drifting off into a preoccupation or obsession.

• Look at underlying fears — growing old, being poor, being
sick, being out of control, looking foolish, failing, succeeding,
being imperfect.

• Pinpoint the precipitating situations that overwhelm you and
tip you into obsessive worries and preoccupations. For example, a
fight with your husband makes you feel unloved and unattractive.
This plays into your fear that you are growing old, which in turn
feeds your obsession to look young at all costs.

• Gradually develop more appropriate and healthy ways to deal
with situations. For example, if your boss makes too many
demands, you can speak up about your feelings and needs so that
you don't feel like a doormat. You don't need to escape into
daydreaming. Your boss is not your father or mother.

• Train yourself to stop mentally taking flight when the going
gets tough. Start to brave it out and effectively handle the situation.
Practice using coping skills that are in line with your adult status.

Identifying Fears And Phobias

In fears and phobias, people bypass situations that are too
anxiety-provoking for them. But the dynamics and origins of fears
and phobias are no different than other compulsive patterns. In
classic compulsive patterns around substances or activities, when
you enter an uncomfortable situation you handle any resultant

anxiety by "self-medicating" with your habit of choice. So the anxiety is partially or completely hidden. If you could peel away the compulsive pattern, however, you would find the raw anxiety right underneath. In phobias, on the other hand, anxiety and other feelings are managed by avoiding whatever causes them. As a result, if fewer and fewer ventures are risked, your life becomes increasingly crippled.

Below are some characteristics of fears and phobias:

• You find that certain objects, situations, activities or places make you extraordinarily anxious. The range of precipitants can be wide:

   - dentists, doctors, animals, insects, snakes

   - heights, being closed in, tunnels, bridges, elevators, social gatherings, new situations

   - swimming, driving, public speaking, horseback riding, writing letters, taking tests, closet cleaning, entertaining, flying

   - any task that involves a number of steps such as doing taxes, or that uses a machine — computers can freak out many people, including yours truly, who are otherwise quite brave

   - being alone, intimacy, making commitments

   - asserting yourself, success, making decisions, competing, and so on.

• Your fear is persistent, irrational, and sometimes embarrassing. You are aware that your anxiety is way out of proportion and doesn't make sense. You are frustrated with your inability to "think" your way out of the fears.

• If you put yourself in the feared situation, you become terrified, feeling trapped and concerned that you will lose control. You may also get physical symptoms such as dizziness, heart palpitations, weakness, faintness, and others.

• If you remove yourself from the fearful precipitant, you instantly feel less upset, though maybe quite exhausted.

• If you totally avoid the dreaded circumstances there is no anxiety. But, depending on what fear you have, this can lead to a more and more limited life.

• Your fears may spread. For example, a fear of dogs can

spread to all animals, which in turn can spread to a fear of taking walks where you might meet anything unexpected.

Ways That Fears And Phobias Can Be Camoflaged

Most of us have fears of one kind of another, but we manage to go ahead in spite of them. We might enter a feared situation, but "stiff it out," being miserable, seeing this as the way life is. Or we might pretend to ourselves that we are not afraid and dash into a feared situation, like jumping into the water when in actuality we are scared to death of it. And we may self-medicate with substances or compulsive distractions to tranquilize our discomfort.

In other instances, we have learned to carefully step out of the path of what scares us. For example, if we are afraid of heights, we don't become house painters. If we are terrified of public speaking, we stay out of the limelight. If snakes give us nightmares, we don't work in the reptile house.

Note: It is important to mention that there is a category of phobia that is all-encompassing and quite globally incapacitating called *agoraphobia.* In this kind of phobia a person is so terrified of uncontrollable and unpredictable anxiety and panic attacks, that he or she may venture out less and less. If these individuals are not helped by good therapy and medication, their lives can become completely immobilized and possibly grind to a standstill. This is *not* the kind of phobia that I am writing about in this book.

Strategy For Recovery

Though you may need to get formal group support, I will still spell out a general outline for recovery.

Step I: Take stock of the situation.

Since not all fears are equally incapacitating, you must decide if a particular fear or phobia is worth confronting:

• How much does it immobilize, restrict or otherwise prevent you from leading a full, active life?

• Are you making important personal or professional sacrifices because of it? Examples: You are unable to meet anyone new because all social gatherings make you uncontrollably anxious. You don't ask for a promotion because the new job would require you to fly, and you are terrified of flying.

Step II: Support.
In some cases, strong motivation and an extremely structured plan of attack can enable you to conquer the problem on your own, especially if the fears are neither too pervasive nor central to your life. Don't hesitate to use a supportive friend to get you through the stumbling blocks.

Others have found a quick and effective route to recovery through being part of a group in a phobia clinic, or working individually with a professional therapist skilled in this area. Comprehensive programs of recovery utilize behavioral and cognitive (changing thinking patterns) approaches, teach relaxation, and also give a perspective on the whole problem. Follow-up support groups are helpful. For some people, hypnosis is a useful tool. Therapy can also help you explore what is behind your fears.

Step III: Plan of Action.
• Fear is in the eye of the beholder, not inherent in what is being feared. You need to learn to stop scaring yourself.
• Small fears can be handled with an approach used for procrastination that will be outlined in the next chapter.
• Avoidance only reinforces the problem. You must squarely face your fears — exposing yourself to that which terrifies you, so that you can start to get a feeling of mastery. This reverses the self-destructive fear cycle.

I used to act rather hysterically around uninvited mice. Living in central Cleveland, Ohio forced me to change my ways, as I had to be brave for my young daughter. I pushed myself to the point where I could not only take mice out of traps, but also nonchalantly watch them play together in the kitchen. Occasionally my bravery is still put to good use in San Francisco.
• This process should be carefully planned so as to build in success. Though some individuals choose to jump fully into a dreaded situation without building up to it (called *flooding*) a more

frequently used approach is *systematic desensitization*. This can include the following:

   - Mental rehearsals — imagine the situation and see a positive outcome. Stop fearing in advance. It may help to think: What is the worst that could happen, and if that occurs, what could you do about it? You are not passive. Some people have gotten mileage out of mocking their fears — "You can't hurt me. I'll just show you up for the nothing you are."
   - Break the whole scenario into pieces. As you take each step, stay in the here-and-now of what is actually happening; consciously relax; picture staying in control; reassure and distract yourself when necessary — for example, count people, trees, signs. When your mind is busy, you won't have time to dwell on your fears.
   - Progressively try more difficult situations. If you get anxious, pinpoint what you are feeling and stay with it. You don't need to eliminate anxiety, just learn to deal with it in a positive way.
   - Take trial runs with a supportive companion.

   • With each success comes a positive ripple effect. Overcoming one fear leads to confidence in other life areas. If you again succumb to an old fear, congratulate yourself for recognizing it sooner, and tackle it immediately.

   • Medication, in the form of antidepressants, is sometimes a useful adjunct to other forms of help. However, be wary of any physician who prescribes antianxiety benzodiazepines (Valium, Librium, Xanax) for more than a few weeks. Otherwise you will simply jump into a substance abuse problem, and have even more of a mess on your hands.

   A woman plagued by fears and an increasingly constricted life came to me for help. I asked her how she had handled it before. She answered, "Not very well," though somehow she had gotten by. But now her fear of elevators had spread, and many other things also felt like an entrapment, even her forthcoming wedding.

   So together we embarked on a desensitization program. First we simply got into an elevator, kept the doors open, and looked around. We spoke of what was the worst that could happen. I pointed out emergency buttons to punch and ways to distract herself if she should feel anxious. Standing close beside me, gradually she allowed the doors to close.

In the days to come, she grew braver, first going up one floor, and then more and more. At each point, we looked at her fears and ways she could stay in control and avoid feeling powerless. During our up-and-down journeys, we explored her early life. From childhood on she remembered having tremendous anxiety in any enclosed place, especially if her mother was not with her.

As an adult, it developed into a full-fledged phobia about taking elevators for more than a few floors. Up until this point of her life, she had handled her fears by avoiding any situation that involved going above a floor that she could readily take stairs to, whether it be for purposes of socializing or work. If she tried to take an elevator, she would feel an inner panic and conviction that something terrible was going to happen and she wouldn't be able to get away. So she always made up some excuse to others, arranging to meet at a not-too-high location.

After we spent a lot of up-and-down vertical practice and talked at length about her past, she was finally able to ride an elevator above the tenth floor and felt triumphant. But the fear of a marriage commitment proved to be more intractable, and most likely had other components which she did not want to examine. She phoned me some months later to inform me that she had decided to call the engagement off, though she was pleased that elevators no longer held a threat.

* * *

In sum, preoccupations and phobias can in their own right be compulsive patterns, whether abuse of substances or driven activities cloud the picture or not. In order to get off the merry-go-round, if such thought processes or avoidance behaviors divert you from feeling your feelings and/or living fully in the here-and-now, I urge you to address the situation, following the suggestions in this chapter.

9 COMPULSIVE WORK OR ACTIVITIES, PRO-CRASTINATION, ESCAPES

Rule No. 1 is, don't sweat the small stuff. Rule No. 2 is, it's all small stuff And if you can't fight and you can't flee, flow.

— Robert Eliot, M.D., Cardiologist

I hold down two jobs to save money for trips," he told me. "Oh," I asked, "and do you go on many trips?" "No," he replied. "I don't have time because of my work schedule."

Identifying Compulsive Work And Compulsive Involvement In Activities

The briefcase or portable-computer-carrying, fourteen-hour-a-day, seven-day-a-week, two-drink-lunch brand of workaholic may be the stereotype. But compulsive patterns around work can come in far subtler forms, often undiagnosed or completely missed. Especially in the American middle class, work is a frequent drug of choice. Unfortunately, a workaholic can simply pass as being responsible and productive — highly esteemed social values.

Compulsively working hard may have been a way of life for you since childhood and adolescence. At first, work might have been a constructive part of your life and a good outlet for your energies. Gradually, however, it has become a refuge from dealing with other problems — loneliness, difficulties in relationships, an inner emptiness. Or it may be a habit that you later developed, to provide purpose to your life, to compensate for other areas of living that feel uncomfortable or out of control, or to give you an anchor when you feel lost. It allows you to feel that you are okay, that you are "somebody."

Because you are a good worker, the response from family and associates almost makes you feel good about yourself. But increasingly work has become your total life, pushing everything and everyone else into the background. It is always on your mind — when others are talking, while you are eating or driving, when you are falling asleep, and even during lovemaking. You feel indispensable at your job. Not by chance, you have fallen into the kind of work that is a bottomless pit, absorbing unending time like a sponge. Furthermore, it is the kind of work that in your eyes can only be done by you, and never perfectly enough. You rush back to it from lunch, weekends, and vacations and forever take pieces of it with you.

Leisure time feels foreign and makes you uneasy. Alcohol consumption can well have become part of your relaxing routine. Cocaine, cigarettes, and marijuana may also be highly intertwined in keeping you going.

It is important to clarify that not all of those who get involved in long and involved hours at work or other activities, are workaholics or activity addicts. The involvement may be temporary or externally precipitated by a particular job, boss, or situation. If you are not a genuine addict, when you sense that it is taking too much toll on your personal life you eventually disengage yourself from the long hours or from the job or activity itself. You can readily shift gears and become involved in other pursuits. In other words, you are controlling your life, not the other way around.

I should also mention that highly gifted or talented individuals may get so absorbed in their work or activities that they genuinely have a lesser need for others. Unfortunately, people close to them may have a comparably high emotional cost to pay as do those involved with true workaholics.

Your work obsession may be focused on gainful employment. But it also can take the form of obsessively cleaning, straightening, doing chores, over-structuring leisure time, or just staying busy. An absurd example of this was written up in a San Francisco newspaper about a woman who was a bonafide puzzle addict. Her greatest nightmare was that someday the puzzle market would dry up. She did puzzles with a frantic obsessiveness that many reserve for work, giving them priority over relaxation and other interests, and even her husband, who eventually left.

Being obsessed with a sport or staying in a rigid exercise program would also fall into this category of compulsive pattern. Instead of truly relaxing, workaholics and "born-again" recovered substance abusers just adopt a new obsession.

Many people get caught into skiing, hiking, bowling, swimming, golf, fishing, playing tennis or racquetball, jogging, constantly entertaining, going to restaurants, or even taking trips. In the latter type, you can stay busy planning the journey, making reservations, buying things for it, packing, unpacking, and talking endlessly about the adventures of the last one and anticipation of the next, to the exclusion of other areas of your life — rather a glamorous form of compulsive behavior.

If the travel bug gets too out-of-hand, people can get caught into full-blown addictions and become permanent expatriates. In *The Italians* written in 1964, Luigi Barzini wrote, "They (foreigners) can no longer face the harsher world where they came from, where they see things perhaps too clearly, and where every word in their familiar language has a precise meaning. They have become hopelessly addicted to the amiable and mild ways of Italy."

Rome almost hooked me. Many years ago, after finishing medical school and an internship, I decided to take a break. I arranged to work as a consultant in the Pediatric Clinic of the University of Rome for five months, intending to then come back to San Francisco to take my psychiatry residency. As the five months drew to a close though, I found myself overglamourizing everything good about Italy, blocking out of my mind anything positive about the United States, telling myself that maybe the residency wasn't really important, perhaps it was foolish to get so much training. After staying an extra month and going through some painful soul searching, I did return. But I visit Rome every time I have a chance, and always experience a "withdrawal depression" when I leave.

Behind those obsessed with work and many other compulsive patterns is what has been delineated by Meyer Friedman, M. D. as Type A Behavior, with telltale signs: You are impatient and waiting feels like forever. If you can't make something happen right away, it feels like it never will. Hurdles and the seeming inefficiency or incompetency of others are especially infuriating. Long lines and not getting treated with special dispensation feel like agony, especially when those who wait on you appear to be plodding along at a Type B, or Type C or D, pace.

You are always on "fast-forward," trying to be super-efficient, often doing two or more things at once — on the phone and sorting papers, finishing other people's sentences, racing through meals, turning every avocation into serious business, and never being comfortable with just sitting and relaxing.

You feel that you must do it all, and all by yourself — flawlessly and in record time. You are unable to say no to reasonable or unreasonable requests, and are incapable of adequately delegating and asking for help. The length of time needed to do a project is often underestimated, so you habitually find yourself rushing and increasing the liklihood of mistakes. As a result, you may well become overextended, chronically tense, and irritable. And I don't need to mention all the indulgences you grab to placate yourself.

If any of this sounds familiar, indeed you are Type A. Incidently, not all Type A's are workaholics, but I have yet to meet a workaholic who isn't at base a Type A personality. It should also be stated that some Type A's carry on their compulsivity in far subtler ways. Or the condition may lie dormant until deadlines arise, like getting a manuscript to your editor on time.

There are also people who do things at the last minute who are *not* Type A. Unlike Type A's, these individuals don't pressure themselves to death nor feel that meeting deadlines establishes their worth. They simply aren't that concerned with whether or not they are on time. Being married to such a person can drive a Type A individual crazy.

Strategy For Recovery

To shift out of this category of habits requires a major life change, for you are attacking close to the root of compulsive living. You must literally move out of the fast lane and into the slow lane of life. This involves a conscious shift of your energy focus. You will need a whole new yardstick to gauge whether your life is successful, one that is not measured in quantities, minutes and dollars.

Step I: Take stock of the total situation.

Weigh the cost-effectiveness of what is going on in your life — what you are gaining as opposed to the price you are paying for it. Reflect on all of it — the constant busyness and pressured existence balanced against neglected family, friends and your own needs; never dealing with the daily upkeep of life; regularly being angry at routine obstacles such as stop lights, waiting in line; never stopping to stay with an appreciation of life's fleeting moments of beauty and joy. Don't be fooled because you are *not* the stereotype of a workaholic. Notice the compulsive way in which you jog, clean house, attend meetings, and attack each day.

Look back over the years at what has been meaningful to you. Honestly assess whether your frenzied pace has added to or detracted from the quality of your life. Do the ends of where you are trying to go justify the means you are choosing to get there?

A high blood pressure or high cholesterol level and warnings from your doctor can motivate you to change. The loss of friends can also pierce your denial and sharpen your determination to better pace your life.

Step II: Support.

Curing yourself of Type A Behavior, workaholism, and activity addiction will be largely up to you. Little formal support exists other than specific programs found in some hospitals. A few cities have Workaholics Anonymous groups, but more available than those are places where you can learn various forms of meditation and relaxation.

I urge you to enlist friends and family members to encourage you to slow down. Those who are naturally *not* Type A can be most helpful.

Formal therapy may be indicated to help you look at why you need to produce in order to feel good about yourself, and how to build your self-esteem from within. You must deal with issues around always having to be in control, your fear of being dependent on others, your needing to please everyone, and your discomfort with having nothing to do.

Step III: Plan of action.

• Get clarity regarding the quantity of work or activities that you regularly attempt to do, and whether this is realistic. A typical Type A day allows no time to eat, sleep, be inefficient, make a mistake, talk to a friend, or even go to the bathroom. You may have to radically change your goals and your schedule. If your present work and activity load pulls for your being too driven and frantic, consider overhauling the entire situation.

• When you define yourself by accomplishments at work or in a specific activity — such as "I'm a runner and I have to run ten miles, seven days a week" — renovations are in order. You will need to cut your overinvolvement with *doing* and learn to get your sense of self from *being*.

• Consciously modify your approach to tackling projects. Instead of attempting to do everything all at once and at breakneck speed, the challenge will be to tackle individual projects with reasonable expectations and truly savor each endeavor. When you are on the phone, be *just* on the phone. When you are at a meeting or sharing an activity with a child, *don't* do anything else.

• Set aside specific time to be with friends and family members. Short of total emergencies, consider this time sacred. Truly listen to and appreciate these people. Learn to let them do things in their own style without constantly upstaging and orchestrating them. Make reservations and commitments to others that seal you into pleasant happenings. Get tickets way in advance. Cancelling at the last minute must not be an option.

• Be selective regarding where you put your time and energy. This will mean staying aware of what you can and what you want to do. Just say "No." It is time to stop meeting commitments to everyone but yourself.

• Leave unscheduled time, specific hours and days when you will *not* work, or engage in any other compulsive activity. Don't cheat. Develop new habits of slowing down, relaxing, and doing nothing. Read books and engage in activities which are enjoyable and totally "nonproductive." But watch that hobbies don't become yet other compulsive activities. Take frequent ten-minute to one-hour breaks each day. Spend weekends, evenings and other times uncluttered by urgency. Allow more time to get to places and to do projects. Stop counting the days, racing the clock, or even looking at it so often.

• Dare to be ordinary. As a workaholic, you have bought into the myth that you are a superhuman being, put on this earth to move mountains and to accomplish far more then mere mortals. It is time to climb off your throne and join the human race. This means that just like everyone else, you have to stand in lines; do mundane chores; telephone and be put on hold; spend hours getting the car fixed; schlepp your children here and there; wait the whole day for the plumber.

When you can allow yourself simply to live each day without feeling burdened to be so special, it will feel like a big weight has been taken off your shoulders.

Step V: Mental outlook.
Be alert to all the "little voices" in your head — or "voice-overs" as a friend of mine likes to say — telling you what you "could" and "should" be doing. Most of these messages are quite unreasonable and must be ignored.

Do everything you can to stay clear about what *is* important to you. Remind yourself that twenty years from now, how much or how fast you got things done will matter little. Become comfortable with every day and every project remaining somewhat undone, as is true of all of life. Enjoy what you do, frequently settling for B's and C's, rather than killing yourself to always get A's.

Search for what is special in life. Keep in better touch with music, nature, and other reminders of how our lives are but a small part of the universe. We're only dancing on this earth for a short time. Don't rush it. It will be over soon enough. Rereading St. Exupéry's *The Little Prince* and Anne Lindbergh's *Gift from the Sea* always give me perspective.

There may be moments when you become overwhelmed by that old urgency that you *have* to work and meet a deadline because time is running out. Remind yourself that the project or activity can wait, loved ones can't — or maybe won't.

Identifying Forms Of Escape
Procrastination

Now the flip side of an obsession with work or activities can take the form of *avoiding* doing them with a comparable passion, all of it disguised in a packaging of procrastination. This might mean delaying applying to school, paying bills, writing letters, making necessary phone calls, getting projects done, making repairs on the car, going to the doctor or dentist. Or it may involve putting off leaving an unsatisfactory work or relationship situation.

As part of procrastination, there is often an addiction to what people refer to as "brinkmanship" — letting everything slide to the last minute, always being late and forever meeting deadlines in a photo finish. For many, the hidden agenda is that of hanging onto the fantasy that if you had more time, you could produce Pulitzer Prize material, but you haven't done badly at all for a last minute preparation. And since you can settle for nothing short of perfection, you never have to be put to the test and risk the judgment of others. Those of us who have been in lengthy school trainings are past masters at this activity, known to students as "cramming." But if you look closely, even *you* aren't fooled by the way in which your behavior resembles the defiant "no" of a two-year-old who feels coerced and in danger of being over-controlled by others.

All procrastination can serve as a subtle way of defying authority and negatively staying in the spotlight. Some find that behind it lies the undying wish that someone else will come and take over — a magic rescuer, the long overdue, "good" all-purpose mother, a bit late but still alive and kicking. Not to be forgotten, is that keeping things forever undone is a sure fire way of avoiding ever having time and energy to get onto other matters. It also hides fears that you may not want to admit. For example, you put off applying for another job because you are terrified of interviews.

Strategy For Recovery

As opposed to combatting workaholism, in order to battle procrastination, instead of doing less and pondering life more, you need to do more and ponder less.

Step I: Take stock of the current situation that has resulted from your procrastination.

- Physical — projects not started, house a mess, clothes un-mended.
- Financial — bill collectors hammering at the door.
- Emotional — guilt, worry, depression, sleepless nights.

Note: It is important to distinguish procrastination that stands for not doing what you deep down feel is inappropriate to do, such as making telephone calls for your husband that you really feel he should make for himself, as opposed to twiddling your thumbs about what you sincerely must do or want to do, paying your bills or writing a letter to a close friend. Contemplative soul-searching may be needed to separate these two groups. The first can be handled with a clear, if not tactful, "No." The second requires that you rev up your own motor.

Step II: Support should be utilized.

Informally it may be possible to enlist the help of a sympathetic friend or family member, and let that person know how to give you non-nagging encouragement. Also, therapists and grass roots peer support groups can help you get going, though beware that you don't set up others to act as controlling parents.

Step III: It is imperative that you develop an active approach in order to reach success.

- Find a physical setting conducive to work without distrac-tions, not attempting to pay the bills in the middle of the kitchen when you'll be sure to be distracted by dirty dishes, the refrigerator, and so on. Unplug or don't answer the phone.

• Break down work into humanly do-able portions.

• Just *start* — at the beginning, middle or end. Don't wait for brilliant inspiration or the "right" moment. Simply get in the habit of chipping away at the task.

• Plan to use times of the day or week when you have the most energy.

• Take breaks. Look back at what you have done, no matter how small it may be. Reward yourself.

• Stop before you are burnt out. Enough is enough.

Step IV: Keep a positive mind set.

• Expect to be somewhat uncomfortable when you first push yourself to get going.

• Consciously hammer away at your unreasonable three-year-old conscience that makes you feel guilty if you don't do it all, perfectly.

• Stay realistic about what you can accomplish in a given time period.

• Accept the fact that some times you work better than other times. Often you will waste time or not be able to use it efficiently. So what?

• If you fall back into old habits, actively attack them immediately. Use the "Two-Week Detox Program" of Chapter 6.

Patterns that Mark time.

Another way to react against both internal and external pressures is to become *hooked onto a specific escapist diversion,* or onto a whole bunch of them. When you feel inundated with "shoulds," you find yourself spacing out into minimal energy pastimes. This could be *television, video games (*"Tetris" is especially addicting for some of my relatives and friends*), movies, sleeping,* detective or romance *novels,* talking endlessly on *the phone,* unnecessary house cleaning, and so on. Your good intentions of getting going with projects fall to the wayside. Hours, days, or months pass. You feel stuck, guilty and more and more behind in life. If you are a bonafide television addict, you may know all the escapades in the soaps, stats of sports figures plus details of their lives, and the nuances of each newscaster, but you are out of touch with what is going on in your own daily world.

Compulsively saving can become another escape. You still have clothes from way back when — long since outgrown and/or out of style. You're always saving newspapers and magazines for the "some day" when you'll get a chance to read them. Boxes of items, no longer used, fill every closet.

Whenever you try to sort through or throw out anything, you are overwhelmed by a heavy feeling of inertia, as if you'd be giving away part of yourself. Soon you literally or figuratively give up, closing the door so that you won't have to look at the unending piles of clutter. You feel like you are suffocating in your "collections" from the past. But you are unable to unload enough excess baggage to move freely into the present.

Strategy For Recovery

As with all compulsive living patterns, the fuel to change will come from a combination of motivation and clear plans.

Step I: Take Stock.

Become keenly aware of ways you are using the activity as an escape. Keep a one-week diary of the quantity and quality (or lack of it) of escapist television watching, newspaper or novel reading, movie watching, telephone talking, working cross word puzzles, bridge or poker playing, and so on. Take a look at all the other aspects of your life that have been put on hold. You may have closed your eyes for so long that you have forgotten what they are. When you can recall them, write them down so that you have tangible evidence right in front of you.

Rather than actively being involved in life, you are seeking refuge in a state of passivity, distancing yourself with your compulsive escape. Again it is not *what* the activity is per se, but *how* you are using it in your life that makes it hazardous to your mental health.

Step II: Support.

If you have trouble budging by yourself, you may want to use therapy to help you explore why you are settling for being a spectator in your own life.

Step III: A recovery approach must have two main thrusts:

• A plan to cut down on the compulsive escape, thereby weaning yourself from using it as a form of avoidance.For example, in regard to television, you may choose to go cold turkey by unplugging the television set, throwing it out or giving it away. Or you may find that you can regulate yourself to specific times and programs. It works best to carefully preselect the exact programs you intend to watch, and turn the set off *immediately* when they are over.

• Pushing yourself to deal directly with the avoided life issues — making phone calls, paying bills, cleaning the house, getting started on projects, or whatever it is you are not doing. Use the approach outlined for fighting procrastination.

* * *

Compulsive busyness — productive or escapist — and its first cousin, procrastination, are forms of avoiding living fully in the present. Whether your compulsive busyness or stagnation is admired or frowned on by those in your life matters little in the long run. Just don't fool yourself

RELATIONSHIP AND SEXUAL FIXATIONS

I loved not yet, yet I loved to love... I sought what I might love, in love with loving.
— Confessions of St. Augustine

*I*n this category of patterns, on the surface it may look like you are in a relationship that fills adult needs. You are not. Instead you use other people as objects in your life, to compensate for your own insecurities and for not feeling good enough inside. When you regularly relate to others in an inappropriately clingy or needy way, it is an addictive relationship. When you constantly relate to others in an inappropriately flirty or seductive way, it is a sexual addiction — whether you end up in bed or not. Most people who have problems in this general area have an element of both of these kinds of compulsive patterns.

Identifying Codependent And Relationship Fixations

Codependency is a condition in which you become obsessively involved in the lives of other people — mates, dates, parents, children, friends, bosses, colleagues, the world — and end up losing yourself. You feel defined by and overly responsible for these people, who may have a whole host of problems that make them emotionally unavailable. You go to unreasonable lengths to influence their behavior and/or their reactions to you, hoping to "fix these people up," gain their approval, avoid displeasing them, be an extension of them.

There are no boundaries. You are not clear as to where you end and other people begin.

You may well put up with another person being emotionally or physically abusive to you, or neglecting you altogether. This could entail tolerating lies, broken promises, infidelity, betrayal, alcoholism, drug abuse, absences, battering, gambling, someone sponging off of you, immaturity, and so on. Your life is increasingly centered on this other person and what you think he or she needs and wants. You feel like an unlucky victim.

You live on dreams and blind faith that the other person will change — addicted to what you think is his or her potential, and always try to orchestrate the unfolding of it. You want that person to be more attentive; to stop abusing alcohol or drugs; to stop gambling and become more responsible with money, etc. You make excuses to yourself and others for his/her indulgences and emotional distance. Or you take over the consequences of the problem as if they were your own, always on a rescue mission. Like hoping against hope to start a car with a dead battery, you keep trying long past your awareness of the futility of the situation.

As you lose yourself further and further into the relationship, you feel totally responsible for any physical or emotional difficulties that exist. That the other person seems to be stuck, you take personally as a reflection of your not being clever enough, attractive enough, or competent enough. So you try to become even more available to and involved with that person. This means incessantly working overtime to please and be helpful — in the bedroom, in the kitchen, in the office or wherever. Nothing feels like too much as you are terrified of failing your partner and risking being abandoned.

It is important to see that all of your self-sacrificing and rescuing is in many ways a false caring and kindness. It keeps the other person dependent on you. This is a role reversal of what happened to you when you were growing up.

You feel unable to stop seeing or thinking about the other

person. In fact the thought of living without this person feels unendingly desolate — life would lose all its color and forever be grey. Every sorrowful love song feels like it is written for you. Others may tell you that the relationship is no good for you, but you feel that they just don't understand. You don't care that you are neglecting your own needs and interests as well as putting so much of your life on hold — you are too much in the grips of your addiction.

If carried to an extreme, your behavior becomes a variation of "stalking." Stalking can exist in mild forms of simply showing up at places where you expect your "loved one" to be, or it can become dangerous intrusiveness into another person's life, carried out by mail, phone calls, or illegal house entrances.

If you are able to finally get out of such a relationship, you end up feeling that there will never again be another love like this one. Yet chances are high that you will eventually go right into another similar relationship. You keep picking emotionally crippled partners and denying their limitations. You forever close your eyes to the inherent problems underlying the emotional unavailability of the other person, and hang on to the illusion that you can remedy the situation. As you saw in "The Source of Compulsive Living" (Chapter 3) this is similar to the ways in which you denied the limitations of your parents long ago.

And so it is not surprising to find that there also exists the precursor for this kind of relationship addiction — one that was the original culprit, but for many, persists in a fairly unadulterated form. A continued *preoccupation with an unfulfilling family attachment* is so common that its compulsive nature often goes unnoticed. You may try so hard to get love and praise from family members that you remain at their beck-and- call, meeting all demands and putting up with intrusive contacts. In fact you've grown up with so much intrusiveness that you accept it as being normal.

A variation of being hooked on your parents or siblings is putting your children, other relatives, friends, co-workers, teachers, bosses, or someone else in a comparable position of power over your life. Instead of living your own life, you are forever worrying and preoccupied with your involvement with that individual and what is going on in his or her life. For example, you find yourself doing endless reruns of your last conversation with someone: "Was Jeff hurt by what I said?" "What does Marsha *really* think of me?" "Is Dad angry with me?" "Will Veronica still want to be my friend?" You feel *indispensable* in that person's life — but sadly, not enough in your own.

In a similar way, an obsessive involvement with a pet can control someone's life. I knew a man who took his dog everywhere on the excuse that his dog would be too lonely without him. Needless to say, his social life was rather encumbered. Many people, incidently, are also addicted to a relationship per se, or to a particular job. As in the above examples, these situations are used as a source of security no matter how boring or unfulfilling they are. Those in them are comparably stuck and terrified of leaving to go out into the unknown.

Regardless of which form your relationship addiction takes, as you bury your feelings and forfeit your needs, you become drained. To lessen your inner pain, you may escape into other self-destructive patterns, ones related to substances — alcohol, drugs, food; activities — compulsive working, exercising, shopping; or preoccupations — obsessive worrying.

In healthy relationships, as opposed to compulsive ones, there is a reciprocal respect and vulnerability, but not an overwhelmingly needy quality to the involvement. "I can't live without you," may sound romantic; more likely it is symptomatic of a compulsive relationship.

Strategy For Recovery

Relationship addictions have deep tenacious roots in childhood. For solid recovery, these roots need to be exposed for what they are and thoroughly excavated. The initial problem, however, is to extricate yourself from the unhealthy relationships themselves, or from the unhealthy parts of otherwise salvageable relationships. You must get back on your feet and move on to interactions in which you don't lose yourself.

Breaking out of compulsive relationships can be as fraught with agony as is any other withdrawal. Carefully design your program for change.

Step I: Take an honest look at how your present relationship is counterproductive.
Make extensive notes of the predictable scenarios triggered by the not-good-for-you person, whether it be a partner, friend, parent, child, neighbor, coworker, or all of the above. Keep these fresh in your mind as well as on paper. Remember all the frustrations and disappointments; the broken promises and the thoughtless actions; the mere token gestures done for you; how often your wishes were disregarded, undermined or discounted; the difficulties in communication and trust. Recall the countless times you put your own feelings, needs and interests aside — how you gave up being "you." In essence, you have been busily pursuing "nonrelationships."

Assess the high personal price that all of this is costing you. It may show up as depression, general unhappiness, having no energy, being easy to anger; the abuse of alcohol, drugs, food, money, work, television; or being in poor health.

Stay clear regarding the actual percentage of time that is or was positive with the particular individual. Remind yourself that you deserve to be treated better. You don't need this nonsense in your life. You can take care of yourself and survive on your own. Mobilize some appropriate anger.

Step II: Prudently pick your support system of friends.
Arm yourself and them with an ample Kleenex supply so that you can regularly cry on their shoulders. Twelve-Step CODA groups for codependents are springing up everywhere. Being a part of one can help you disengage yourself from your present catastrophe. When you are involved with someone who has a specific addiction — alcohol, drugs, gambling — there are Twelve-Step "anon" groups for co-addicts that can be useful to you.

In addition, if you are immobilized by this relationship or if you have a long track record of falling into addictive relationships, seek professional help. Take the time to get to the bottom of your problems so that you can finally be free of them. Relationship fixations point directly to unresolved childhood issues that must be addressed and given proper closure.

If staying in your present situation is too counterproductive to your breaking the codependent cycle and outpatient therapy isn't enough, you may want to consider an inpatient treatment modality. A number of such programs exist around the country offering stays ranging from five days to several weeks.

Step III: Plan of action.

• *Schedule alternative activities* so that you won't sit by the phone, drive by the place where he/she lives or works, or wrap your life around the mailman's deliveries. Push yourself, at a pace that you can tolerate, to throw out reminders of the person. Some people like to look at and hold old momentoes first; cry a bucketful; put them all in a box out of sight; and when ready, burn them or stuff them in the garbage can where they belong. You don't necessarily have to be so radical, but try to move in this direction.

• *Become clear about your boundaries and responsibilities regarding other people.* Realistically appraise individuals currently in your life — relatives, friends, work associates — in terms of their emotional limits and problems. Then you won't continue to expect more than they can deliver.

You are in charge of you. It is not your job to manage and control someone else. You haven't caused others' problems, nor is it up to you to solve them. You must truly see and accept who someone else is, and stop trying to choreograph that other person's life. Let go of being his or her parent, rescuer, or therapist.

• *Get back in touch with all the "old you" that was lost* during this self-destructive relationship — interests, activities, friends, your sense of humor. You must stop running away from yourself and your insecurities through centering your life around trying to fix up another person. Have you forgotten that there is a "you" that can exist separately? As part of the healing process, you will have to learn to act out of your own needs and not just react to the needs of others. This entails establishing who you are from inside yourself — not using others as a mirror for self-validation.

• *Examine your discomfort with real intimacy,* and why it

makes you feel out of control. Trying to get close to unavailable people camouflages fears about being vulnerable to available people. These issues can be explored in therapy.

• *Make physical modifications in your life that commit you to starting a new chapter.* Change around your room, your apartment, your wardrobe, your hair style, your schedule.

Step IV: Watch out for relapses.

If you are in the presence of the "intoxicating" individual long enough, the old pulls can come back, possibly in full force. Sense when you again start to put aside your own needs, to become obsessed with thoughts of this other person, or to be at the person's beck-and-call, tolerating the inappropriate. Unfortunately, no amount of determination or actual changes in you and your life can ever one hundred percent insulate you from such vulnerabilities. This applies whether you are weaning away from an unhealthy relationship to a mate, a friend, a parent, or some one else. You will need to maintain a slightly detached and guarded stance. Or it may be wiser to stay away altogether.

Perhaps even more subtle and seductive will be ways that repackagings of unhealthy relationships can occur — different people in new sheep's clothing but an identical quality to the interaction. If you start to feel those same desperate crazy feelings, pay immediate heed. Cut your losses and get out of the situation.

Identifying Sexual Fixations

A sexual addiction is a close cousin to a relationship addiction, and in fact frequently serves as a defense against becoming too dependent on any one person. Though being a Don Juan or a gigolo may not be as frowned upon as being a nymphomaniac or a promiscuous woman, it is all the same thing.

If you are caught in a sexual addiction, you indulge for every reason *but* a true sexual one. When you're feeling tense, bored, pressured or empty, your mind frequently wanders off to sex or the thought of a new conquest. You then have difficulty concentrating on anything else. Your addiction may be anywhere on the spectrum, from obsessively day dreaming, to "looking," to being preoccupied with pornography, to flirting or to being obsessively provocative. Or you may be engaged in compulsive sexual activity which can range from masturbation, to frequent promiscuous relationships, to philandering. Or you might have crossed into something less socially sanctioned such as flashing, window peeping, or even compulsive rape. Pursuing your behavior gives you temporary relief from tension, but then leaves you feeling guilty and disgusted, and afraid of being discovered.

Sexual addictions can also come in far subtler forms:

• You may constantly sexualize relationships that should be neutral — to your boss, to the postman, to your friend's spouse, and others.

• You might remain so fixed on wanting your partner to have predesignated physical attributes that you avoid deeper levels of intimacy — "How can I love her, she's gained fifteen pounds."

Whatever form your sexual obsession takes, it gets in the way of being vulnerable and having genuine intimate relationships. In fact your preoccupation with sex provides a safe distance from other people that insulates you from needing anyone.

You may well find yourself doing "it" more, regardless of the consequences, and enjoying it less, with increasingly shallow and meaningless encounters. If you are engaged in forbidden or embarrassing sexual interactions, you may become more and more secretive about your indulgences, and frightened that someone will be aware of them. You might or might not be married, but this doesn't curtail your compulsive activities. It only makes them more hidden and better rationalized.

Again it is important to clarify the difference between compulsive sex and healthy sex. Healthy sex can be frequent, but it is integrated into a total relationship, closely bound to feelings of respect and tenderness for a specific person. A sexual addiction, on the other hand, is basically anonymous and impersonal, and used in a relationship that has only transient validity.

Strategy For Recovery

Step I: Take a good look at ways you have misused sex, compromised yourself and taken advantage of others.

Remember the times you flirted or had sex just for sport or to pacify your insecurity. You may have flitted from flower to flower to avoid closeness and potential dependence on any one person. Sex has clearly been used like a drug for self-medication. You are not a "bad" person, but you have done much to be ashamed of. Sincere apologies to your "victims" may be in order, though in some instances, it may be best to leave the past in the past.

Step II: Get adequate support.

If your sexual activities are way out of line, you must waste no time in getting help to stop your impulsiveness. If available, a Twelve-Step Sex and Love Anonymous group can enable you to start to get control. Other groups are called Sex Addicts Anonymous and Sexaholics Anonymous. If there are no convenient or suitable meetings nearby, as a last resort, attend an Anonymous group that deals with other compulsive problems that you have — abuse of alcohol, food, money or something else.

At the same time, consider being in psychotherapy. Here you can understand your needs and insecurities, and why you have used sex to compensate for them.

My prejudice is that you should *not* share your sexual exploits with friends. Sex is a private matter that should not be spoken of in a locker-room public style. Much of your problem is that you have been inappropriately involved in sex in an anonymous way. Information about your sexual stunts can be saved for fellow Twelve-Step participants or a private therapist.

Step III: Plan for success.

• *Set up your life so as to avoid temptations.* Be aware of places and situations that trigger your getting out of control. Purposefully avoid them. No more cruising. When your mind wanders off to sex and conquests, think of other things. If you find yourself flirting in anonymous situations, stop! You are not helpless. You are responsible for all your actions and their consequences. Force yourself to think of the embarrassing and possibly humiliating scenarios that your sexual exploits have gotten you into. You have hurt enough people, especially yourself. Keeping sexually active and in a high state of excitement will not solve anything for you.

• *It is time to move on to real life satisfactions*. You must find healthy ways to relate to other people, respecting their boundaries and learning to use sex as a part of genuine intimacy, *not* as self-medication for anxiety and insecurity.

* * *

In sum, there is a vast difference between *wanting* as opposed to drivenly *needing* someone in your life. If there is an all-consuming hunger to mate, this is a compulsive pattern which should be dealt with; it is *not* "true love." Healthy relationships involve two separate individuals who are able to be vulnerable to each other and yet each stand alone.

You mean you can have fun without food?
—A struggling compulsive eater

*O*vereating patterns and preoccupations about weight are common. The food-weight obsession is extremely easy to fall into, and extremely difficult to leave behind. There are a number of reasons for this:

• Eating is the earliest form of nurturing, the proverbial comforter, hence it becomes unconscious and automatic. Food remains heavily intertwined into all aspects of our lives.

• Slim is "in," particularly in Western cultures. It is equated with attractiveness, confidence, and self-control. Being fat is felt to be a sign of shame and moral failure.

• Unlike alcohol, drugs, or cigarettes, you cannot go "cold turkey" to cure your compulsion, you have to eat. And daily food cues are unavoidable.

Identifying Food-Weight Obsessions

Since I was a little kid, I got into a weird pattern. In front of others, my eating habits are not unusual. But when I am alone it's a totally different story. I'm always snacking, eating leftovers out of the refrigerator when I'm cleaning up, tasting as I'm fixing myself a meal. Especially when I'm trying to push myself to get going on an unwelcome chore or feeling a bit at loose ends, there I am, wandering into the kitchen. I start munching on a bit of this or that, a cracker, something sweet, just about anything—rationalizing away that it won't hurt. Pretty soon I'm eating more and more. It gets ridiculous. Others have no idea of the constant daily turmoil I go through regarding my food and weight. No one ever sees me overeat.

This from a fifty-one-year-old patient of mine.

In food-weight obsessions, eating is regularly used to fill in the spaces of life. If pounds start to accumulate, you frantically attempt to rectify the situation with fasting, rigid dieting, obsessive exercise or some other unhealthy practice. You may feel unable to lose five to twenty pounds. Or you may be someone who is doing battle with far more extra poundage— thirty to one hundred or more pounds.

Here is a typical dieter's profile: You incessantly search for a magic diet — a cure-all to your woes. You devour each new magazine article on being slim, hoping that it will help by osmosis. You try all the diet groups around — some where you weigh in daily, others that meet weekly, seminars that offer a totally new outlook in one evening to six weeks. You dip in and out of doctors' offices, hypnosis, therapy, exercise programs and other groups. You might even have gone under the surgeon's knife for stomach stapling or some comparable procedure. Occasionally you may get down to or close to the weight that you'd like to be, only to watch paradise slip away as you gradually climb back into your fortress of fat and your old familiar weight obsession.

You might stay at your desired weight part of the time, but obsessively worry when you gain even a few pounds and your clothes don't properly fit, feeling everyone is aware of your size. You then hide in baggy outfits without belts, and avoid looking into mirrors that show you below the neck. And when you feel too fat, you may shun any active social life, barricading yourself at home with pity and more food. At these times, you may discount yourself as being a worthwhile person.

The idea of eating three meals a day may make you laugh. You've only been eating one — granted, the one meal starts when you wake up and finishes when you go to bed. If the food-weight obsession is too center-stage in your life, each day may feel like a relentless battle —"to eat or not to eat"— a nightmare of trying to stay in control. You may find yourself using any excuse possible to avoid being home alone so as not to be near the ceaseless and irresistible magnetism of the kitchen. Or you might stay away from potentially enjoyable events because social gatherings with food feel like overwhelming obstacle courses.

Many of those attempting to control their weight have told me about innocently starting to purge themselves, using laxatives or other medications, or forcing themselves to vomit regularly. They eventually became trapped in vicious cycles, unable to stop, even though they were well aware of serious health dangers secondary to their habits — eroded tooth enamel, cardiac arrhythmias, altered blood chemistries.

Regardless of whether you are over, under, or at the right weight, if you are food-weight obsessed, you are probably a calorie expert and know the exact value of each food. But even though you are well informed, endless attempts to gain control and free yourself from the power that food has over you only bring frustration and a feeling of failure. You have started to wonder what is wrong with you — whether there is something radically amiss in your psyche. You realize that the only times the food-weight obsession has not been center stage in your life is when you are overwhelmingly depressed, in love, juggling exciting dates, drinking too much, or involved in a demanding project.

In sum, if any of this sounds familiar, a food-weight obsession has you in its clutches.

To set the record straight, just because someone overeats or puts on excess weight, does not mean that he or she is necessarily a compulsive eater. Many overweight people are neither obsessed about their eating nor upset about their weight. They simply may have gotten into the habit of eating a great deal since childhood.

Or individuals may overeat during emotionally difficult periods of life. However, unlike compulsive eaters, their self-worth is in no way tied to the scales nor to the size of their clothes. Nor do they beat themselves unmercifully when they overeat or have difficulty taking off weight.

Strategy For Recovery

There are three main phases of recovery which must be tackled. To some extent, these phases overlap:

• Developing healthy eating habits by taking charge of your eating and weight. You need to consistently stay aware of what and how much you eat, and keep away from foods that set off out-of-control eating.

• Getting to and stabilizing at an appropriate weight. You also must become comfortable with your new eating patterns and learn to tune into your own natural hungers, while gradually introducing difficult-to-handle foods.

• Letting go of the food-weight obsession and moving beyond this preoccupation.

Step I: Have tremendous clarity about your current eating-weight patterns.

• How much are you actually overweight?

• What are specific emotional triggers that lead to your over-eating? Being tired? Anxious? Bored? Angry? Lonely?

• Mentally, where are you blocked — when do you regularly shoot yourself in the foot? In the evening? After work? On weekends? At other people's homes? When food is free? When you are alone? When you are in love? At your parents' house? At parties?

What self-defeating beliefs keep sabotaging you? "I can never permanently lose weight." "I'll offend people if I don't eat what they serve me." "If I get too thin I'll get sick." "Throwing out food is a waste." "I've gained again so to hell with the whole plan."

• What life patterns need changing? Staying out of the kitchen in the evenings? Getting more activities into your weekends? Not bringing into the house foods that set off overeating? Not tasting leftovers or while cooking? Not nibbling during unstructured time? Not eating directly from the refrigerator while standing up?

Step II: Set up adequate support to enable you to break out of the cycle and to build in success.

Which people in your life could positively influence your efforts to lose weight? How can you better communicate your needs to them? "Please don't offer me extra food. It's too tempting and I can't handle it at this point." Which people sabotage your plans? How can you avoid them or their undermining messages?

Doing it alone is possible but difficult. What kind of formal support would be conducive to your success?

- A situation where you are weighed daily or weekly?
- Attending regular group meetings?
- Getting frequent medical checkups?
- Temporarily being on a special food or liquid program?
- Being in therapy?

Different kinds of support can be useful at different stages of your weight struggle.

Since being overweight is unpopular and the frustrations of dieting are immense, weight loss programs abound. Many of them have much to offer if you can place them in the context of a total attack on the problem, and stay focused on your overall strategy for recovery. Otherwise it is all too easy to get off on a tangent and never reach your goal, which is to both lose the weight *and* the obsession with it.

Let me highlight what I feel can be gained, or more aptly stated, "lost" from different kinds of programs:

- *Private group support programs that have you weigh-in weekly*; examples are Weight Watchers and Diet Workshop. I myself prefer Diet Workshop, if it is available in your community. It has a greater emphasis on behavioral changes and looking at the attitudes that perpetuate your cycles. These kinds of groups offer clear boundaries and tangible goals by having you weigh in. The main focus is on good diet plans, with some attention to your eating patterns. The quality of guidance given in these groups vary. Many of them are open-ended, allowing for people to drop in, and may become too large and/or impersonal to sufficiently motivate you to change. Some of these programs also have smaller, short-term groups. In my estimation, working in a small time-limited group, with the same people each week, maximally provides incentive and encouragement to change.

Some hospitals offer comprehensive short-term as well as long-term and maintenance programs. More and more exercise centers include weight programs, though these tend to be heavily geared toward calorie counting.

• *Private weight loss centers where there are daily weigh-ins and weekly nutritional and behavior guidance lectures.* Since you are forced to face the scale each day, these help break the cycle. But in most cases, the programs minimally deal with the faulty thinking and self-defeating beliefs that compulsive eaters have, nor do they properly address the causes of overeating.

• *Programs that provide prepackaged foods plus offering weekly weigh-ins and meetings.* Nutri/System and Jenny Craig are examples of this type. Eating only programmed food can be both a positive and negative: positive for those who like clarity and simplicity and who welcome a chance to radically change what they usually eat; negative for those who find themselves craving the forbidden and sneaking extra food.

My reservation regarding these monitored programs is that they do not adequately teach participants to understand addictive eating nor how to effectively move out of a compulsive living style. Many programs chastise participants if they do not stick to the letter of their particular diet, or when there is a weight plateau or backslide. This plays into your good/bad thinking and sets the stage for rebellious overeating. Hence the weight-food obsession persists, with the likelihood of regaining the weight.

• *Programs that provide liquid supplements exclusively in-stead of food.* These may exist within hospital centers or are sometimes dispensed by private physicians. For some people, such programs are essential for breaking out of self-destructive eating patterns when nothing else has worked. In highly controlled liquid supplement programs, what is acceptable to consume is clear-cut. And there is the possibility of the kind of rapid weight loss that we who are "quick fix" addicts love to have. This may be especially valuable for individuals with much weight to lose. Weekly nutritional information and behavior guidance lectures are usually given. Unfortunately, as with other highly structured weight-loss programs, the psychological understanding of compulsive problems is often inadequate. Hence participants can easily relapse.

Note: If you are on a liquid supplement it is essential to have competent medical supervision. there are potential health dangers that can involve your heart and even your life.

• *Overeaters Anonymous Programs.* Having and regularly utilizing a sponsor and calling in your food plan each day greatly increases your chances for success. Because there are no weigh-ins, this type of program alone may not offer you enough incentive for change. However, O. A. can complement and enhance other support you are getting. You may want to glance back over the "Adequate Support" section in Chapter 4 for a fuller discussion of Twelve-Step Programs.

• *Privately run groups or seminars that meet regularly to deal with the dynamics of the food-weight problem, why it has controlled people's lives, and how to move on.* Look for groups that have a limited number of participants and combine behavioral, attitudinal, and insight-oriented approaches. The best ones include nutritional guidelines and the opportunity for follow-up support. If ThinWithin exists in your area, it is excellent for helping people get an overview of the total recovery process.

In sum, I have found few resources that have it all. In addition, individual needs vary. You may prefer being weighed-in regularly. Or you might be the kind of person who feels that such monitoring is akin to being stuck with another parent. You have to decide what circumstances are conducive to your gaining control. This may necessitate creatively combining several programs together. For some people, therapy can provide the necessary glue to make it work.

Step III: Set up a reasonable food plan.
In order to lose weight, you have to take in fewer calories than you burn — 3,500 fewer calories to lose one pound. You already knew this, though you were hoping for a better solution.

Unless you are in a program with a predesignated food plan, I strongly urge you to design your own. Then you won't feel deprived, and cheat on yourself with foods you have labeled as forbidden. *Any* reasonable food plan or diet will work if *you* stick with it.

I have had best results for myself and in working with others using the following basic guidelines:

• Figure approximately 1000 to 1200 calories a day, depending on your height, build and activity level. Include a balance of protein, fruit, green vegetable, and dairy products. Get a good calorie reference book so that you know exactly how many calories specific quantities of food have. Eating nutritiously with a minimum of junk food is more satisfying and filling, though I myself fought this truth for years.

• Make the whole eating plan as simple as possible. Include foods that need minimum preparation. For bona fide food addicts, even five minutes of waiting for something to cook can feel like forever.

• *Be sure* to include foods that you can't live without, though be careful about quantities. If a cookie a day keeps you happy, make it part of your plan and enjoy it.

• Stay wary of foods that set off overeating, particularly in early days of taking charge. Either eliminate them or only have them in the house in restricted quantities — an ice cream cone as opposed to a half-gallon of ice cream. These "difficult foods" can gradually be reintroduced into your life when you are feeling strong. For many years, I felt safest with small rather than large jars of peanut butter around.

Most people have the greatest success by initially using a controlled plan to break out of the unhealthy habits that have imprisoned them. This can be mapped out for the week or designed each morning for that particular day. Other people prefer to focus exclusively on changing eating patterns, which will be described shortly, and not to think so much about calories and specific foods. See what works for you. If you are losing weight on your own, consider sending for Richard Simmons' "Deal a Meal." It is a surprisingly well-put-together food plan, coupled with excellent self-motivation tapes and reading material.

Gradually you can find out which eating patterns and amounts of food allow you to lose or maintain a certain weight level. *Remember, one hundred extra calories consumed each day — 36,500 calories a year — add ten pounds to your weight each year.* Sobering, no? Like having a limited amount of money to spend, it's up to you as to what you want to buy. I suggest that you use a structured plan in the early stages of getting control, though eventually you can learn to trust your own real food hunger as a pilot, untainted by emotional issues.

Whatever your food plan is, see it as a guide and *not* a fixed proclamation. You don't have to follow it to the letter. But if you take liberties, be careful that you don't play self-sabotaging games: juggling the quantities; trying too many substitutions; depriving yourself and later overeating to compensate; and so on.

Step IV: Develop an active, sensible approach toward eating so as to stay in charge.
Most people with food-weight obsessions have gotten in the habit of mindlessly eating for all the wrong reasons in all the wrong places.

To put eating in its proper context in your life, it is important to at long last establish healthy, calorically-realistic eating patterns — a bit like learning to walk all over again. Use food for real hunger and nurturing — not as a tranquilizer, source of excitement, recreation and/or escape. *You must finally begin to eat for the right reasons in the right places. This entails staying 100% conscious of the eating process, and being totally responsible for everything that goes in your mouth*:

• Preplan what you will eat. Don't be irresponsible and just "let it happen" because you are tired or lazy.

• At first, though it is a royal pain in the neck, measure and weigh *all* food so that you don't fool yourself regarding the quantity of calories you consume.

• Arrange the food attractively on a small plate.

• Relax before you eat so that you can really enjoy your meal.

Don't eat when you are tired, anxious, rushed, bored, angry, or "down."

• Sit in a proper eating place, not standing in front of the refrigerator.

• As you savor each bite of food, mentally okay or say "yes" to it. Keep the food in the front of your mouth so that you truly taste it —don't inadvertently gobble it up.

• Eat slowly, taking at least twenty minutes for a meal. If you don't have twenty minutes, wait to eat until you do. Otherwise you will simply wolf food down and still be hungry.

• Put your fork or spoon on your plate between each bite.

• Focus your full attention on the food and the process of eating it.

• Don't simultaneously eat, talk, read, drive, watch television, or engage in other distractions. Eat *or* engage in the other activity. You can go back and forth between the two.

• Stop before you are full. Leave the rest. Cover it with salt if this helps. "When in doubt, throw it out!" Your leftovers will not benefit the starving of the world.

• Wait before having more. *Think twice.*

• Gracefully say "no" to anyone who pushes you to eat.

• Don't nibble, eat leftovers, or eat off anyone else's plate. Food eaten quickly still has calories.

• If you start mindlessly overeating, break a sweet binge with salty food and vice versa.

• After finishing, move away from the table — out of the eating area. Start doing something else. Brush your teeth. Walk.

• Record *all* you have eaten — nibbles, tastes, binges, whatever. This will eventually enable you to make sensible choices for yourself that will give you control of your weight.

• Drink lots of water — six to eight glasses during the day. Set up a pitcher in the morning. Eat vegetables, drink tea and low calorie beverages when you are hungry between meals.

• "Fat proof" your home so that it is not a mine field of pig-out foods. Put tantalizing food in closed containers out of sight or out of the house. Don't even take a taste of foods that cause you difficulty in controlling your eating.

• Anticipate problem situations. Visualize and rehearse staying with your food plan and in control of your eating in difficult situations like parties, other people's homes, restaurants, weekends, evenings.

• Prepare meals ahead of time allowing for when you will be tired or rushed. That way you can avoid automatic and hurried snacking and stuffing.

• If necessary, change your schedule so that you don't fall into automatic eating or unecessary overeating. Eat at a different hour or perhaps alone, before other family members eat.

• Preplan grocery shopping, make a list before you leave home. Eat *before* you go.

• Give yourself credit when you successfully avoid bad eating habits.

• Reward yourself daily in nonfood ways for all your hard work.

• Don't be down on yourself for not being perfect — for "dumb" food choices, slips on your eating plan, or not following all these behavior suggestions all the time.

• Your weight will fluctuate. Stop jumping on the scales all the time. Once a week is more than enough.

In sum, the kitchen can't give you love.

Step V: You must become comfortable feeling attractive, sensual, independent no matter what your size.
This is critical Your self-worth can no longer be dictated by what you eat and weigh. *Already* start to dress tastefully and become more active. In this way you can begin to enjoy your physical being, rather than viewing your body as an enemy. Unless you accept yourself in the shape you have right now, you will hold on to your food-weight obsession, yo-yo-ing yourself into eternity.

Long before you are at your goal weight, visualize yourself as slim. Get a clear image. What are you wearing, doing, feeling? What is your life like? How are you utilizing the calmness, the freedom, the feeling of being in control? It is essential that you look at all the positives and the negatives of being slim. You may discover some surprising concerns. The fear of becoming promiscuous is a common worry of men as well as women who set out to lose weight.

To have control of your weight and appearance means to belong to yourself. You must give up your need to be taken care of by others and your feeling that you are responsible for everyone else. Once you stop being the codependent caretaker of everyone else, you may have to stand up to their criticism. They might love you and still express anger and envy. Gradually you can learn to be less obsessed with external approval, and become more guided by your own feelings and needs.

Losing weight will not solve all your problems. But you owe yourself the joy of weighing what you want to, so why not go for it?

Step VI: Avoid relapses.

You are undoubtedly a master game player. You just *happen* to walk into the donut shop; *happen* to bring home four dozen of your favorite cookies; *happen* to stand near the food table at a party; *happen* to find corn chips in your shopping basket; *happen* to nibble on the leftover cake; and so on, and so forth. You taste something, knowing full well it will lead to out-of-control eating. You walk into the kitchen when you can't get going on a project. And *no one* is more surprised than you when things roll out of hand.

Be keenly aware of ways you live dangerously — playing with food situations that at some level spell disaster.

Your immediate goal is to stay with a food plan until you reach your desired weight. The long-range challenge is to let go of the food-weight preoccupation. This is what separates the amateurs from the pros. After all, this has become a boring obsession in your life. Aren't you ready for bigger and better adventures?

Identifying Anorexia

At the other end of the scale from being too heavy are those who have gotten so preoccupied with controlling their weight that they have pushed themselves into a dangerous level of anorexia. If this is the case for you, you may have started by struggling to lose some extra plumpness, only to get caught up in the attention you got for getting slim and the power that you felt when you resisted eating. You then became lost in a whole new war. Rather than a prisoner of obesity, you are a hostage of a fear of fatness. Your need to weigh as little as possible is something you do at all costs.

You may be so obsessed with getting thin and thinner that you eat very little, but in each mirror you pass, you glance for a judgment of whether you stick out too much anywhere. And when you eat anything that in your eyes might round out your bare bones, you frantically burn it off through a desperate exercise regime or something comparable. So your food-weight obsession keeps you emaciated, though you may not see it that way, and overshadows your concerns about other areas of your life.

Some years ago, lunch with a teenage anorexic turned out to be unexpectedly memorable. She spent over half an hour picking away at one boiled egg, didn't even finish the yolk, announced she had eaten too much, and abruptly left to run off the calories. It was a pathetic scene to me. But I sensed that for her, the terror of gaining weight was real.

Strategy For Recovery

Anorexia, though seemingly different from other problems of food-weight obsession, is part of the same condition. However, since control dominates indulgence, several issues are more exaggerated and must be addressed:

• The tremendous loss of weight that comes with this condition brings your body to a near starvation state. You lose critical muscle and alter your body chemistry. These physiological changes may cause you to be unaware of what you feel and confused as to when you are actually hungry. In some instances, this can lead to a psychotic delusional state that interferes with your judgment and insight. If there is enough disorientation you may lose touch with reality.

• In addition, your food-thinness obsession covers over deep concerns regarding autonomy and control. Underlying problems stem from your trying to be separate from your family, which may now be replayed out in a marriage or other relationships.

Step I: Take stock.

The following three areas must be assessed and balanced in order to figure out what kind of treatment plans are best for you, and if hospitalization and/or immediate medical intervention is necessary:

1. Your medical status. You need a thorough workup and evaluation by a physician, hopefully one who has experience with anorexia and can spot problems and potential dangers from loss of normal body tissue.

2. Your capacity to function at work and maintain relationships in spite of your anorexia and food-weight obsession.

3. Your family and how intertwined and enmeshed you are with them. You may choose to be away from them during treatment.

Step II. Support.

While you deal with the emotional issues of your problem, don't put your physical health at risk. At minimum, you should be under the care of an internist and a psychotherapist who work as a team. In addition, in many areas there are Overeaters Anonymous groups specifically for anorexics, or anorexic groups associated with a hospital.

At maximum, it may be wise for you to be in an inpatient setting for a period of time. An increasing number of hospitals have inpatient programs that deal with anorexia. A hospital or live-in treatment center will assure that your nutritional needs are met and give you the opportunity to start your emotional healing on your own, separate from your family and others close to you.

Step III. Plan for success.

• Again, the number one priority is your physical health and that you get out of danger of starving. You may be terrified of gaining an ounce, scared that you will become out of control. But you must trust your doctor, once you find one that doesn't push you too hard. As you start to feel more in control in other areas of your life, you will be less afraid of reaching a normal weight.

• Psychotherapy will help you take responsibility for your own recovery and, the result will be that you feel more powerful and in charge of your life. Gradually you will tune into what you feel; learn to distinguish "food hunger" from other needs; value yourself for being *you*, not for how thin you are; gain confidence in your decision-making abilities.

You got confused messages as you grew up, but now you must accept the fact that you own your own body; you own your own feelings; and you own your own life. You have the right to be a self-motivated independent person, and not an extension of other people.

Being in therapy may at first make you anxious that your therapist, like your parents, will take over. On the other hand, you may feel that if you stand up for yourself you will be abandoned. Working through these issues will be an important part of your recovery.

• If you are still living with or emotionally overinvolved with your family, your recovery will move much faster if family members have therapy of their own, and possibly have some sessions with you. Families of anorexics invariably mean well, but have tremendous difficulty giving their children "wings" and validation as separate beings. Good outpatient and inpatient programs try to involve the whole family.

Unfortunately, some families are unwilling or unable to change their dynamics or the way they interact with you. You will then have to get well without them. And you can.

* * *

It is not food per se nor caring about your weight which is the culprit, but the preoccupation with food and weight used to fill non-food hungers. If not recognized and faced, these preoccupations can derail your life and give you mugh grief.

MONEY ADDICTIONS — SPENDING, GAMBLING, SHOPLIFTING

12

Well, I spent half of it on gambling, drink, and romance, and I guess I squandered the rest.
  —George Bosque, who robbed Brinks, when asked how he spent a million dollars in a year and a half

*I*f you have a tendency to misuse money and be preoccupied with buying things, daily life presents a mine field of temptations and seductions.

Identifying Compulsive Spending And Shopping

There is a saying, "When the going gets tough, the tough go shopping." The nature of compulsive spending is that in one way or another spending money makes you feel better. You often buy things that you don't need and can ill afford. Your spending can take many forms:

- to make yourself look better—clothes, cosmetics;
- buying gadgets and "toys"—cars, cameras, computers;
- buying "escapes"—travel, long distance phone calls;

- trying to impress others—spending too much on a new romantic interest, picking up the tab at a restaurant; and
- possibly, but not necessarily, consistently living beyond your means.

Some purchases may sit at home — unused, unopened or even hidden away. You feel a real high when you charge things on your card, open up a new account, or just minimally make ends meet. Whether money represents self-worth, power, or acceptance, you attempt to buy an elusive something that feels missing inside.

Your spending may or may not put you into debt, depending on your available assets. If you are living way beyond your means, most likely you are obsessed with trying to catch up in paying off debts, in constant fear of creditors and repossessors. Your plans are usually well-intentioned but frequently unrealistic. When expected funds don't arrive, your payments drop off, checks may bounce, or you have to tell people to wait to cash them so that they will be covered. There is a big excitement from risk taking as you forever challenge fate with your careless handling of money. Vainly you hope that riches will magically materialize or that someone will bail you out or let you off the hook. Occasionally this does happen, which further feeds into your irresponsible spending patterns.

You are always juggling and hiding your financial picture, feeling worthless, guilty, and sometimes hopeless and despondent about it. (As noted previously in Chapter 3, this is in sharp contrast to a sociopath, who is *not* genuinely bothered by debts.) These patterns can take a heavy toll on your work, your relationships, and your ability to concentrate on anything else, as well as possibly getting you into legal problems. The pain and shame may lead you to take desperate measures—forging checks, even attempting suicide.

Spending and shopping addictions are unfortunately a by-product of the society in which we live:

- We too readily accept the notion of living beyond our means, living on credit and just barely paying off our accounts. If you are not in serious debt your compulsive spending sadly stays well hidden. As a result, it is easy to deny that you have a problem and delay remedying the situation.

• Effective treatment of the problem is difficult because there is no way you can go cold turkey and totally eliminate your need to deal with money or some equivalent of it.

• You will continue to be bombarded on a daily basis with advertisements, commercials and other enticements to buy, that skillfully link how you look and what you own with who you are.

As is true in other categories of compulsive patterns, just because you overspend or spend foolishly from time to time, this doesn't necessarily mean that you have a compulsive spending problem. It is only when it becomes a chronic, out-of-control pattern that pervades your life, damages relationships, and begins to define your self-worth that it is considered unhealthy.

Strategy For Recovery

The approach to taking charge of your financial situation parallels the approach you take to control eating patterns. Solid recovery requires that you address the following:

• Developing healthy habits of spending, running your money, not allowing your money to run you.

• Rectifying any debts or legal problems caused by past irresponsibility. Listen to the wisdom of Victor Hugo in the novel, *Les Misérables:* "A creditor is worse than a master; for a master owns only your person. A creditor owns your dignity and can belabor that."

• Putting money-spending issues into the background of your life and the past, where it belongs, behind you.

Step I: Take stock of the total financial-spending situation, and its consequences on your life.

• In what ways is your life revolving around money — spending it, thinking and worrying about it, scrambling to repay it?

• Take a personal inventory of the average amount of money that you bring in each month. Write down your unavoidable fixed monthly expenses and those that are not absolutely necessary expenses.

• Take the bills and due notices out of the drawer, the closet, the glove compartment and start to assess the damage. As painful as this might be, you have to put it all on the table.

Though it may take days or weeks to do it, if you are to make changes, you have to pinpoint the areas that are out of hand. The big question is, where is the money going? Are you making a feeble attempt to buy what you feel you aren't? This is sometimes referred to as "retail therapy." It's when cameras, cars, clothes, companionship, computers, cosmetics, and condominiums become the medicine to cure disappointment, insecurity, poor self-esteem.

Again, compulsive spending can exist in the absence of debts. You may be playing elaborate games of "catch up," frantically struggling to make ends meet each month. Or you may have sufficient wealth to never get into debt. The key point is whether you are spending for all the wrong reasons.

• Look carefully at the triggers that lead to your difficulties. When and in what situations are you losing control of your spending?

   - In the evenings, on weekends, on holidays?
   - When you are anxious, angry, lonely?
   - After stressful situations at work, a call from your parents, during difficult times in a relationship?
   - In the stores, the restaurants, the travel agencies?

• Examine the chain of events that inevitably roll to their predictable awful conclusions. Clearly see your patterns. Do you spend frantically and mindlessly? Do you feel a temporary high, followed by feelings of shame, guilt, depression, and hopelessness? At the same time you ask yourself these questions, look at what is being neglected in your life, and the consequences of this neglect.

In order to give up this "fun" way of coping, you must become clear about the high financial and emotional price you are paying.

Step II: Support.
• Accurately access, perhaps by trial and error, how much and

what kind of support you need. For a few people, honestly facing the problem and all its consequences is enough to start them on the road to reform. For others, a helpful friend can keep you honest with yourself, and on top of your tendency to hit the stores when the going gets tough. Just be careful that you don't set someone up to treat you like a child, doling out an allowance to you. For the majority of people though, much more help is needed.

• The only reliable support group I can recommend is Debtors Anonymous, even if you have no debt. Their basic approach and literature is sound and can help you gain financial control. If you have difficulty finding a group, persist.

Some cities have privately run groups that specifically deal with compulsive spending or compulsive shopping. Many are on the up and up, but be cautious in your selection.

• Financial counseling may help. Use a consultant or consumer credit counseling agency with *bonafide credentials*. Do be careful that you don't fall into the greedy hands of one of the many rip-off artists lurking about. I have heard too many horror stories of people's dreadful experiences with so-called "financial advisors," even those who have practiced for a number of years. Examples abound of people receiving inaccurate advice about paying back the I.R.S. or other debts, which led to a heap of later trouble. Individuals have given over money to someone to pay for filing bankruptcy, only to find out that the money had instead been pocketed, and so on. Check with the Better Business Bureau and even with your local District Attorney's office. If anything feels strange, stay away.

• If you have a long-standing problem with spending, address underlying personal, work and relationship issues with a competent therapist who understands addictions.

Step III: Plan for success.

• For now and the near future, you need to *make all spending conscious*, and in your control. This won't happen overnight. The rule of thumb is, "If in doubt, don't buy it."

There is no substitute for getting a small notebook and writing down every single expense. On a daily basis, start to keep track of your money, where it goes and how much. This is your business and should not be shown to anyone else. The whole point is that you are an adult and it is entirely up to you to use your money responsibly. Do not hand over the reins to a partner or to your parents, or you will stay in the child role.

• Religiously *preplan* what you will spend during the month. If you feel offended by the term "budget," call it a spending plan. Many people negatively associate being confined to a budget with being "good." Yes, you should also set aside money for fun and entertainment, and start saving to buy things that are important to you. But you must no longer use spending as a highlight and/or escape valve in your life.

• If *stores* are your Achilles tendon, the following may help: Shop only when you feel calm and are using a list; take time to carefully mull over each purchase, waiting to buy it on another day if you are not sure; take a careful-shopper friend with you; have someone else shop for you if you are feeling weak or if certain stores are too "high risk" for you; watch that sales don't lead to out of control "bargainitis." If television's "home shopping" programs do you in, don't even turn them on.

• If you are abusing *credit cards*, take the scissors and cut them up so that you stop tempting yourself. (Yes, you can leave home without them!) For too many people, charge-now-pay-later life-styles feel like Monopoly® games. This is not a game. This is real life.

• If *checking accounts* lead to out-of-control spending, close them. Carry travelers checks. Pay by money order.

• If *spending too much on others* is a frequent problem — giving gifts that are more than you can afford or always picking up the tab — figure out what you are really trying to buy. Friendship? Approval? Power? Forgiveness? Love? Attention? Control? Revenge?

• The *holiday season* and special occasions have many pitfalls for compulsive spenders. Advertisers purposefully draw us into the belief that the price of a gift is the measure of our love of the recipient. Don't go for it.

- We sometimes overspend on loved ones to make up for our neglect of them during the year.

- We may overspend on special occasions to compensate for financial hardships that we experienced as children.

- The holidays bring on depression as well as heightened spirits. We may compulsively spend as self-medication for these feelings. Be careful.

• *Declaring bankruptcy seems an attractive solution to some compulsive spenders, but for most, it is inappropriate.* Your immediate financial pressures might be relieved but it does nothing to treat your irresponsible spending pattern. Declaring bankruptcy is much like a compulsive eater taking laxatives or throwing up to avoid gaining weight. Getting your parents to pay off your debts is a comparable nonsolution. Remember, there are no shortcuts to recovery. Restitution is your responsibility and an important part of starting to feel good about yourself. Some people prefer to gradually pay off all debts. Others get a mental boost by first paying off the smaller manageable ones.

• Get some *order in your life.* When you are feeling brave, pull all your extra purchases out of their hiding places, sort through them, and give away all that you don't use or need. To heal yourself, it is important physically and symbolically, to travel lighter.

• If you start obsessing about money and are feeling overwhelmed by that old familiar *urge to splurge*, STOP. Wait one half-hour before you enter a store or stay away altogether. Breathe deeply; take a walk; call a friend; put on some music. Remind yourself of the horrible scenario that will unfold if you give in to your addictive urge. Sit down and ponder or write so that you can get in touch with what is going on. Try to pinpoint what you are feeling and weather it through.

• Be sure to *take care of yourself;* allow for reading, music, nature, friends, flowers, time to do nothing. You need healthy ways to have fun and to slow yourself down. It is also important to get comfortable spending a little money on yourself without feeling guilty. If you unreasonably deny yourself, it is a setup for trouble.

Step IV: New mental outlook.

• You need to switch outdated mental tapes: "I'm just no good with money," to "I can become a responsible spender." "I'll never get out of the red," to "I'll just persist until I get my money matters in order." Watch for the old monkey on your back of expecting immediate perfection. Also, be wary of such rationalizations as "Everyone else is in debt," "I don't want to deprive my children," and so on. These are excuses you can well do without.

• Give up the unhealthy excitement of forever living on the edge.

• Enjoy your freedom and independence. It is time to stop setting up others to excuse, rescue and parent you.

• You will have to get and stay in touch with what counts to you in life, none of which can be bought. True, you can buy the image of happiness and mastery, but you are only purchasing an illusion—a transparent cover-up for an emptiness inside. It may temporarily impress and fool others, but in your heart-of-hearts, it will never fool you.

* * *

Did you ever pay attention to the words of W. R. Mandale's "Pop Goes the Weasel" that we used to sing when we were children? "Up and down the City Road, in and out the Eagle. That's the way the money goes, pop goes the weasel."

Don't be a weasel.

Identifying Compulsive Gambling

Kenny Rogers' gambler may know when to "hold 'em" and when to "fold 'em," but if you are a compulsive gambler, you don't. Like most who get caught into this problem, chances are you are intelligent, you are competitive and love a challenge, you are easily bored in social situations, and you are in or bordering on being in serious difficulty. Your past may include a big win. So, against all odds, you hang on to the hope of repeating it.

The bottom line of compulsive gambling is simple: You could be a teenager or a senior citizen; your compulsive gambling might take place in a formal establishment, at the tracks, in the bingo halls, in a friend's recreation room, or at the stock exchange. The trappings may vary, but common to all is that you are playing a losing game with Lady Luck.

Though you might not want to admit it, "investing," especially speculative investing, can also be a form of gambling. After all, a bet is a bet, whether the transaction takes place in a "Wall Street Casino" with a stock broker and an easy line of credit, or in a gaudy casino with a croupier.

In spite of your compulsive gambling, you can remain solvent if you have sufficient resources. Or you may have borrowed extensively and have debts pending or, if it has gone too far, even threats against your life. Those close to you might have financially and emotionally bailed you out for quite some time.

To set the record straight, gambling that is *not* compulsive is something that you can take or leave. For a social gambler, it is integrated into entertainment and companionship. For a professional gambler, it is highly disciplined and entails keeping elaborate records. But for a compulsive gambler, the action precludes interests in food, sleep, friends and common sense. And it is filled with guilt and shame.

Strategy For Recovery

Conquering compulsive gambling has many similarities to those we'll discuss in the next chapter for handling substance abuse addictions. Unlike substance abuse, however — even when the problem has moved into an extreme form — people outside of your immediate family may be unaware of your difficulties. Unfortunately this can play right into your denial, where you rationalize that all you have is a "money problem," not a gambling problem.

Step 1: Take stock of the situation.

Where are you in the downward progression of damage? Do you still have work, your family, any credibility or dignity left? Are there outstanding debts? Have you used illegal means to get money, the consequences of which now place you in jeopardy? Are there pending legal problems? Has the "roof fallen in"? Are you feeling depressed, hopeless, or even suicidal? Is there anything in your life besides gambling?

Step II: Support.
If you can do it alone, I'll wager heavy odds that you don't have a real addiction. Consider yourself fortunate. Quit while you are ahead and before you are totally in a jam.

More likely, getting support will be indispensable. Gamblers Anonymous is your best bet. Locate one near you and start to go regularly. Family members should go to Gam-Anon so that they can play a positive part in your recovery.

Though the number of female gamblers is on the rise, unfortunately there are still few women in Gamblers Anonymous groups. As a result, women have a harder time admitting their problem and getting help. But the problem for them is just as real. Elderly widows may be especially vulnerable. Like other compulsive patterns, compulsive gambling does not respect gender, age, class, religion, or racial origin.

As helpful as Gamblers Anonymous is, it may not be enough. This is because, as is true in other Twelve-Step Anonymous groups, its main focus is on the symptoms and not on the faulty self-image and coping patterns underneath them.

• Consider getting psychotherapy to help you deal with underlying problems.

• You may need a more comprehensive treatment program, especially if your life is too much in shambles. Several of the nationwide programs are part of Veteran's Administration Hospitals. Some are inpatient, similar to substance abuse detoxification programs. Good programs integrate Gamblers Anonymous, Gam-Anon for family members, group therapy, individual therapy and family therapy. They teach relaxation techniques and how to reduce stress. If no such comprehensive program exists near you, put together your own, integrating Gamblers Anonymous and group and/or private therapy.

Step III: Plan of action.
• To get control of your life and begin recovery, you have to

completely abstain from all forms of gambling. This means staying away from any potential situations and people that might draw you back in. Beware of office football pools, drawings, bar dice, lottery, and so on.

• Make realistic plans for restitution of any outstanding debts and follow through with them. Immediately deal with any pending legal problems.

• Stop yielding to the temptation to instantly gratify yourself. Life is full of frustrations and you must learn to tolerate them.

• Find healthy sources for pleasure, self-fulfillment and relaxation. Develop interests and find activities in your life that provide enough challenge and legitimate excitement.

• Engage in respectable employment that gives you confidence and makes you feel in charge of your life. You must become proud of what you legitimately earn, and relinquish feeling run by luck and unrealistic dreams of instant wealth. Though it is socially acceptable, beware of shifting your addiction from compulsive gambling to compulsive work. Real recovery means getting beyond all forms of compulsive living.

Step IV: A new mental outlook.
Concentrate on developing a more realistic self-image so that you can emotionally grow up. You are special but not omnipotent. You are an imperfect, vulnerable human being like the rest of us. You are not above a nine-to-five job.

• Become honest with yourself and you will gradually earn self-respect and the respect and trust of others.

• Find ways to feel good about yourself — to feel loved and validated from within as well as by others. If you don't, you will continue to take rejections and disappointments personally and allow them to trigger you into self-destructive cycles.

• Often the constant excitement of a gambling life is used to mask an underlying depression. Consider what kind of support and treatment you will need to deal with that.

• Balance other people's needs and feelings against your own, so that you are neither run by inappropriate guilt nor by an insensitivity to others.

• To heal yourself, you have to gain confidence that you can be an independent and productive member of society, standing on your own two feet. Relationships must be based on healthy give and take, devoid of power struggles. Family involvement in the treatment process is extremely important, but there needs to be clear boundaries between you and others, so that everyone stays responsible for his or her own business.

In sum, you must believe that you can change, and persist until you do. This transformation can take several years, so don't despair. Each gain in your struggle will give you strength and a feeling of well-being.

Step V: Preventing relapses.
Stay aware of your level of control. Don't play games by unnecessarily testing yourself with tempting situations that seduce you back into the gambling action, especially when you are feeling vulnerable.

Identifying Compulsive Shoplifting

Compulsive shoplifting is a regularly used way of impulsively handling tension. It provides excitement that may be missing in other areas of your life.

The problem usually comes to a head when you are caught, bringing to a dramatic climax a long history of petty pilfering. At minimum — unless your wall of denial is impenetrable — there is embarrassment, shame, and the realization that you are just a common thief. At maximum, there may be loss of a job, and/or real or threatened prosecution. As serious as the situation is, it can provide you with a long overdue opportunity to come face-to-face with yourself.

Strategy For Recovery

Step I: Take stock of the whole situation.
Get sufficiently past your well-deserved guilt so that you can realistically assess the damage. If you are in legal trouble, you'll clearly need a lawyer. Most first offenders are not put in prison, but you must take your problem seriously.

Step II: Support.

I am aware of no official support groups, but do consider getting into therapy. It is important that you fully understand what your stealing is compensating for. Are you feeling inadequate, bored, lonely, depressed?

Step III: Plan for success.

• Find a photograph of prison bars to put on a wall or somewhere to remind you of how near you have come to disaster.

• Level with close family members. Admit that you have a problem and you are working on it.

• Stay out of stores when you are feeling tense, upset, or depressed. The purchase can wait. When you do shop, go with a list, buy what you need, and make a quick exit. When you are feeling unsure of yourself, bring along a supportive friend.

• Even after you haven't shoplifted for months or years, don't take your recovery for granted.

• Find healthy sources of excitement and ways to take risks, combat boredom, and fill time.

• Don't forget to be kind to yourself. Get comfortable spending money on yourself in legitimate responsible ways — a dinner or evening out, saving up for a trip, and so on.

• Keep working in therapy until you feel good about yourself.

* * *

In sum, an obsession with having material possesions, winning large sums of money, or taking items that aren't yours, marks underlying pain and insecurities. The behaviors must be brought under control so that you can go on to deal with the more basic conflicts.

13

SUBSTANCE ABUSE — ALCOHOL, DRUGS, CIGARETTES

First the man takes a drink, then the drink takes a drink, then the drink takes the man.

—A Japanese proverb

Identifying Substance Abuse

Substance abuse is the most commonly recognized compulsive pattern. The hallmarks are classic:

• You actually take a chemical like alcohol or some other drug into your system.

• Toleration for the substance develops, and you find yourself increasing doses to get the same effect.

• Physiological withdrawal symptoms occur when you attempt not to use the substance.

What makes it compulsive is not whether you indulge or occasionally overindulge. The question is, do you regularly use substances to handle the issues of life and are you no longer able to control your indulgences? As with other compulsive patterns, friends and loved ones may recognize your problem long before you do.

Substance abuse can involve:

• Drugs illegally obtained from the street, where dangers are compounded by potential impurities in the chemicals, the physical danger and violence associated with the underworld, and the potential for police arrest;

• Drugs prescribed by physicians, where a medical sanction can lead you to believe there are no health hazards;

• Drugs and substances bought over-the-counter, where availability gives the illusion of safety.

Cutting across all three of these groups, drugs fall into a number of specific categories:

I. Central nervous system depressants

• Alcohol

• Sleeping medications — barbituates (Seconal, Nebutal, Placydil, Tuinal); barbituate-like (Quaaludes, Miltown, Equanil); and over-the-counter medications with scopolamine

• Antianxiety medications — benzodiazepines (Xanax, Valium, Librium, Ativan, Dalmane, Serax)

II. Central nervous system stimulants

• Cocaine, "crack"

• "Speed," "Ice," Amphetamine, Ritalin

• Some over-the-counter nasal sprays, anti-asthmatics, weight-reduction drugs.

III. Opiates and analgesics, which dampen pain

• Opium and by-products (morphine, heroin, codeine, Percodan).

• Analgesics (Demerol, Darvon).

IV. Mind altering hallucinogens are less addicting but dangerous

• LSD, psilocybin, mescaline, peyote, ecstasy.

V. Marijuana and hashish

VI. Miscellaneous: laxatives, solvents, P.C.P., amyl nitrite, steroids have now also entered the addictive ranks.

VII. Nicotine, which will be addressed separately below.

One substance is frequently used hand-in-hand with another, to enhance or offset the other's effect: Many people smoke cigarettes while they drink alcohol. Sleeping pills may be used to help someone on cocaine calm down. Countless cups of morning coffee can help an alcoholic wake up.

Substance abuse is also interwoven with other compulsive patterns. For example, a workaholic may regularly drink in the evening to relax. A "foodaholic" smokes to avoid overeating, or habitually uses laxatives to prevent weight gain. Many people indulge in alcohol and drugs so as not to be swallowed up by an addictive dependency on relationships. Other individuals abuse substances to dilute guilt resulting from debts or procrastination. And a great many people drink or use drugs to try to overcome fears related to social situations.

It may be difficult to tell which compulsive pattern is primary and which one is secondary.

Strategy For Recovery

Regardless of the drug abused, there are several stages to recovery:

• The immediate course of action is to stop taking the substance into your body, unless, as noted in Chapter 4, going cold turkey is dangerous. I want to emphasize that *if you have become physically dependent on large doses of alcohol or even small doses of benzodiazepines for over six months (e.g. Librium, Valium, Xanax), you can face seizures or other life-threatening withdrawal symptoms if you suddenly stop.* Get competent professional help. Do *not* try to handle this on your own.

• Once abstinent, you must develop healthy coping skills for daily functioning so that you can stay sober and/or clean. This entails getting comfortable with painful internal emotions as well as accepting the often difficult realities of life.

• To fully heal, you need to continue your personal growth, better resolving childhood issues that interfere with getting real satisfaction in the real world.

Step I. Taking stock.

If alcoholism and/or drug abuse has evolved over a period of time, its effects may have infiltrated every part of your life. How much your well-being has deteriorated will depend on what age you started to drink or use drugs, which areas of your life are coming apart at the seams, and what else you have going for you. There may well be a number of different substances that you are abusing — alcohol, cigarettes, prescription drugs, marijuana, cocaine, and so on.

Substance abuse patterns are invariably kept in place by family dynamics that allow the patterns to flourish, and by elaborate systems of denial — underestimating the quantity of substance ingested; overestimating its positive effects; having the illusion of being in control.

In order to hit an effective "bottom," something must pierce your denial and stop you in your tracks. Some kind of physical or emotional crisis, that you see as intolerable in a *personally relevant way,* must make you opt for sobriety and/or becoming clean. This might be a drunk or drug-related driving ticket or accident; sexual difficulties or marital problems; becoming aware of the depth of one of your children's suffering; a family member confronting you; problems at work caused by your indulging; a public embarrassment; realizing that you are becoming dishonest and/or using poor judgment; feeling you are losing your identity; or just waking up one day with a hangover and bloodshot eyes and finally seeing yourself in the mirror. It is not important what specific event wakes you up and shakes you up, only that it sufficiently does.

It should be mentioned that cocaine addicts frequently see their habit as one that is exotic and provides status. Unfortunately some health professionals use the same rationalization and deny the seriousness of the problem. This is nonsense. Cocaine users are common junkies — nothing more, nothing less.

• Think about things you have said and done while under the influence that you wouldn't have said or done otherwise, and all the consequences of this. Contrast what your life was like before alcohol and/or drugs took over, as opposed to what it is like now. Solicit feedback, especially from those who have complained about your indulging.

• See how difficult it has been for you to disengage yourself from drinking and/or drugs. Don't be fooled by the fact that you have been able to stay sober or clean for short periods of time, though past stretches of abstinence are a positive sign that you *can* move into permanent abstinence.

• Admit to yourself that you are hooked and that it is time to stop.

Step II: Support.
With few exceptions, it is not a question of *if* outside help is needed, but rather how much and what kind. Several routes to abstinence exist and can be combined: Twelve-Step and other support groups, outpatient and inpatient programs, and group and individual psychotherapy.

There are also therapeutic communities for recovering substance abusers where individuals can stay for three months to a lifetime, depending on the particular community. For some people these communities can make the difference between life and death.

After you are comfortably in sobriety and/or clean, you may greatly benefit from being in a professionally run therapy group that is specifically for those in recovery — either run privately or associated with hospital programs — and/or getting private therapy with a therapist familiar with addictions. Many who need such help and don't get it end up forever being "dry drunks" or edgy addicts, "white knuckling it" to the next relapse . . . or to the grave.

Women And Substance Abuse
Women's substance abuse often follows different patterns from that of men: Women are more likely to get their drugs through legal

channels, from physicians and drug stores; women are less likely to be involved with the criminal justice system; and women are more apt to use alcohol in combination with other drugs. Furthermore, women with substance abuse problems more often come from histories of sexual or physical abuse. They may feel unable to have sexual relations *without* using alcohol and/or drugs.

In addition, women feel especially stigmatized by being identified as alcoholics and/or drug addicts, seeing this as meaning that they are failures, "bad," and outcasts to society. Because of this, women alcoholics and addicts frequently feel so ashamed about their addictions that they socially isolate themselves. They may go to such great lengths to hide the problem that by the time they get into recovery, their condition has progressed to a dangerous state. This can be tragic as women are more physically vulnerable than men to develop alcoholic liver disease. And of course there can be gynecological and obstetrical problems, including infertility, miscarriages and an increased risk of birth defects.

Another consequence of the stigma women substance abusers carry is that their husbands frequently leave, as opposed to wives of male alcoholics and drug abusers who stay and become codependent. The reality of childcare needs can compound the problem of getting into recovery. Hence a woman may be afraid that if she seeks help she will be left alone and/or lose her children.

Substance abuse treatment programs that are sensitive to women's needs are increasingly available. Comprehensive programs not only address the problems directly related to substance abuse, but also offer vocational training, financial assistance, legal counseling, and child care. In this way women can find tangible ways to get control of their lives.

Many women are more comfortable being in support programs for women only. Twelve-Step Programs and inpatient programs exclusively for women can sometimes be found. And though not as widespread as A. A., Women For Sobriety is an excellent resource for women alcoholics, particularly once you achieve sobriety.

Step III. Plan for success.

The basic philosophy of recovery is nicely spelled-out in sayings of Twelve-Step Programs:

• "One day at a time." Stay focused on sobriety or staying clean for the next twenty-four hours. This may sound like an insurmountable goal but, you can handle it, one day at a time.

• "First things first." Avoid that first drink, or drag or hit of a drug. If you don't start with the behavior you won't be tempted to continue it. This is your number one priority for right now. Don't sabotage yourself with worrying about all the other problems in your life.

• "If you don't want to slip, stay out of slippery places." You will have to look at all the potential booby traps of life, and plan ahead in order to stay clear of your habit.

Note: For recovering drug addicts, get rid of your paraphernalia—bullets, scales, pipes, needles, and so on. When drug addiction involves illegal purchases, in addition to stopping the drug itself, you must bail out of your dealer system. This entails completely cutting your connection to former cohorts and sources as well as paying off any outstanding debts.

• "Live and let live." "Easy does it." Pay attention to your own living of life; it is all you can hope to have control over. Stop trying to arrange other people's lives or expecting to change the world.

• "Stinking thinking leads to drinking thinking," and drugging thinking. Watch out for feeling sorry for yourself, for being preoccupied with grievances, or for the return of old patterns of denial — "One drink won't hurt"; "Being sober and/or clean isn't making me happy anyway"; "I'm older and wiser. Maybe now I can handle liquor/cocaine/Valium/uppers"; "It's just cough syrup"; and more.

Nicotine Addiction

Nicotine is one of the most addictive of all drugs. It modulates moods and provides a high degree of euphoria, making it an all-too-comfortable security blanket. Peer pressure, and the desire to look sophisticated further fix this habit in place. In addition, in spite of the well-publicized health hazards of cigarettes, it continues, kept afloat by the money of the tobacco industry. As a result, many people who might *not* get caught into other areas of compulsive living become hooked on cigarettes.

Strategy For Recovery

Recovery rests on a strong desire to quit smoking and having structured plans for doing so. You need much hoopla and ceremony befitting the difficulty of this rite of passage. Since you may well be quitting on your own without using formal support, I offer the following four-week program, based on suggestions from many former smokers. It can be adapted to your needs:

Week I: "One for the money" — Awareness
• To help get appropriately motivated, stop denying the long-term disasters that result from cigarettes. Cancer programs often have excellent materials on the consequences of smoking. They will graphically illustrate the tangible, terrifying reality of what cigarettes do to your body which can eventually lead to your death. Images of premature aging, damaged lungs and damaged lives lost to emphysema, heart attacks and cancer will help you face reality and get you through many temptations.

As the future may seem distant, also focus on short-term benefits of quitting: more stamina; food tastes better; getting rid of your smoker's cough; no stained teeth or fingers; no burned clothes or upholstery. Write and post this list of benefits as an inspiration.

• Buy a small notebook and attach it with a rubber band to your cigarettes. Every time you smoke, write down a few words about what you are feeling and when and why you are smoking — to add excitement, to get going, to calm down, or purely out of habit. If you have time to smoke, you have time to write. Keep a daily and weekly tally of the *number* and the *cost* of cigarettes you smoked.

Week II: "Two for the show" — Positive plans
• Continue with the steps of Week I.
• If it helps, find a support system:
  - Choose a buddy to quit with you.
  - Attend Smokers Anonymous meetings.
  - Go to a hospital program or an institute like American

Cancer, American Heart Association, or Seventh-Day Adventist Five-Day "Breathe Free" program. Or enroll in SmokEnders or another comprehensive commercial program

• Set a date, about two weeks ahead, for quitting. Select a day where quitting can be top priority, make an event of it. This can be rescheduled if you need more time to prepare.

• Practice taking ten-minute relaxation periods several times a day where you are away from distractions.

• Take two half-hour walks each day and make plans for other kinds of exercise programs. Join a health club.

• Start other habits with your hands, mouth, and mind. Drink more water; eat regular and healthy meals. Take Vitamin C daily. Spend time on new enjoyable vocations.

• Make a dental appointment in a month for a teeth cleaning.

• Plan specific short- and long-term rewards — clothes, movies, dinners out, weekends away, big trips — that you pay for with money saved from cigarettes.

• Talk to your physician about the possibility of using nicotine gum (e.g. Nicorette). If you decide to use it, get a supply on hand to last three to six months from the day you quit smoking. See notes about how to use it in Week IV.

Week III. "Three to get ready" — Specific tips for tapering
• Continue writing in your diary and the steps you covered in Weeks I and II.

• Switch to a lower tar and nicotine cigarette brand. Buy only by the pack, *never* by the carton. Throw out all cigarette lighters.

• Don't carry cigarettes with you. Leave them in a specific place.

• Stop asking for or accepting cigarettes from others. Be firm with "pushers," say "No thank you, I don't smoke."

• Each time you reach for a cigarette, force yourself to wait ten minutes and first engage in some other activity.

• Smoke using the opposite hand, between different fingers. Put your cigarette down between puffs. Only smoke in pre-designated areas.

• Discipline yourself to smoke less and less often. Start by smoking exactly on the hour or half hour, a maximum of twice an hour. If you miss a time, don't make it up, just skip it. Be aware of every cigarette smoked.

• Have established clean times — one hour after awakening and one half hour after meals. Brush your teeth instead. Don't smoke while driving, being in bed, drinking alcohol or coffee, watching television.

• Save all cigarette ashes and butts in a jar with a screw on top. Cover them with water to avoid the temptation to fish butts out in 3:00 a.m. moments of desperation. *Save this jar to gaze at as a trophy of triumph.*

• If you don't feel ready to quit on your "due date," keep repeating Week III until you are.

Week IV. "And four to go" — Quitting time.
• Review Week I and Week II.

• Announce to family, friends, and coworkers that you are quitting.

• Throw all of your cigarettes away. One friend of mine who was finally able to successfully quit, though, said he owed his victory to having always carried his "enemy" around with him. He would frequently take out the dreaded cigarette and talk to it: "You are nothing but a stupid cigarette and I'm stronger than you." And he was. As is true for all recovery programs, find out what works for you and do it.

• Send your clothes to the cleaners to get rid of the smoke smell.

• Overstructure the first few days so that you have minimum stress, boredom, inactivity, loneliness. Consider transition times, such as work-to-home, that make for difficult moments to avoid smoking through them.

• Stay away from coffee, alcohol, and others who smoke. Be firm with "pushers": "No thank you. I don't smoke."

• Drink six to eight glasses of water a day.

• Chew sugarless gum, cinnamon sticks — not candy or other sweets.

• Keep vigilant about your tendency to retreat to your habit when you are tired.

• When you get an urge to smoke, take a deep breath through your mouth and slowly exhale; take a shower; take a walk. The urge will go away.

• Call helpful friends for moral support.

• On a daily basis, buy yourself small rewards. Treat yourself to a taxicab ride. Follow through with other nice plans.

• Remember your positive thinking. Re-read "An Updated Mental Outlook" in Chapter 5. It includes affirmations, but here are some additional ones, as well:

- "I am quitting for me. I'll feel better."

- "I can quit. I'll take one hour and one day at a time." Most smokers find the idea of never smoking again to be too hard to swallow.

• If you use nicotine gum, use it correctly:

- Carry it with you all the time.

- When you first quit, use at least one piece an hour, whether you feel withdrawal symptoms or not.

- Each piece should sit in your mouth for a half an hour and get an occasional chew until your feel a tingling, then stop until the tingling goes away. Spit out saliva rather than swallowing it — it can irritate your stomach.

- Do not drink beverages immediately before or while chewing the gum.

- Use the gum for at least three months before starting to taper off.

• In some cases, clonidine is being used as an adjunct for nicotine detoxification. Check with your physician.

Stay Wary Of Relapses
Re-read "Not Shooting Yourself in the Foot." Here are some critical areas to work on:

• Think of yourself as a nonsmoker. Keep seeing all the benefits.

• For months, handle associative activities — such as drinking alcohol or coffee — with trepidation.

• Watch out for rationalizations and temptations to test your new healthy status — "One cigarette won't hurt." Yes it will.

• Celebrate each month's abstinence.

• If you slip and smoke a cigarette or two, or three or four, just STOP. Don't compound the problem with self-incriminations. Slipping is not a sign of weakness, failure or moral degeneration. Remember, nicotine is highly addicting, a treacherous foe. Respect the difficulty of the task at hand and try again. If necessary, go back to Week I. A close friend of mine quit twelve times before he finally quit for good. That was twenty years ago.

Note: In some cases of severe nicotine addiction, it is best to be in a hospital for one to two weeks to help with withdrawal. This is especially true when there is a marked underlying depression. Check with your physician if you feel this applies to you.

* * *

In sum, substance abuse, legal or illegal, has physiological as well as psychological components and consequences. Sometimes recovery can be undertaken alone or with twelve-step or other group support. If in doubt about the severity of your situation, get a good medical consultation.

14 | *BEYOND COMPULSIVE LIVING*

I was never myself before I got sober. I was my parent's daughter, then my husband's wife, then my children's mother, but I was never me.
> — A recovered alcoholic

A patient who had struggled hard and victoriously to let go of self-destructive patterns pondered on her current life:

I feel like I have no history. That's one of the reasons I sometimes like to get together with particular friends who have also weathered childhood storms. We exchange dysfunctional family shop talk and tales of compulsive catastrophes. These people become the birth family that I never had. I don't want to contaminate my good marriage with all the garbage of my past.

A Second Act

If you have given up whatever compulsive pattern you were using, consider your accomplishment nothing short of outstanding. You did it! You have every right to feel extremely proud of yourself.

When you are newly abstinent from self-destructive habits, thoughts about staying in control will undoubtedly concern you. This is to be expected in the beginning, but be aware that if the feelings stay too central to your thinking, you won't be able to move on with your life. You will be like a divorcee who forever mourns the death of a past marriage and never goes on to try out a new relationship. You have worked hard to let go of your old patterns. Don't sell yourself short by nesting in this stage and roosting there into old age. You will only end up creating a whole new collection of problems. Don't deprive yourself and regret more lost opportunities.

See giving up compulsive patterns as the beginning of an adventure, *not* the end of fun. Channel your energy into previously neglected arenas. F. Scott Fitzgerald said, "There are no second acts" on the stage of life. He was wrong. His life was destroyed by alcohol and compulsive spending, yours doesn't have to be. There is still the possibility of a whole new act for yourself, one that is beyond compulsive living.

> *It has been almost twenty years since I quit smoking. But every once in awhile over a cup of coffee, I'll get that old familiar urge to light up. I guess I could smoke a day or two without getting hooked. But I would truly be playing with fire. I could so easily get back to square one. Life is too precious for me to take that risk. I only hope my past smoking hasn't irreversibly hurt my health.*

That said by a recovered smoker.

> *I never in a million years could have imagined that my size and shape wouldn't be the most important thing in my life. I feel I have finally managed to escape from being a food junkie and so obsessed with my weight. I now pretty much eat what I want and food is only on my mind when I'm really hungry.*
>
> *What's amazing is that I'm actually about ten pounds more than I thought I'd like to be and even that is okay. And what I'm pleased with is that when I am upset, I can just stay upset. Only rarely do I overeat to get away from feelings, and not even very much when I do.*

So shares a compulsive eater in recovery.

Becoming "You"

Your life has been so centered on self-destructive habits and recovering from them, that this has in many ways defined you and given you an identity — "I'm an alcoholic," "I'm a gambler," "I'm a workaholic," "I'm a procrastinator," and so on. At best, you have lost your way on your life path. At worst, you may never have discovered it. Since you have been busy publicly being who you thought you should be while privately rebelling, it will take time to get acquainted with who you really are. In fact a great deal of "you" may be quite underdeveloped.

The only way to repair your self-image and inner wholeness is through patiently getting to know yourself, including exploring your hopes and your dreams, your likes and your dislikes, your values and your priorities. You will have to experiment with new ventures, dare to make waves and look ridiculous, and sometimes do things badly.

So much of your life has been put on hold with compulsive living that you may have only rarely, if ever, paused to ask yourself a key question, "What counts in life?" Is it certain activities or adventures? Is it time spent with particular people? Have you taken for granted your spouse, children, parents, friends? After her little girl had died someone once told me, "If I had known she was going to die, I would have hugged her more." The time to hug is now.

There are no absolutes of good or bad, nor right or wrong ways to live your life. But, as Carlos Castaneda said, if you follow a path with "no heart" and too many unfilled dreams, you'll have reason to be sad.

> *I was waiting in a long check-out line at the supermarket. I got talking about this and that with a very nice woman about my age in front of me. The conversation was pleasant and easy — we had a sort of instant rapport.*
>
> *In former times, I would have let things go their limit, and possibly ended up in bed. This time, I made myself think of my wife and children and all we shared. I also thought of the predictable scenario that would unfold with this woman — I know myself and my patterns pretty well.*
>
> *So I smiled at her, walked away, and felt a momentary*

pang of emptiness. Then I continued on home to my family feeling like a cat who had just eaten a canary.

This was told me by a recovering sex addict.

Last week, I was late to an appointment and drove around and around like crazy looking for a parking place — which I finally found quite far away from where I wanted to go. I then went into my usual pout and rage, furious at humanity for putting obstructions in my way. I felt victimized. The world owed me a rescue.

After I had run a couple of blocks towards my destination, a curious thing happened. A sudden flash of insight hit me. Though I was still livid, at some level I realized I was enjoying this feeling with it's adrenaline rush.

I started to smile and my fury gradually melted away to I don't know where. I think I've been wasting a ton of energy battling windmills.

A Type A man in recovery recounted this story.

Sadness For What Was And What Is

I have found for myself as well as for others who have climbed out of dysfunctional backgrounds, that from time to time, leftover feelings from childhood may haunt you. When you least expect it, vestiges of past sadness intrude. You start out feeling blue. But occasionally you find yourself catapulted backward into a black, awful feeling from which it is hard to extricate yourself.

Sometimes the reasons for the sadness are clear — a touching scene in a movie; someone going beyond the call of duty and being particularly nice to you in a way that you wish had happened when you were a child; the loss of a friend who moves away, a child that moves on, or a stage of your life that you leave behind.

Other times, whatever it is that sets off the sadness is far subtler and more difficult to detect. Perhaps it is something minor that piggybacks on a whole bunch of frustrations. It might be a series of situations where you have to be brave and strong, and then a final one represents the straw that breaks the camel's back.

But there you are, feeling alone and vulnerable, wanting to be somewhere where no one and nothing will make any demands on you. You wish you could fall asleep or just be held and rocked. Life feels melodramatic — you are easily reduced to tears and your sense of humor vanishes. In former days, you would have immediately comforted yourself with compulsive patterns of one kind or another. Now you just wonder if the pain will ever go away. It will.

> *I feel a pervading sense of sadness — like I'm real fragile, disconnected. I go back in my thoughts to reassure myself that all is okay — to keep perspective that I'm not going off the deep end. I want to cry. I desperately want reassurance that everything is all right — that I'm all right — that I'm good enough — that I'm liked enough — that I'm not alone. I want to get away — escape. Food formerly served to make me feel okay — or getting drunk, or being busy or throwing myself into some exciting relationship.*
>
> *But right now I'm going to stay with this dreadful feeling and not run. I can beat it. What does it serve? I feel isolated, angry, terribly alone, bitter, resentful — but of what? Like I'm no good for anything, or anyone. If people knew how down I get, they'd leave — have to keep up a front. Eating or drinking would cover this awful feeling. I refuse to go that way — I don't want to get zonked. And I'm not sure I like the effect that much. Do I want more attention? Do I want people feeling sorry for me? This is insane.*
>
> *I look back on what I wrote yesterday and I almost can't believe it was me writing. My life is really not all that bad. In fact it is quite good. I guess the daily grind pulled for that old "empty-caught-lonely-hopeless" feeling that was my constant companion as a kid. I haven't felt it for a long time. But I didn't give into it. And it didn't kill me. And this morning I'm neither fatter nor hung over nor kicking myself for having made an ass of myself with someone. Feeling rotten is the pits. I'm glad it doesn't hit me like this very often. I guess I am finally growing up.*

A woman in recovery from a variety of compulsive patterns showed me these notes that she had written in her journal, after a series of disappointments.

Life indeed can hand out too much pain. It is hard to stay vulnerable and not end up dissolving or unduly hardening from it. That is part of the difficult art of being fully alive — getting comfortable with the rough texture of existence and yet remaining open and flexible. There are delicate balances: To stay with the impact of the moment and yet be in touch with the passing of time; to belong one hundred percent to yourself and yet feel connected to the human race. Sometimes it is excruciating and overwhelming. At other times, it is all worth the effort.

As you gain experience staying with your feelings — whether it be sadness, loneliness, anxiety, anger, or some other — these times of darkness will become less scary and hopefully less frequent. You'll learn to take them in stride, seeing them as reminders of how far you have traveled.

New Strengths

If you'd have asked me ahead of time how a phone call from him would affect me, I would have told you, "Not that much." After all, the whole relationship was so long ago. Though I was still touched by intense love songs, my heart no longer bled uncontrollably. I saw him for what he was and is — a lot of potential, but not much more; too scared of closeness. Not only could I not change him, but I would always be vulnerable to being hurt by him.

When he did call, I thought I was cool and calm, that I took it in stride. I was wrong. I could barely breathe afterwards. I kept reminding myself that he wouldn't follow through when he said he'd visit. Sure enough, he didn't. Temporarily I was sucked back into that same hollow place. But it was different than it had been two years previously. I now felt more secure about who I was.

One week later he called again. I told him I wished him well, but not to phone anymore. I felt a genuine sadness for his tragedy, but realized that I no longer needed to be part of it. We said good-bye and I hung up. For ten solid minutes I felt frozen and unable to do anything. Then I got up and went about my business. I'm free. I can go on. I've had so much

pain in my life. It's not worth hurting any more. I deserve better,
and I'm willing to wait for it.

I heard this from a recovering "relationship junkie."

Notice that the people in recovery who are quoted here maintain a healthy respect for their former tormentors, and tread carefully when around them. Much of the time recovery becomes second nature to these individuals, but not always. When necessary, these people have the ability to walk away from situations that seduce them without feeling a great sacrifice has been made. Temptation still appears on the scene, but it no longer steals the show.

It's at the extreme lows and highs when I most miss a
good drink — the times when the world falls apart, or the times
I'm on top of it. But the past was just too horrible. I don't ever
want to go back to booze. It's ten years since my last drink.
Every once in awhile I'll drop into a meeting. It keeps me
humble in the right ways.

So spoke a recovering alcoholic.

After a chaotic twenty years of debts, I had finally gotten
my finances in pretty good order. It required radical surgery
— I gave up my checking accounts, stopped using credit
cards, and even chose to live in a place that didn't get Home
Shopping on television.
I thought I had passed that era of my life and could handle
anything. I got a new credit card last year. Well, I guess I'm
still not safe. Christmas did me in. Back I was with my credit
card run up to the max. But unlike the old days, once I realized
I couldn't control it, I just cut up the card and now I've almost
paid off my debt. Some day maybe I can handle credit, but
not yet.

This was told me by a former compulsive spender. Even a relapse was taken in stride and quickly cut short.

When my personal life doesn't go well, work still tempts
me. I can so easily bury myself at the office. Hours and days
go by and I'm safely hidden from all the stress. But I don't
want to do that any more. I've got a good marriage, my

*children are growing up quickly, and I don't want to risk losing
out on any of it. So I force myself to stay conscious of what I
am doing. When I sense that I'm escaping into work, I quickly
shift gears and come back to the here and now.*

A recovering workaholic shared the above.

*I know at base I am and will always be a procrastinator.
But I refuse to give in to it. When I see myself falling back into
old patterns and the desk begins to pile up with all that's
undone, I make myself start anywhere. Initially it is sheer
agony to get going. But with a half-hour work here and there,
gradually I can see daylight. It is worth it. I feel so much better
about myself than I used to.*

That from a procrastinator in recovery.

Incidentally, the story of our cats, Michaelangelo and Sasha,
last seen in Chapter 3, continues. If you recall, their relationship
was frozen by Sasha's continuing need to nurse and
Michaelangelo's codependent habit of playing surrogate mother. I
am happy to report that there has been a decided change in their
behavior. A few days ago, my children pointed out that they hadn't
seen Sasha "nurse" on Michaelangel's belly fur in weeks. Indeed
the two cats shifted from the parent-child role playing to a more
appropriate male-female interaction, with lively exhibitions of their
romantic affections. As is true for many late bloomers, though, their
need for public display of newfound talents often outweighs any
decent sense of discretion.

Wonders never cease. Perhaps Michaelangelo and Sasha read
my manuscript.

Healthy Detachments

Stay clear about the limits of your will and resistance and have
an appropriate detachment from others. Care for people and help
them when you can, but don't be drawn into situations where you
habitually rescue them from their problems and weaknesses.

Full recovery means outgrowing the unhealthy aspects of your
family of origin and your identification with their problems,

without feeling that you are being disloyal or betraying them. If you don't go on with your own life, you will end up betraying yourself.

> *Now that I'm in recovery, I feel wonderful. But my parents are still stuck in their own juice. And I can't do a damn thing about it. I love them and they are not bad people. But I know if I get too close for long, they can drag me right in. Sometimes I feel as if I've abandoned them, and that makes me sad.*

So spoke a friend after successful therapy and beginning a new fulfilled life.

When family and friends continue to be unwilling or unable to address problems, there is little you can do about them. But you can do something about you. You may need to set limits. For example, with a still-drinking parent you might have to say, "I'm sorry. But when you are drinking, I won't visit you or allow my children to be with you." You have a right to protect yourself and to protect those for whom you are responsible.

You will be stepping into the virgin territory of emotional maturity. So, you may experience outgrowing your parents, being alone yet complete, handling life without self-destructive crutches. Your parents may be unable to guide you. But that is no reason for you to deny yourself happiness and an enjoyment of your accomplishments.

Moving On

An important part of getting beyond compulsive living entails genuinely saying good-bye to what has up to now been an unfinished childhood. This is not an easy good-bye to say, but it is a necessary one. You need to stop lamenting for what your life lacked; let go of the anger at your parents for not taking better care of you; and let go of your illusions of what life should be.

Nothing can make up for the past. You missed a lot and it wasn't and isn't fair. But who should take the blame? Was it your parents, their parents, or who? Each generation is obviously the product of the one before. Where does the blame end? At some point you will run out of scapegoats and must claim responsibility for your own life.

Your parents were products of their own childhoods, and were often flawed and scarred as a result. Given their strengths and limitations, consider that they did the best they could. You *were* affected by what happened while you were growing up, but you don't need to continue to be victim.

> *So many bad things were in my past — too many nightmares in childhood that never should have happened. Thank God I had the strength to climb out of the snake pit of my family. My brothers and sisters weren't so lucky.*
>
> *It took a lot of therapy, but I guess it takes what it takes, and I refuse to keep carrying the pain of the past with me. For awhile I thought I'd never be able to give up the anger — but I have. Sometimes I flash on sadness when I think of all I missed, but I don't want to lose any more time being bitter about the past. Life is much too good to me now to waste a single minute.*

A patient formerly obsessed with bitterness told me this.

You have "promises to keep and miles to go before (you) sleep," Robert Frost said. Instead of compulsively attempting to make yourself feel better from the outside, you must finally allow yourself to heal from the inside.

As you move on to new interests and activities, stay aware of the fine line between appropriate vs. compulsive involvement. There is a difference between being enjoyably absorbed in satisfying involvements, as opposed to being driven and caught in fleeting gratifications. In the latter case, you are clearly escaping from dealing with other life issues.

When you are beyond compulsive living, you are not preoccupied with thoughts related to a particular habit. You eat when you are hungry and don't worry about your weight. You spend appropriately and don't obsess about how much you've spent. The proof of the pudding is whether you can easily disengage yourself from a pattern and focus on other areas, when *you* so choose.

Obviously not all addictions are equally malignant. To be obsessed with reading does not effect your liver like alcohol does. But at some level, compulsive living is compulsive living. All forms of it rob you of being maximally "you."

Back On Track

To be fully alive and adult entails dealing with universal existential truths:

• *Death is an eventual reality. Time is passing and we are all getting older.* You don't have forever to do whatever you want to do with your life. As many have said, "This is it," life is not a dress rehearsal. You may deny this truth by staying unaware or numb or mindless through compulsive living. But there is no way that you can freeze time. William Saroyan fervently wished, "Everybody has got to die but I have always believed an exception would be made in my case." There are no exceptions.

• *We each have a given amount of freedom which we can use, or not use, to be active participants in our lives.* This means constantly taking full responsibility for yourself and all of your choices. Even if you are in good relationships, you are ultimately alone.

There are no precedents, no firm guidelines, no guarantees, and no perfect answers. Your only true validation must come from within. You will never have it all completely figured out. But at the end of your life journey, you must answer to yourself as to whether or not your life has been meaningful, and if you became all that you wanted to be.

Compulsive living is a last vestige of parts of your childhood that were not good enough. It represents an attempt to find simple answers to the complex questions of your existence. In order to truly step off the compulsive merry-go-round, you need to give up this self-destructive way of life — or should we call it a self-destructive way of death? It is time for you to reengage with the world.

WHEN TO GET PSYCHOTHERAPY

15

Thanks to therapy I realize I have choices.
— A former patient

*A*s you struggle to get off the compulsive merry-go-round, you may ask yourself, "How do I know whether I should get into therapy?" If you are reading this book and asking the question, the matter of getting into therapy is most likely not a life-or-death issue. Let me give some criteria, however, that can help you decide at what stage of your recovery psychotherapy could help:

• *You continue in a compulsive life-style, knowing how self-destructive it is, but you are unable to motivate yourself to change.* A fifty-six-year-old married father of four grown children, well known in his community, came into therapy only because the court had ordered it. He had had a brief meaningless liaison with a woman who threatened to bring the affair out in the open and professionally destroy him. She filed charges against him and only agreed not to press for a settlement if he got immediate treatment.

When he met with me, it became clear that though he had a conscience, he had managed to ignore it. As a result, he had no motivation from within himself to stop his behavior, only to get out of his current mess.

I don't understand why I do this. Sex with my wife is good enough, though sometimes a little humdrum. But when things are strained between us or work pressures are coming down heavy on me, I start to feel restless and I can't stand it. And there I am back with some pickup relationship. I've even gotten desperate enough to go to prostitutes. I then end up lying to my wife about where the money went.

After a conquest, momentarily I feel peaceful, nothing bothers me. But soon I start to feel pretty horrible about what I've done. I've just been using these other women. What kind of human being am I? What kind of rotten husband am I? I love my wife and wouldn't want to hurt her in any way.

I keep promising myself that I won't do it again. But I know full well that I will. When I get the urge, it's like I go into a trance, and I can't stop myself. I wish I could tell you that I would have sought help on my own, but that's not true. I think this particular woman will eventually leave me alone — I've been through something like this before.

I agreed to work with this man only if he would immediately get into a Twelve-Step Program for sex and love addicts. I knew this would be key to helping him gain control. He went to five different groups before finding one in which he felt comfortable. He had used other Twelve-Step Programs in the past to handle problems with alcohol and compulsive spending.

During the course of therapy he recalled his mother as having been both overprotective and overly controlling, and his father as publicly being a giant but quite weak at home. He thought his father had most likely been involved in numerous extra-marital affairs, which as a boy he was probably aware of. He remembered much fighting between his parents which he thought centered around these extra liaisons.

The more we worked together, the more this man was unable to silence his conscience. There was a critical session when the full impact of what he had done and how he had hurt other people hit him. He sobbed for a solid half hour. This marked a turning point. From then on he was highly motivated in therapy and started to get his life straightened out. With time, he was able to reconstruct the origins of his problem.

Having been sort of an ugly duckling as a child — I wasn't that good in sports and was rather a bookworm — I had a lot of pretty miserable years. Then in junior high, the girls really took to me and overnight I became "Mr. Somebody," suddenly getting a lot of admiration from the guys as being a local stud. Every girl became a challenge, a conquest, and then an event to boast about to my friends. As I got older, my conquests became more numerous, more flamboyant and far more risky.

The more danger there was about being found out and the more I had to sneak about to get someone in bed, the greater was the excitement. Hence any woman who was at some level forbidden became a high prize — married, too old, too young, etc.

In my late twenties, I met a wonderful woman, the answer to all my dreams, and I thought my wild days were now behind me. And they were — for a few months. Then that old impulse took over again, only now I had to lie to my wife to cover my absences, a skill I gradually perfected to a tee. Wherever I went, I cased the crowd for someone to fill my needs. There seems to be an endless supply of available women, women who want a sexual liaison with no real involvement. But I notice over the years I get less and less choosy about who I'm with, and obviously more careless or I wouldn't be in the current jam I'm in.

Fortunately, he was in a marriage which was basically sound, one that could stay intact through the crisis. In fact, as he worked through his problems, his marriage became far stronger.

It has been three years since I last saw him. I hear from him now only at holiday times. His life appears to be going well. From time to time he continues to drop into Twelve-Step meetings to safeguard against falling into old patterns. And, indeed, I think he would have difficulty staying in recovery without having intermittent support.

As was the case for this man, issues relating to identification with an out-of-control parent and with an overly controlling parent may need to be addressed in therapy. There is often a mixture of both wanting to be similar to family members so as to belong, and fears that if you are like them you will be trapped. The more you are conscious of these conflicts, the better you will be able to resolve them.

• *You have too many relapses and you feel unable to get on top of the problem.* Though in Debtors Anonymous for several years, a thirty-six-year-old woman never could remain solvent for long. Her efforts to contain her overspending stayed central in her life. This compounded the difficulties of an already troubled marriage. Reluctantly she decided to get therapy. This eventually enabled her to turn her life around.

Within a year she not only settled her debts, but also got into a reasonable money management plan. She stopped hiding her spending behind her husband's back and getting her parents to financially bail her out. She worked hard in therapy and was able to reach a point where she no longer attempted to buy security and confidence with material things. She increasingly was able to develop it from inside herself. Her marriage remained problematic, but she opted to stay in it and to confront the differences between her husband and herself more directly.

• *Your habit itself is no longer out of control, but you find that you still expend too much energy obsessing about the situation.* Let me relate what happened to a patient I saw some years ago who was struggling ferociously with a food-weight obsession:

She was in her thirties, in her eyes still a few pounds overweight, and had already been in a number of weight loss programs — Weight Watchers, Diet Workshop, Thin-Within, Overeaters Anonymous, and a private group where she had been weighed each day. She told me that before entering these programs, she had been more than fifty pounds overweight, so progress clearly had been made. In fact, she felt that all of the programs had been helpful — temporarily. But she was discouraged by her ongoing weight preoccupation. Even when she was exactly at the weight she liked, she remained obsessed about food and her looks. By the time I saw her, she already knew many skills of changing her self-defeating patterns. These were helpful *when* she used them, but she usually didn't.

In her two years of therapy, we focused on a number of areas:

- What feeling heavy symbolized.
- How the weight obsession was obscuring other life issues.

- How to help her get comfortable being thin.
- How she could reinvest her energy, freed up from the weight obsession.

After she was in therapy for one year, she also started attending a weekly support group for women concerned about their weight. This continued for six months, until her weight stabilized to one that was acceptable to her.

Therapy dug up many issues of current relationships and past family life. Being thin risked vulnerability, which brought up fears of becoming dependent if she were to be intimate with someone. She also had concerns about being attractive and sexual, and that this would lead to her becoming promiscuous. In addition, weighing what she wanted to and no longer being preoccupied about it meant letting go of her past. She had come from a food-weight obsessed family where there were double messages: "You should be thin." But, "Being thin is too sexual, and that is *not* all right."

Through much sweat and tears, she was finally able to let go of her dilemma. She left therapy weighing a few pounds less, but far more important, much lighter in spirit, having unloaded present and past emotional baggage.

• *You continue to jump from one habit to the next.* When one patient told me that compulsive working had followed compulsive relationships, which in turn followed being addicted to marijuana, I pointed out that he was still on the compulsive merry-go-round. He answered, "I think it's more a compulsive 'weary-go-round'." P.S. With therapy, he finally got off of it.

• *You are safely out of your compulsive pattern but not fully going on to other issues.* Relationships and an enjoyment of life's challenges may be frozen by fears of being vulnerable and of becoming intimate. It's bad enough that these fears limited your childhood. It is worse when they keep crippling your adulthood.

A recovered alcoholic found that since he no longer drank, his anxieties in social situations severely hampered him:

> In the "old days," I was painfully shy, which is really an understatement. I was terrified of socializing when there might be an attractive woman available. It didn't show. Instead, I

appeared to be easily bantering with any new women, smiling and laughing. What others didn't see was the quantity of vodka I routinely drank before I came to any social gathering. Since I'm in recovery, I break out in a cold sweat every time I meet a new woman. Because of this, I often avoid social gatherings altogether.

Therapy focused on him remaining in such feared situations and gradually working through the anxiety related to them.

Though you might be abstinent from your self-destructive habit, you may still have a fragile capacity to enjoy healthy excitement and your own achievements. It may feel as though you are further betraying your family because you are enjoying and solving what they haven't been able to enjoy and solve. If not worked through, your feelings and guilt about this can lead you to shoot yourself in the foot and never get on with your life.

• *You are no longer living compulsively but you continue to have a problematic relationship with your parents.* Learning how to have a healthy relationship with your parents that does not pull you back into dysfunctional childhood patterns is critical for your mental health. This means not regressing in their presence and not allowing yourself to feel inappropriately responsible for them. There should be clear boundaries between you and other family members and a mutual acceptance of the individuality and separateness of all concerned.

Since you only have one family of origin, even if the relationship has weak points, hopefully there are big portions of it that can be salvaged. However, if it remains too detrimental to your wellbeing; if maintaining contact means forfeiting your emotional growth; if interactions with family members keep digging up areas that catapult you back into compulsive living, you may have to entertain the possibility of severing the relationship altogether. If this is necessary, there is always a real sadness and mourning that goes with the process. It is a genuine loss. But unlike childhood, you no longer need parents to survive.

• *Your life may be going along, now unencumbered by self-destructive patterns. However, you remain emotionally frozen by unresolved feelings about your childhood.* As discussed in the last chapter, in order to be whole, with perspective and understanding you must finally reframe your childhood through adult eyes; accept what was and what can never be; and move beyond anger and resentment. Most people who come into therapy have problems in this area which have not been adequately resolved.

Therapy provides a safe arena in which to tell your story and have it be heard and validated. When childhood has for whatever reason felt incomplete, reexamining it can offer you the opportunity to integrate the past into the present so that you can continue to move forward. Otherwise you will forever be bogged down in the hopeless task of trying to rewrite yesterday.

Some months after terminating two and a half years of regular weekly therapy, but still dropping in for occasional 'booster' sessions, a patient called me one evening. What she said stands out less in my mind than the fact that she spoke haltingly through ten minutes of crying. I said little other than giving some general words of support. At the end of the call, she reconstituted herself and thanked me profusely for helping her.

When we met the following week for an appointment, she went over why the phone call had been so helpful.

> *It's not really anything you said — it's just that you were there and you care. I know I have the strengths within me to go on and handle my own life when someone is in the wings standing by.*
>
> *It felt like no one was there for me when I was growing up. My parents definitely made significant contributions to our community, but it was another story at home. They were always preoccupied or too busy to tune into where I was. So I spent my childhood pretending I didn't feel as bad as I did.*
>
> *When I called you the other night, you really listened to me. I could just let go and feel awful and get it out of my system. Kids from good families don't realize that they get gold every day.*

This story also illustrates how the therapeutic process has many facets. The therapist not only offers insights and suggestions, but also is a real person who is emotionally present and available. He or she can be your ally as you gradually wean away from unhealthy parts of your attachments to your family and their beliefs, or from other inappropriate partnerships.

• *Compulsive patterns are no longer a problem, but you are often exhausted, or you have a low-grade feeling of being in the doldrums and wondering, "What's the point of it all?"* And no physiologic cause has been found by your doctor.

If you find that each day entails expending too much energy and not having enough fun, this may indicate the presence of some degree of depression. To oversimplify, depression is a warning that you are neglecting yourself — that in an unconscious way you have decided to feel miserable instead of standing up for what you need. Compulsive living often covers over depression. This depression should be dealt with or you will forever feel incomplete. In therapy, you can get at the roots of what is not right and learn to handle it in ways that make you feel better. If indicated, effective, safe anti-depressant medicines are available.

• *You have moved beyond compulsive living, but you find yourself increasingly overwhelmed each day.* You are more and more confused, very anxious, prone to extreme highs and lows, withdrawing from family or friends, reacting way out of proportion to situations, unable to cope with daily activities at home and work, and/or feeling hopeless. For some people, compulsive patterns have actually kept them going, compensating for serious mental illness. If you think this may apply to you, get psychiatric help as soon as possible. With proper treatment, you can turn the tide and start back on the path to mental health.

* * *

In sum, if you feel stuck, you probably are. Though you might have taken giant steps to get yourself off the compulsive merry-go-round, you may not yet be free. At some level, you are still not facing life directly and being one-hundred percent in the present. Your responses to feelings of discomfort may remain at base compulsive — denying it with busy activities, dulling it with substances, diverting it onto preoccupations, or avoiding it by staying away from uncomfortable situations.

If any of this rings true, I suggest that you explore a few sessions of therapy. You have nothing to lose and everything to gain. Look back over the "Adequate Support — Informal and Formal" section in Chapter 4, regarding selecting a therapist.

Let me close this section with an unsigned poem I ran across a number of years ago:

> *A psychiatrist is like a poet.*
> *He creates images for the unimaginative to see,*
> *and if he is really good*
> *he helps THEM become poets —*
> *and to dream again.*

A Last Two Cents Of Advice

In the time of your life, live — so that in that wondrous time you shall not add to the misery and sorrow of the world, but shall smile to the infinite delight and mystery of it.

— William Saroyan

Being at base a Jewish mother, I can't resist giving you a last two cents of advice, a final kick in the pants.

Ultimately, what you do or don't do in your life will have little effect on the lives of others. You may be seen as an inspiration or not particularly memorable; a shining light or a person of unfulfilled potential; a good example, a bad example, or, very likely, not an example at all.

If you have children, of course, you will have far more in-fluence — for you are an integral part of their history and will forever be etched into their memories. With them you have the opportunity to break the legacy of all of the dysfunctional dynamics that have been handed down from generation to generation for much too long.

What your parents couldn't share with you, you *can* share with your children. You *can* be the parent that you never had. You *can* give your children "roots" and "wings." You *can* stay clear as to what your needs are as opposed to what theirs are. Your children shouldn't have to repress their feelings and needs and get caught on their own compulsive merry-go-rounds.

But whether you have children or not, what happens in your life makes *a great deal of difference for you*. You can keep fooling the world, coping on the outside and hurting on the inside. You can continue to be a "good" person with "bad" habits, throwing one precious hour away after another, never enjoying life enough. Or, you can fight your way out of compulsive living, and become an authentic, whole person. For this you must be accountable to yourself in every respect, and no longer hide in self-defeating patterns that detour you.

Particularly in times of stress, the compulsive merry-go-round will beckon. It may tantalize you with a seemingly harmless way to pass the time, especially if you are hesitant to follow your own dreams. Don't be fooled. The glitzy horses will break you before the ride is over. The trip is guaranteed to go nowhere. Walk away. Walk away before it's too late.

We have traveled together through some pretty rocky terrain. Now it is time to go our separate ways. The rest is up to you. As you continue on your pilgrimage of self-discovery, may you have the courage to choose wisely for yourself. Enjoy your life. Good luck!

APPENDIX

Additional Resources

The following are resources which I have found to be useful, personally and professionally. These are books that I consider to be substantive and "reader friendly."

I feel that books written by authors with firsthand experience with a particular pattern are especially valuable — an asterisk is placed in front of those. My apologies for any important sources of support that I have overlooked. I recommend *The Recovery Resource Book*, by Barbara Yoder (Fireside, 1990), for additional resources.

Coming To Terms With Your Past

*Bradshaw On: The Family, A Revolutionary Way of Self-Discovery, by John Bradshaw (Health Communications, Inc., 1988), is based on his television series of the same name. He communicates with heart and soul the stark impact of dysfunctional backgrounds on growing and adult children.

*Bradshaw On: Healing the Shame That Binds You, by John Bradshaw (Health Communications, Inc., 1988). Further explorations of the dynamics that evolve from dysfunctional families and how to climb out of them.

*When You and Your Mother Can't Be Friends: Resolving the Most Complicated Relationship of Your Life, by Victoria Secunda (Delacorte Press, 1990). Beautifully written. Provides a means to understand and better resolve your relationship with your mother.

*Toxic Parents: Overcoming Their Hurtful Legacy and Reclaiming Your Life, by Susan Forward (Bantam Books, 1989). Gives perspective on childhood pain with useful suggestions for dealing with family members — though you may not want to follow all of them to the letter.

Growing Beyond Emotional Pain: Action Plans for Healing, by John Preston (Impact Publishers, Inc. 1993). Explains the complex nature of emotional pain. Provides personal action plans for working through distress.

Driven Preoccupations And Thought Patterns

How People Change, by Allen Wheelis, M.D. (Harper and Row, 1973). An excellent little book, well worth searching for. It illuminates the process of personal change and growth that is possible in therapy.

The Road Less Traveled: A New Psychology of Love, Traditional Values and Spiritual Growth, by M. Scott Peck, M.D. (Simon and Schuster, Inc., 1978). This book well deserves its popularity. Thought-provoking suggestions about dealing with life's difficulties.

Overcoming the Fear of Success: Why and How We Defeat Ourselves and What to Do About It, by Martha Friedman (Seaview Books, 1980). Excellent understanding of the inner roadblocks that encumber us.

Fears And Phobias

Managing Your Anxiety: Regaining Control When You Feel Stressed, Helpless, and Alone, by Christopher J. McCullough, Ph.D. and Robert Woods Mann (Tarcher, 1985). A good overall guide to understand the problem and the road to recovery.

* * *

Work And Activities

Treating Type A Behavior and Your Heart, by Meyer Friedman, M. D. and Diane Ulman, R.N., M.S. (Fawcett Crest, 1984). The book is insightful and full of excellent suggestions.

Work Addictions: Hidden Legacies of Adult Children, by Bryan E. Robinson (Health Communications Inc., 1989). Exceedingly readable and wise. Tastefully combines a professional and personal approach.

Enough is Enough: You Don't Have to Be Perfect, by Carol Orsborn (G. P. Putnam's Sons, 1986). Humorous perspective on ways women overstretch themselves, and some thoughts on breaking the pattern.

Combatting Escapism

Procrastination: Why You Do It and What to Do About It, by Jane B. Burka, Ph.D. and Leonora M. Yuen, Ph.D. (Addison Wesley, 1983). Gives a thorough understanding of the condition and good suggestions as to how to overcome it.

How to Get Control of Your Time and Life, by Alan Laiken (Wyden Press, 1973). An immensely practical cookbook approach to the problem.

The Plug-In-Drug: Television, Children and the Family, by Marie Winn (Viking Penguin Inc., 1977). Food for thought about what television does to the minds of children and adults and how to break away from it.

Relationships Fixations

How to Break Your Addiction to a Person by Howard M. Halpern (Bantam-McGraw, 1982). Excellent and sympathetic.

Women Who Love Too Much, by Robin Norwood (Tarcher, 1985). Reads like a novel. An in-depth look at problems which women can easily identify with.

Love and Addiction, by Vincent Peele (Taplinger, 1972). An early pioneer in the field which examines the addictive nature of unhealthy love relationships.

Codependent No More: How to Stop Controlling Others and Care for Yourself, by Melody Beattie (Harper/Hazelden, 1987). An encouraging look at climbing out of the codependent pit.

Lost in the Shuffle: The Co-dependent Reality, by Robert Subby (Health Communications Inc., 1987). A thorough exploration of childhood roots of codependency.

Letting Go: A 12-Week Personal Action Program to Overcome a Broken Heart, by Zev Wanderer and Tracy Cabot (Dell, 1978). Practical suggestions.

How To Survive the Loss of a Love, by Melba Colgrove, Harold H. Bloomfield, and Peter McWilliams (Leo Press, 1976). Nice little book—humanly touching and easy reading.

Married People, Staying Together in the Age of Divorce, by Francine Klagsbrun (Bantam, 1985). In contrast to the other books listed, this gives a clear picture of healthy relationships.

* * *

Write to CoDependence Anonymous, Inc., P.O. Box 33577, Phoenix, Arizona 85067-3577 for literature and local group referrals. Tel: (602) 277-7991

Sexual Addictions

Out of the Shadows, by Patrick Carnes (CompCare, 1983). This book offers an excellent understanding of the problem of all sexual addictions. I feel it is an invaluable learning tool for those struggling with any form of this problem.

* * *

These organizations can offer information on other helpful literature and local groups:

National Association on Sexual Addictive Problems, (NASAP)
P.O. Box 696, Manhattan Beach, CA 90266

Sex Addicts Anonymous
P.O. Box 70949, Houston, TX 77270
Tel: (713) 8869-4902

Sexaholics Anonymous
P.O. Box 300, Simi Valley, CA 93062
Tel: (805) 581-3343

Eating, Food, And Weight Obsessions

There are shelves of books with more arriving every minute. Here are a few that I especially like:

Fat is a Family Affair, by Judy Hollis, Ph.D. (Hazelden, 1985). Shows how the whole family plays into producing an individual's unhealthy relationship with food.

Successful Dieting Tips, Compiled by Bruce Lansky (Meadowbrook Press, 1981). Loaded with practical hints—for example, "What to do when your willpower wilts."

*Feeding the Hungry Heart, The Experience of Compulsive Eating, by Geneen Roth (The Bobs-Merrill Co., Inc. 1982). Painful stories with which you can easily identify.

*Breaking Free from Compulsive Eating, by Geneen Roth (The Bobs-Merrill Co., Inc. 1982). Excellent understanding of the dynamics of recovering from the food-weight obsession.

*Forever Thin, by Theodore Isaac Rubin, M.D. (Bernard Geis Assoc., 1970). Sheds light on the difference between "fat" and "thin" thinking.

*Overcoming Overeating: Living Free in a World of Food, Jane R. Hirschmann and Carol H. Menter. Well thought out suggestions of ways to have a healthy relationship with food.

The Slender Balance: Causes and Cures for Bulimia, Anorexia and the Weight-loss/Weight-gain Seesaw, by Susan Squire (G. P. Putnam's Sons, 1983). Clear exposition of how all of these are on the same spectrum.

Bulimarexia: The Binge-Purge Cycle, by Marlene Bosking-White Ph.D. and William C. White Jr. Ph.D. (W. W. Norton and Co., 1983). Zeroes in on fighting bulimia.

*Living Binge-Free: A Personal Guide to Victory Over Compulsive Eating, by Jane Evans Latimer (LivingQuest, 1988). Very first-hand and very insightful.

* * *

Overeaters Anonymous literature on compulsive eating is excellent. Check local telephone listings or write to P.O. Box 92870, Los Angeles, CA 90009.

Anorexia
Anorexia Nervosa: Finding the Life Line, by Patricia M. Stein R.D., M.S., M.A. and Barbara C. Unell (CompCare Publications, 1986). Revealing stories told by recovering anorexics with a good medical and social perspective.

The Golden Cage, by Hilda Bruch M.D. (Vintage Books, 1979). An enlightening examination of the family dynamics that produce anorexia.

Treating and Overcoming Anorexia Nervosa, by Steven Levenkron (Charles Scribner's Sons, 1982). An in-depth look at the kind of therapy that is appropriate for anorexia.

Compulsive Spending And Shopping

As of this writing, there are few books available relating to compulsive spending. I'll list what I have found.

*How to Get Out of Debt, Stay Out of Debt & Live Prosperously (Based on the Proven Principles and Techniques of Debtors Anonymous), by Jerrold Mundis (Bantam, 1988). A no-nonsense practical look at the problem and the solution, learned the hard way. Cuts through excuses and denial.

Quick Fixes and Small Comforts, by Georgia Witkin (Villard Books, 1987). Good coverage of the range of ways we try to buy security and comfort, and what this does to us.

Wealth Addiction, America's Most Powerful Drug — How It Weakens Us. How We Can Free Ourselves, by Phillip Slater (E. P. Dutton, 1980). Perceptive look at how money controls and distorts our lives.

Shopaholics: Serious Help for Addicted Spenders, by Janet E. Damon (Price/Stern/Sloan Inc., 1988). May be useful for those wanting to start their own support groups.

* * *

Gambling

Compulsive Gamblers: Observations on Action and Abstinence, by Jay Livingston (Harper and Row, 1974). Excellent sociologic study regarding who gets caught into compulsive gambling, what happens in Gamblers Anonymous, and the process of recovery.

When Luck Runs Out: Help for Compulsive Gamblers and Their Families, by Robert Custer, M.D. and Harry Milt (Warner Books, 1985). Offers a thorough understanding of backgrounds of compulsive gamblers, how their problems spread into current family relationships, and the work necessary to get into recovery.

* * *

Gamblers Anonymous. Check local telephone listings or write to P. O. Box 17173, Los Angeles, CA 90017.

For in-patient programs for compulsive gambling, contact the National Council on Compulsive Gambling, Inc., 445 West 59th St., Room 1521, New York, NY 10019; Tel: (212) 765-3833 and 3834 or 800-522-4700.

Substance Abuse

To locate physicians versed in substance abuse, write the American Society of Addiction Medicine, Inc., 5225 Wisconsin Avenue, Suite 409, N.W. Washington, D.C. 20015. Tel: (202) 244-8948.

Locate therapeutic communities in your area by contacting the state or county health agency.

Alcohol

Of the many books in the alcohol area, here are some I've found helpful:

*The Courage to Change, Personal Conversations about Alcoholism with Dennis Wholey (Houghton Mifflin Co., 1984). Insightful stories of famous people who share their pain and triumphs.

Broken Promises, Mended Dreams, by Richard Meryman (Little Brown, 1984). Fictionalized biography of a woman's journey through hell and back—in denial, in an inpatient hospital program, and again in the family.

*Good-bye Hangovers, Hello Life: Self-help for Women, by Jean Kirpatrick, Ph.D. (Atheneum, 1986). An autobiographical exploration by the founder of Women for Sobriety of ways alcohol is embedded in people's lives, and the road to healing.

Drugfree, A Unique, Positive Approach to Staying Off Alcohol and Other Drugs, by Richard B. Seymour and David E. Smith, M.D. (Facts on File, 1989). Based on many years of experience at the Haight Ashbury Free Medical Clinic, it thoroughly covers the range of substances that can be abused.

* * *

Alcoholics Anonymous books and pamphlets are excellent. Check local telephone listings or write to A. A. World Services, Inc., Box 459, Grand Central Station, New York NY 10163. The "Big Book," and booklets titled "Alcoholism a Merry-go-round Named Denial" and "Living Sober" are especially useful.

Women for Sobriety's address is P.O. Box 618, Quakertown, PA 18951. Tel: (215) 536-8026.

Adult Children Of Alcoholics (A.C.O.A.)

The literature on Adult Children of Alcoholics is immensely helpful to individuals from *all* kinds of dysfunctional families, whether alcohol has been present or not.

*It Will Never Happen to Me, by Claudia Black (M.A.C., 1982). A pioneer classic for Adult Children of Alcoholics. Very readable.

*Adult Children of Alcoholics, by Janet Geringer Weititz (Health Communications Inc., 1983). Describes well the emotional and psychological toll of surviving an alcoholic family background.

*Choice Making, by Sharon Wegscheider-Cruse (Health Communications Inc., 1985). Clearly delineates the connection between unresolved A.C.O.A. issues and the later development of addictive patterns.

*Guide to Recovery: A Book for Adult Children of Alcoholics, by Herbert L. Gravitz, Ph.D. and Julie D. Bowden, M. S., (Learning Publications Inc., 1985). Good picture of the total process of recovery for Adult Children of Alcoholics and children of all other dysfunctional families.

*A Time to Heal: The Road to Recovery for Adult Children of Alcoholics, by Timmen L. Cermak, M. D. (Avon Books, 1988). A good look at how dysfunctional family dynamics play out.

A Life Worth Waiting For: Messages from a Survivor, by Dwight Lee Wolter (CompCare, 1989). A poetic and moving presentation of the stark realitites of being an adult child of alcoholics.

Safe Passage, by Stephanie Brown (John Wiley, 1992). In a warm readable style this book demystifies the passage from pain to freedom. It explains "growing up, growing out, and coming home." Full of gold.

* * *

There are a growing number of Twelve-Step and professionally run Adult Children of Alcoholic *groups*, as well as therapists who are tuned into these issues.

Drug Abuse

800-Cocaine, by Mark S. Gold, M.D. (Bantam, 1984). An extremely straightforward and sober look at the problem of using chemical solutions to life, with practical suggestions for change.

Cocaine, Seduction and Solution, by Nannette Stone, Marlene Fromme, and Daniel Kagun (Pinnacle Books, 1984). Stark stories of cocaine abuse that tragically illustrate cocaine's power, along with overall guidelines for recovery.

* * *

Call 800-COCAINE for treatment and referral numbers.

Literature from Narcotics Anonymous (World Service Office, Inc., P. O. Box 9999, Van Nuys, CA 91409), and Cocaine Anonymous , P.O. Box 1367, Culver City, CA 90232).

Prescription Drugs

I'm Dancing as Fast as I Can, by Barbara Gordon (Bantam, 1980). Depicts the nightmare of Valium addiction and how the medical world plays into it.

Cigarettes

You Can Stop, by Jacquelyn Rogers (Simon and Schuster, 1977). Firsthand account of the smoking struggle — an excellent book to help strengthen your motivation to quit.

Quit Smoking in 30 Days, by Gary Holland and Herman Weiss, Ph.D. (Bantam, 1984). Excellent short booklet. Get a copy if you can.

*How to Stop Smoking, by Herbert Brean (Vanguard Press, Inc., 1958). Includes some practical suggestions by someone who knows all the rationalizations.

*The Stop Smoking Book by Margaret Kraker McKean (Impact Publishers, Inc. 1987). Candidly revealing her own struggles and sharing her 25 Ways of winning, McKean's book lends a gentle helping hand to the non-using smoker.

* * *

Literature from the American Cancer Society, 1599 Clifton Road N.E., Atlanta, GA 30329; American Health Foundation, 320 East 43rd St., New York, NY 10017; Office of Cancer Communications, National Cancer Institute, Bethesda, MD; and the American Heart Association, 7320 Greenville Avenue, Dallas, TX 75231; *Smokers Anonymous* (check local telephone listings).

Abandonment, as part of emotional cycle, 44
Adolescence, in development of compulsive behavior, 76-77
Affirmations, 145-146
Agoraphobia, 186
Anorexia, 223-226
Authority, rebellion against, 40
Avoidance, as reason for compulsive behavior, 37-38

Barzini, Luigi, 192
Behavior cycles, 51-52
Boredom, 36-37, 132
Bulimia, 87

Codependency, 202-208
Compulsive living, 7-12
life after recovery from, 252-262
Compulsive patterns
cycles of, 42-43
defending the status quo, 53-59
dominating your life, 23-29
effect of on your relationships, 19-23
functions they fulfill, 30-41
games we play, 59-60
identifying how serious they are, 12-29
as integral part of your existence, 14-19
origins of, 64-80
roles we pretend not to play, 60-63

Coping skills for recovery, 125-126
breaking emotionally fueled cycles, 131-135
changing old patterns into new ones, 138-140
handling potential pitfalls, 127-131
incorporating exercise into your life, 137-138
relapse prevention, 164-176
setting goals for yourself, 126-127
updating your mental outlook, 149-149
weathering "emergency urgency," 135-137

Defensive cycles, 52-53
Depression, as reason for compulsive behavior, 36-37
Detoxification (drug or alcohol recovery), 116-117
Detoxification program for compulsive behavior, 150-163
Diet Workshop, 216-217
Driven thought patterns, 179-184

"Emergency urgency," 135-137
Emotionally fueled cycles of behavior, 43-49, 131-135
Escape activities, 197-200
Excuses, 146-147
Exercise, 137-138

Family structure, as part of
　origin of compulsive behavior,
　65-79
Fears and phobias, 184-189
Fitzgerald, F. Scott, 33
Food obsessions, 212-223
Friedman, Meyer, 193
Friends, as informal support
　network, 108-109

Gambling, compulsive, 234-238
Genetic sensitivities, as origin
　of compulsive behavior, 72
Group therapy, 118
Guilt, 75

Health issues, compulsive
　concern with, 182-183

Identity needs, as reason for
　compulsive patterns, 32-34
Inpatient hospital treatment
　programs, 115-117
Insecurities, as reason for
　compulsive patterns, 32-34
Insulation, as origin of
　compulsive behavior, 70-71
Intrusion, as part of emotional
　cycle, 43-44

Jenny Craig, 217

Lindbergh, Anne, 197

Men
　support groups for, 109-111
　unreachable standards for, 83
Mentally fueled cycles of
　obehavior, 50-51

Nicotine addiction, 246-251
Nutri/System, 217

Outpatient programs for
　recovery, 115
Overeaters Anonymous, 218

Parents, relationships with, 74-75
Peer pressures, compulsive
　behavior and, 74
Peer support groups, 114-115
Procrastination, 197-200
Psychopaths, 75-76
Psychotherapy, 117-119,
　263-272

Rationalizations, 146-147
Rebellion, as reason for
　compulsive behavior, 38-40
Recovery, 90-91, 119-124
　coping skills, 125-149
　getting into gear, 100-107
　relapse prevention, 164-176
　seven-day program to take
　　stock, 91-99
　support systems, 107-124
　two-week detox program for
　　compulsive behavior,
　　150-163
Rejection, as part of emotional
　cycle, 44
Relapse prevention, 164-176
Relationship fixations, 202-208
Relationships, effect of
　compulsive patterns, 19-23
Relatives, as informal support
　network, 108-109
Relaxation or recreation, 35-36,
　133
Rescuers, 61-63
Risk-taking behavior, 181
Role-playing, 60-63

Saboteurs, 60-61, 108
Saving, compulsive, 200
Seducers, 60-61
Self-nurturing, 31-32, 131-132
Self-sabotage, 105
Seven-day program to take
    stock, 91-99
Sexual fixations, 208-211
Shoplifting, compulsive, 238-239
Shopping, compulsive, 227-234
Smoking, 246-251
Societal pressures and
    seductions, 80-89
Sociopaths, 75-76
Spending, compulsive, 227-234
Stein, Gertrude, 33
Stress, compulsive behavior
    and, 73
Substance abuse, 240-244
    women and, 244-246
Suffocation, as part of emotional
    cycle, 43-44
Support systems, 105, 107,
    108-119

Thinking patterns, reworking,
    142-145
Tranquilizing behavior, 34-35
"Trigger" situations, 130
Twelve-step Programs,
    111-114, 118, 121, 210, 246
Type A behavior, 193

Weight obsession, 212-223
Weight Watchers, 216-217
Women
    dilemmas of, 81-82
    substance abuse and, 244-246
    support groups for, 109-111

Work and activities,
    compulsive behavior around,
    190-197
Work environment, stresses of,
    84

MORE BOOKS WITH *IMPACT*

We think you will find these Impact Publishers titles of interest:

Please see the following page for more books.

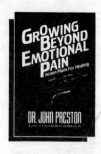

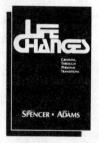